Return to Oneness:

A Course

As Revealed to Eddie Lee

Table of Contents

INTRODUCTION

This is a course to help you Return to Oneness. Just as Love cannot be taught, neither can the meaning of unity and oneness. This course is not designed to teach that which exists in abstractia. Its aim, however, is to assist you in preparing for the experience. For through direct experience, you will come to feel oneness throughout the whole of your being. Oneness is meaningless to the mind, and is therefore unknown. However, to the heart, oneness is as it has always been. It is why we now communicate through feelings. Although your mind is reading and searching its past, in order to understand these words, it is your heart that feels them and translates them to the appropriate thoughts for which the mind and its power can be utilized with regards to its proper function, which is extension rather than projection. It is from the union of the mind with the heart, between the soul and spirit, which brings you into Self Awareness and the Realm of Divine Existence. For without this union, oneness, like Love, will remain alien to you. And, your True Self, which is both Love and one, will continue to be hidden behind the veil of dreams. Peace is your treasure. It is your inheritance, given by the Father to His Beloved Son. Yet, to experience your birthright, you must come into oneness with All That Is.

Therefore, this course can simply be summed up as follows:

> Love and oneness are your natural state. They are not separate aspects of God. They are God, without which nothing that exists would exist. You exist. Therefore, you must be Love and One, nothing more, but certainly nothing less. For in oneness lies the power to create the new, and to bring Heaven to Earth. This is your function. This is your Joy, which is but the realized True Self, the Self of God, the Self that is but Awareness.

Part I:

THE MAKING OF HELL

CHAPTER 1

Your True Self

I.1.1   Now We begin. This is a most joyous occasion. For We now speak to you in the Voice of Unity. You share this Voice with Us. It is Our Voice. It is your voice. Become comfortable with it. For We are with you as We have always been. We have come to speak to you of unity and oneness. This is the next step in conscious expansion. Although it may have appeared that you were on a journey, now you will discover that you have journeyed not. There was only the opening of your heart. The stone has been rolled from the tomb you once made in self-imposed exile. The time of your awakening, of your rebirth, has come. And, We are here to assist you in the most glorious expansion of consciousness. It is time to arise. You have heard the call Home. And, you have answered. We welcome you to that which is Our Home, Our birthright, Our Inheritance.

I.1.2   As you have come to know, you are an individuated self of the One, the Creator, Who is the Source of Our Being. You are not an individual, who lives a separate life from those around you, those whom you can see with the body's eyes, as well as those you cannot see. Trust Us, in this most Holy Moment, when We say that there are many more of Us, Who are unseen

9

by you that you are as of yet unaware. We move and work around you, offering you the help for which you have asked, but have so often refused. Yet, you have called Us and We are here with you right now, in this moment, the only moment that exists.

I.1.3   We are one, one with everything that exists in all realms, or dimensions, of creation. This is Our Truth. This is Our Reality. While you have come to shift your belief system from one of separation to oneness, you have yet to experience oneness in any real sense, which would have removed the last vestiges of doubt that still exists within your mind. And, this doubt is as pervasive as the belief in separation. For you cannot say you believe in oneness and doubt it at the same time. Doubt, even if it is merely the size of a grain of sand, is still doubt. And, to your mind, it will be seen as that of the tallest mountain on the blue marble you call Earth.

I.1.4   Doubt is nothing but another word for fear. And, where there is fear, Love remains unknown. For as you have been told, Love and fear cannot abide together. However, fear is not real; it is of your making and must be undone by you. It is this little bit of fear, which remains hidden within your mind, that must be exposed and dissolved by the Light of Grace. Until this fear is released, you will continue to experience separation, and oneness cannot be experienced in its fullness, which is the only Way for which it can be experienced.

I.1.5   Until you experience the joy and peace of oneness, it will remain unknown to you. How could it be different? For you believe only that in which you see and experience. Is this wrong? Certainly not! For it is, after all, nothing more than the power of your mind in motion. It is the natural effect of the Spiritual Laws. Remember, you were told in *A Course In Miracles* that you are under no Laws but God's. Although you have forgotten these simple Laws, your forgetting them did not negate them. They are you. Yes! Since you are one with everything, you are one with the Laws, as well. They do not exist outside of you. In truth, the Laws live within you. They do not control you, because that would oppose the first Law, the Law of Free Will. Instead, the Laws simply maintain unity.

I.1.6   The Laws will be mentioned throughout this Course. While this Course is *A Course in Oneness*, its only focus is on that which will allow you to experience the oneness, which is your true state of Being. Yet, to experience oneness, you must remember the Laws. For after all, you are their co-creator.

Lesson 1

Words are Powerful, for They are Creative Agents

I.1.7 It is here where We will introduce the first lesson contained within this Course. For even the word *co-creator* is one that symbolizes separation. While the word carries with it a sense of loftiness and worthiness, it nevertheless maintains the belief of separation within your mind.

I.1.8 Allow your mind to still itself, even if but a moment. Rather than think of the word *co-creator* and its meaning, feel the vibrational frequency created by the word. Yes! Feel the word. Be honest with yourself. For if you are being truthful, you will feel a distinct sense of separation, not one of unity. The very word implies *two-ness*. And, where there is a belief that there is more than one, there will be fear held within the mind. For only in oneness is Love truly felt and experienced.

I.1.9 This brings us to the first lesson: *words are powerful, for they are creative agents.* They either project judgment and fear or they extend, or create, Love. While you were told that *words are but symbols of symbols twice removed from reality* in *A Course in Miracles,* you were never told that words weren't powerful. For words, derived from the power of the mind, are the intention set forth by desire itself. Every word carries with it a frequency, an energy signature, which interacts with the Infinite Field of Potentiality, what you call God, to bring forth, or manifest into form, an experience you have chosen to create. As of yet, you have been unaware of the very power that words have. Recognize, words are not magical, although some on your planet have spun myths around their purpose, they are one with you, just as all things are. They carry the energy of the very beliefs you hold sacrosanct regarding yourself and the world around you.

I.1.10   Furthermore, words manifest form. And, form allows you to experience your beliefs. While both the form and the experience are neutral, the words, with which you speak silently to yourself or out loud for others to hear, are not neutral. For words are thoughts in motion. Until now, your thoughts and words were used to create the experience of separation. Now, the time has come for them to create experiences of unity and oneness.

I.1.11   As discussed by Us in *A Course of Love,* you are moving from the time of learning into the time of sharing. The time of sharing has dawned. For this time ushers in a time of unity to be discovered, explored, and ultimately shared by All. And, the understanding of the immense power given unto you will now be experienced moment-to-moment. As previously stated, words are the energy signature of the very thoughts you entertain. And, the power of words comes from the feelings generated by every thought you allow to be planted within the hallowed soil that comprises the garden of your mind.

I.1.12   Words do not exist from just the thoughts you think. Words are, in truth, derived from the thoughts you think and the feelings each thought invokes. If this sounds familiar, there is a good reason for it. We are sharing with you the workings of two Spiritual Laws: the Law of Cause and Effect as well as the Law of Belief. And, these are the Laws which allow words to ultimately manifest into form and experience.

I.1.13   We would like to take a moment to share the importance of these Laws on the fabric woven into the tapestry that you call life. This is a moment that requires unification of your mind and heart. For the sharing to be complete, you must join Us in the unity of true communication. *Communication is creation,* as was shared in *The Way of Mastery.* For creation to be whole and complete it must be communicated, which is to say that it must be shared. Without sharing, without unity, there is only projection. And, projection is nothing more than the misuse of the power given unto you. Where projection remains in the realm of those who sleep and dream of separation, creation exists in the Divine Realms, because communication is extension. They are the same. Communication, creation, sharing, and giving are all words which carry the same energy signature. Not only are they synonymous, they are the same. It is here that We now speak to your heart. For it is here that We communicate via the *feeling* of Love.

I.1.14   We not only share Our thoughts with you, but We share our feelings. This, O Brother and Sister, is true communication. We now extend the truth of our Being, the truth that is oneness. Do not just read these words, feel them. Allow yourself to experience the energy they carry. Allow yourself to once again become acquainted with the frequency associated with the words. That is what is meant by *feel* them. For this is your power, this is your Self, this is the Joy of Heaven.

I.1.15   Therefore, this first lesson has nothing to do with learning, which implies nothing but a transfer of thoughts from a teacher to his or her student. Instead, this lesson is really a sharing of what We, thus you, already know: that *words are powerful, for they are creative agents.* This lesson isn't difficult at all. In truth, you will experience great joy as a result. For joy is your birthright. And it is your Being.

I.1.16   This lesson requires no thought. If you begin *thinking* on it, then stop and return to it at a later time. For this lesson simply requires you to *feel.* This is not a new concept, for you are quite adept at feeling. However, you have believed that your feelings were separate from the feelings of others, just like you once believed that your thoughts were private and held part from those around you. In oneness, all things are shared. For We are but One.

I.1.17   As you move through your day, begin to *feel* each word. Feel its energy. Become reacquainted with the frequency, or energy signature, of each word that visits your mind. Do not think of the word's meaning. For that is pointless. Rather, feel the word. For it is in the word's energy field that its true meaning is relayed and understood by All. Play with this lesson. For it is one in which you move ever closer to experiencing oneness and unity each time you play with it. Do not limit your play to just words that you think or deem appropriate. For then you are judging some words worthy at the expense of others. No! This is a time to play. It is a time to return to the childlike play you once cherished. Regardless of the word that appears in your thought process, simply *feel* it. Feel its energy. Feel its power. For it is your power. It is the very power of intention.

I.1.18   In your play, begin to allow the recognition of the energies of those words which foster and engender separation from those that extend unity. Some words will have a very pronounced energy attached to them, while others will be more subtle. At first, it may appear difficult to distinguish between these more subtle frequencies. But, with practice, you will begin to be able to detect even the most subtle energy that exists between each word. In truth, you have already mastered this. But, your intense focus on separation has veiled this knowledge from you. However, together in oneness, We will simply refocus Our consciousness from that which appears to separate to that which unites.

I.1.19   Continue to play with this lesson for as long as you choose. And, as you begin to identify more with the feelings and energy found within each word, allow your consciousness to expand and include the statements made by a string of words. For statements act as words themselves. Statements carry the energy found in the overall intention of the seemingly separate, but united, words which comprise them. For example, it is written in your Bible that *"God said, 'Let there be light: and there was light.'"* This example, found in the account of the First Day of Creation, was given you and all of man to demonstrate the very power and energy found within words and the statements that they imply.

Let There Be Light

I.1.20   Look again at the Bible verse. For there is a wealth of knowledge contained within it for those who have chosen to awaken to the Reality of Oneness, rather than to continue the

17

dreaming associated with those who still choose to sleep. Look closely. This time do so with the desire born of the One. Let your intention follow the desire to *feel* it rather than just think of the meaning behind the words. Ask your Self, that Self created in the image and likeness of God, "What do We feel?" Then, simply allow the feelings that arise from within to speak to you. For they are the direct link between you and everything that exists.

I.1.21   Look at the verse with both an open mind and an open heart. For when you feel the intent, born of God's desire, the words will be seen as living. You will see and feel the energy behind the words, every one of them. Yet, look deeper. Allow the words to be seen as one in wholeness.

I.1.22   The verse begins with, "And God said…." Those three simple words imply that He is sharing His Thoughts. He isn't speaking to Himself. Yet, to whom is He extending His thoughts? Feel it.

I.1.23   Yes! Feel it Our Brother. Allow the feeling of those words to wash across your soul and spirit. Those words are shared with Us. Recall them. Feel them. For they were not spoken in some distant past, so long ago that they have become weathered and eroded by time. No! They are being spoken to you in this moment. Hear the Voice of the One as He declares with you, "Let there be light." For O Holy One, He speaks to you of Our creation. We are His Light. We are His Holy Extension. We are One.

I.1.24 In this most Holy Moment, He is calling you into Us, into Him. You, who are His Beloved, feel His Presence. Feel His Power. Feel His Love. For He calls you into Awakening, into Being, into Life eternal. This is His gift to you. This, O Holy Brother, is your re-birth.

I.1.25 With these four words, *Let there be light,* We Exist. Why? Because We are told, *and there was light.* This is the light of man. This is Our Creation. This is Our Awakening. We are One with Him Who extended Himself. And, We are Him, just as He is Us. Feel this to the depth of your Being. This, O Holy Child, is the power given Us by Him, Who is Everything and Nothing.

I.1.26 Feel, now, the power of that statement. Feel the energy not only behind each word, but the energy associated with the wholeness of the declaration, itself. That energy is you. It is Us. And, that energy is Ours to extend. It is Ours to go forth and create from. It is Ours to experience. We are not separate from the energy. We are the energy. We are Its Power.

The Spiritual Laws: An Overview

I.1.27   As Our focus moves into unity, We turn Our attention to the two Laws mentioned earlier. However, before We share with you the two Laws, and how they translate words into manifestations and form, We must share with you the Laws' intentions. For many are blinded to them, as they see and believe them to be an enemy of freedom, rather than the purveyor of the very freedom for which they claim to seek.

I.1.28   First, the Laws were born from Our desire, with that of God's, to ensure that All are united in Will and Love. The Laws do not enslave. They maintain God's Will, which is one with Ours, for they are the same, remain unencumbered and eternally free. Furthermore, the Laws are the Great Equalizer. They maintain the free flow of Knowledge between All. And, they ensure the wholeness of the Kingdom.

I.1.29   The Laws are not given to harm. Instead, they serve to protect. For the Laws are the very reason that *within our defenselessness our safety lies,* just as you were taught in *A Course in Miracles.* The Laws are what is referred to in your Bible as the *breastplate of righteousness* and the *armor of God.* They are your protection. They are your safety. They keep you from harm. The Laws are why dreams cannot touch you. For without the Laws, the nightmare of separation would have consumed you long ago. Yet, the very Laws you seemed to have once denied and forgotten are the reason you *remain as God created you,* whole, unharmed, and free.

I.1.30   In addition, the Laws cannot be usurped or manipulated, nor can they be broken. They are a perfect creation of unity. Although you are free to forget them, or even deny them, you are not free to change them. They govern all aspects of creation. They govern everything seen and unseen. The Laws live in the Mind of Our Source, just as everything does. Furthermore, the Laws determine the outcome, or the effect, of every thought you have. And, it is for this reason that the Laws exist. In other words, nothing, absolutely nothing, occurs by chance or happenstance.

I.1.31   At first, it may appear that the Laws work separately and apart from one another. This would be true if the separation were real. But, it isn't. Only to a divided mind do the Laws seem to stand separate and alone. Yet, this simply is not the case at all. While there are twelve Laws, not only do they work in tandem, they function as one. For how else could oneness be maintained?

I.1.32   In *A Course in Miracles,* you were informed that *there are no neutral thoughts.* Then, later, in *The Way of Mastery,* you learned that *all experiences are neutral.* For you are the one who assigns each experience the meaning it has for you. The Laws are the very reason as to why there are no neutral thoughts. For each thought sets the Laws into motion. But, you must understand that the Laws act only in accordance with the vibrational frequency of the thought itself. While the Laws set into motion the experience, they do so by acting only within the framework of the vibrational signature inherent to that thought pattern.

I.1.33   As mentioned, every thought you have sets the Laws into action. The first Law which is set into motion is the Law of Cause and Effect, which is: *For every cause, there is a simultaneous effect which is created.* To fully appreciate this Law, you must come to realize that every thought is a cause, or causal agent. And, the vibrational signature will simultaneously create a corresponding feeling, which matches the energetic frequency of the thought.

I.1.34   There are only two primary feelings, or emotions, Love or fear. One you created, the other you didn't. Because of man's belief in separation and division, the two primary feelings have been decided, and yet divided again, to such an extent that you believe that Joy is a separate feeling when compared to Love. You have come to believe that Peace is a separate feeling from that of Joy. It is for this reason that We now share with you that you do not *know* Love. For when you come to know it once again, which can be done only through experience, you will feel them only in oneness. They are the same. They are God. The *feeling* of True Love, True Joy, True Peace is God. And, it is through the awareness of the *feeling* in which you experience that you know you stand witness to the Awareness of Love's Presence. You *feel* them as One, for they are the One.

I.1.35   However, just as you have separated the feelings of Peace and Joy from Love, you have done the same with fear, which was but your answer to Love. For you thought fear could replace Love. Yet, nothing can replace Love. For nothing can replace God. Therefore, your creation of fear did not bring joy, it brought *hell* and nightmares. And, just as you did with Love, you divided, and further divided fear into separate feelings. Some of these are anger, depression, irritation, doubt, sadness, grief, hatred, lack, and loneliness. The list of feelings, which you have come to label as distinct and different, is nothing but deception on your part. For regardless of what feeling you choose to call it, if it isn't Love, it is always fear.

I.1.36   You have been told that fear is not Real. And, this is Truth. For only Love is Real. Nothing that isn't Love exists.

Yet, because you made fear, it appears and seems quite real. Fear, regardless of the form you call it, acts on both your mind and body, creating something you call illness, or sickness, in both. Yet, *this need not be.*

I.1.37   Have you yet come to understand that you love fear and fear Love? For the love and relationship you have with fear is simply you attempting to be one with your creation, just as God is one with you, who are but His Creation. However, you cannot become one with what does not exist. For that is impossible. Fear does not exist, because God does not share this feeling with you. He knows it not.

I.1.38   It is your wish to join with the *nothingness* which fear is that creates the internal and external conflicts so prevalent within you and the world. For how can the repeated attempts to join, or become one with *nothingness,* which is what fear is, ever create experiences other than conflict? Do you yet see the insanity you have created for yourself? And, it is this insanity which creates the very illusions you believe real. But, these illusions, created by the mind that believes fear is real, is the hell so often spoken of in your Bible and other religious texts.

I.1.39   Hell is no more real than any other twisted illusion created by a mind who believes that fear is as real as is Love.

And, until the last remnants, the last vestiges, of fear have been dissolved, Love will remain but a forgotten memory, just as unity and oneness have been. For they truly are inseparable.

I.1.40   This is the reason as to why an understanding of the Laws and their function are required. Because until they are understood, you will continue to create experiences which are fearful. Therefore, We do not ask that your mind give any thought to the Law of Cause and Effect. It will never be understood by the mind alone. You must come to *feel* the Law with your heart. For only by feeling the Law will it be recalled into your memory.

I.1.41   Allow your heart to speak to you – which means nothing more than to listen to the feeling – of the purpose of the Law, which is the same purpose given unto you by the Creator. What is this purpose? Your purpose, which is one with the Law, is that of creation, of extending only Love, of extending or giving only of your Self. Since you are *not* fear, you cannot extend or share it. You can only project it, which is nothing but your attempt to create as God does. This is why projection is rightly referred to as *miscreation*. For to extend like the Creator is but to extend only Love, to extend only that which is Real, to extend only your Self as God did in Our creation.

I.1.42   Thus, the Law of Cause and Effect is one with Whom and What We Are. We are Creators, created in the image and likeness of the Creator. Any attempt to create other than what you are in Truth will always lead to conflict, because by its very definition, *fear is conflict.*

I.1.43   Allow the memory of the Law of Cause and Effect to dawn once again upon your mind. Feel it. Feel its purpose. For, then, you will remember but your own. And, this return of memory will usher in the memory of your True Self, the Self which has been so long imprisoned behind the stone you rolled in front of your heart, hoping to erase and blot it out of existence.

I.1.44   As your memory of the Law returns, you will once again know that every thought simultaneously creates a feeling. And, the thought, which is but the causal agent, along with its feeling, the effect, creates an energy pattern of what is referred to as a belief. This, then, leads to the next in the series of Laws. For the Law of Cause and Effect immediately sets into motion the Law of Belief. This Law is given as, *Every thought, with its concurrent feeling, creates the energy of a belief.*

The Energy of Beliefs

I.1.45   The energy field of the belief is what manifests that which is seen and experienced. In addition, every thought, with its feeling, either creates a new belief or strengthens one already held in the mind. Thus, the Law of Belief is why you can only see and experience what you *believe* – think and feel – to be true about you, others, and the world around you. It is impossible to see and experience that which you do not believe. Why? Quite simply, because you have never had the thought and feeling to create the energetic frequency to create it.

I.1.46   As We are always with you, We sense your disbelief. For you but think to yourself that you have certainly had thoughts and feelings which did not lead to an experience. And, to this, We but point you to examine your beliefs even deeper than you have. Since there are no neutral thoughts, and every thought either strengthens an old belief or creates a new one, you can only see and experience the belief which has the highest vibration behind it.

I.1.47   For example, just because you entertain the thought of winning what you call the lottery does not mean that you will experience it, unless its energy signature is greater than those of other beliefs you hold within your mind. *Thoughts leave not their source.* As such, thoughts of lack and thoughts of unworthiness, which are but fear in disguise, that you have had and fed for a lifetime, carry with them a strong enough energetic field to cancel out the energy signature contained within a simple thought or two, what We refer to as a wish or fantasy, of winning the lottery.

I.1.48   As your consciousness is now expanding, We can now share with you the reason as to why affirmations seem to work. Affirmations are not based on some form of magic, they work simply because they call into function the two Laws that have been shared with you. At this point in our sharing, you should clearly begin to see and feel how affirmations work. For each time one is repeated, it strengthens a new belief. When the energy of that belief is greater than its opposing belief still being held within the mind, then you will begin to see and experience what you have been affirming.

I.1.49   Yet, can you see the inherent problem with affirmations? While affirmations are not *bad*, for nothing in Truth is bad, they do not dissolve the opposing belief. For the old belief is still being held within the mind. Affirmations only work when the energy of the new belief reaches the threshold to overcome the energy field of its opposing belief. Our question to you is: why create an opposing belief when simply dissolving the old belief is much more efficient and agreeable? For to create a belief which merely opposes another does not reflect or extend your True Self. In other words, it does not reflect oneness. Rather, in the case of affirmations, they but strengthen the belief in separation and division, regardless of the intention behind the affirmation.

I.1.50   We come to you now in order to collapse time. We are not here with you in this Holy Moment to share with you those things that serve no purpose. For that does not serve the Kingdom, which you are, as well as belong to. And, while We are not with you to share that you are doing anything wrong, We are here to share with you that which will aid you in experiencing oneness.

I.1.51   Therefore, We invite you to release those beliefs whose purpose is to keep the mind enslaved to division rather than unity. And, you have already received the means necessary to accomplish this. For you hold in your hands the means to release your mind from its self-created prison. In *The Way of Mastery,* you were told, *You cannot take fear into Love. You cannot take judgment into forgiveness. You cannot take limitations into unlimitedness. These things must be released at the level in which they were first created.*

I.1.52   In the above quote, the words *these things* are referring to the errors made by the mind. But, because the errors are believed real by the mind, the belief in their reality must first be challenged, then forever released back into the nothingness from which they were born. Yet, more specifically, you are being told that the original errors of judgment, guilt, fear, and the belief in limitations must be released on the level in which they first appeared. But, in order to do this, We must share with you where these errors hide within your consciousness. For until these errors are completely released, there still remains dark recesses hidden within your mind where the Light of Love is not welcomed. And, until Love is welcomed in its entirety, it is not welcomed at all.

CHAPTER 2

The Descent into Darkness: The First Split of the Mind

I.2.1   Now, We ask you to join Us as We shine the Light of Grace on a past that is not there. However, because of the continuation of the errors, the original errors remain behind a veil that appears so thick that the Light of Love cannot penetrate it. Yet, the veil is nothing but a shadow of what once was, but is no longer. The veil We speak of is the veil of separation. But, as you know, separation is not real. For the Atonement Principle is complete. And, you are whole.

I.2.2   In *A Course in Miracles,* it is written, *Into eternity, where all is one, there crept a tiny, mad idea, at which the Son of God remembered not to laugh. In his forgetting did the thought become a serious idea, and possible of both accomplishment and real effects. Together, We can laugh them BOTH away, and understand that time can NOT intrude upon eternity. It is a joke to think that time can come to circumvent eternity, which means there is no time.*

I.2.3   What was the tiny mad idea mentioned in those verses? We are here, now, to help you correct a common mistake often associated with that quote. Although the answer is given within the quote, the mind refuses to see it or accept it. For many students of the curriculum often answer the question with *separation was the tiny, mad idea.* But, to believe that separation was the tiny, mad idea is to ensure that the culprit remains concealed. And, it is this culprit which is the veil that keeps you from knowing and experiencing your True Self.

I.2.4   What is this culprit? It is but *TIME.* Yes! Time is the tiny, mad idea at which the Son of God, also known as the Sonship, remembered not to laugh. For time seems to be greater than you, because it seems capable of accomplishment and real effects. Separation was not the insane idea. Time was. For time allowed for the belief that you had separated from Source to not only take root, but to become one in which you believed happened. This is the meaning behind the phrase *his thought became a serious idea.* For time is taken seriously by all those who have ever walked, or currently walk, your planet.

I.2.5   We ask you, in this moment, the only one in time which intersects eternity, to release all thoughts you have ever had regarding time. You have given time its meaning. And, as We have told you before – time is meaningless, because time does not exist. Now, We are asking you to stop thinking about time, and allow yourself to feel it. Feel time. Feel the energy in the word *time*, itself. Yes! Feel the energy signature in the word *time*. If you are being honest with yourself, you can *feel* the energy of separation in the word. And, whenever there is a feeling of separation, the feeling, thus the experience, of oneness will not be yours. Yet, it must also be noted that the feeling associated with time, or separation, is that of fear. For what else could it be? Since time is not real, the feeling created by the thought of time can only be that of fear, since it too is not real.

I.2.6   This brings us to the second Lesson of this Course. If you will complete this exercise, you will come to feel and see the energy patterns of fear and Love. For when you can sense and recognize the energy of separation being called forth by a thought, you can immediately choose again. You can choose to entertain a different thought, one with an energy signature which calls forth and creates experiences of oneness, or those of Love, Joy, and Peace.

Lesson 2

I.2.7   For this lesson, simply write the word *time* on a small piece of paper or index card. Then, on another small piece of paper or index card, write the word *eternity* on it. Take no more than one minute per word per day, and simply look at it as you have written it. Allow yourself to feel the energy of that word.

33

Allow the feeling to move throughout your entire being. Do this for two weeks. You will quickly discover that this exercise has given you a new sense. Yet, this sense isn't new at all. But, it will seem new as you begin to feel energy patterns within thoughts and words that you think and speak, as well as the energy from the words spoken by others. Recognize, while it may feel new, it is but one of the Divine Abilities, often called gifts, given to you at creation.

I.2.8   Just as you did with the first exercise in this Course, play with this one. Play with it as if you were a child. Do not take it seriously. For to do so will decrease its efficacy. As you play with this lesson, allow the conscious expansion that will come to come without any fear attached to it. You will find the conscious expansion to be quite pleasant and spiritually delicious.

I.2.9   As you play with this exercise, allow yourself to feel the energy associated with time, itself, and not just the word. The more you recognize the energy field contained within the concept and belief in time, you will begin to feel the *terror* associated with it. When this feeling of terror strikes at your heart, do not cower at it. For you have bowed and sacrificed enough at its altar. You have worshipped it, all in the hopes that you will be spared from its effects, which is to wither back into the dust from which you were created. You bargain with time daily. You believe you are subject to its every whim. And, you see time as the great taker. For you believe it will take from you everything you believe you obtained in life.

I.2.10   Furthermore, time is referred to as *Father Time.* Stop here and feel the energy signature which swirls around those two words. For what you are feeling is the belief that *time* is God. And, this is the feeling that strikes terror within the hearts of man. For *Father Time* has replaced the memory of Our true Heavenly Father. And, in your forgetting the Source of All Creation, you have transposed your beliefs regarding *Father Time* onto your Heavenly Father. Is there any wonder that you have fear and terror within your mind and heart when you think of God? For now your Heavenly Father is seen as the One Who is vengeful and determined to visit upon you His Wrath at the time of His Choosing.

I.2.11   Look at your myths surrounding *Father Time.* He is depicted as a shadowy, dark figure, draped in a black hooded cloak, carrying a sickle, the symbol of reaping, in one of his hands. And, hidden within you is the fear that, at some point in the future, he will arrive and strike you down. To further instill fear into your concept regarding *Father Time*, death is envisioned as the same figure. Therefore, time and death have become synonymous.

I.2.12   O Dear Brother, how ridiculous this is. Share with Us in laughing away such foolishness. For neither time or death is real. They are but of your making. Our Father, Who is but Love, knows not of taking. For even the idea that something can be taken is one in which you made. Our Father only gives.

I.2.13   In your Bible, it is written, *The wages of sin is death, but the gift of God is eternal life.* Look at this Bible verse once again. For it is not sin which brings about death, it is time. For everything which enters into time must eventually die, even stars die. Yet, God's gift to His creations is eternal life. And, what God gives is as eternal as is He. In order for death to be real, God must know of death. But, We can assure you God knows not of death. And, since He knows not of death, He knows not of time.

I.2.14   We ask you now to laugh with Us at the nonsense behind both time and death. For only in laughter, which is simply the inspiration of Joy, given by God, can We shine the Light of Grace upon the dark myths which have imprisoned your mind in a cell of absolute terror. Join with Us as We watch the fear within you dissolve into the emptiness of nothing from which it came. Feel the Joy as it flows from the inner most depth of your Being. Feel it as it washes away the last vestiges of terror that have remained within your mind since the moment time was born within it. For until you release the stranglehold that time has upon your mind, every experience you have will still be of separation, of terror and fear, rather than the Love experienced in oneness.

I.2.15   In order to aid you in the collapsing of time from your mind, We turn to the beginning. We do not do this to give power to that which has none and is meaningless. We do so with you in order that We can stand alongside of you and point to the beginning of the reign of terror, which has created the nightmare of hell that you each have experienced. Together, We stand at the end of hell and look back at its beginning. Yet, while this may at first create discomfort and internal conflict, We must look back at the beginning, so that We can watch the collapse of what never was.

I.2.16   Time is the greatest illusion you have perpetrated against yourself. As such, time is the illusion in which all others rest. In other words, time is the base card in a house of cards. When the card of time is removed, the house of cards will come tumbling down. For every illusion projected from the mind is done so on the back of time. Without the belief in time, there could be no projection. Thus, the universe and the world you believe real will simply cease to seem to be when the belief in time is finally released by you. But, how did time come to preoccupy your mind?

I.2.17   To answer this question, We ask that you take our hand as We turn and look at the beginning of what seemed to occur, but in truth never happened. But, because you believe that it happened, it seems real to you. Hell has come to replace Heaven, and in your mind, hell is more real than Heaven, which is what you are. Neither hell or Heaven are places that exist outside or apart from you. Rather, both are states of awareness. Yet, only one is real, the other is but an illusion erected on the back of time. And, it is for this reason, We must look to the beginning, the beginning of the consciousness of hell. For both Heaven and hell live in your mind. And, as long as both remain there, you cannot experience the oneness and beauty that is Love, which is your birthright.

I.2.18   We turn now to that moment when darkness seemed to replace the Light of Truth within your mind. Because the mind is split between two realms, We must turn to the heart. For only the heart has the power to see past the illusions of the mind. These illusions hide the Truth from you. And, they will continue to do so until their spell is broken.

I.2.19   In order for the heart to dispel the illusions created in what seems like an ancient and distant past, We must have the heart speak to you now. While you read these words, do not allow the mind to take over. Do not attempt to recall the memory these words will elicit. Instead, allow the heart to feel these words. For it remembers the events which led the mind to believe that terror had come to replace Love.

I.2.20   We start with a passage in your Bible. For although it has been misunderstood for millennia, We bring what seems to have occurred in some distant past into this moment. Here is where the mind will recoil and attempt to derail this discussion. For the mind is firmly entrenched in the belief that time is real. But, time is not real. It does not exist. Only this moment exists. Therefore, what the mind believes occurred so long, long ago, is but dawning within your consciousness now. Feel these words, don't think of them. For your thoughts are both meaningless and pointless. Your thoughts are what created the hell for which darkens your mind.

I.2.21   In your Bible, the first verse is: *In the beginning, God created the heaven and the earth.* Feel those words. Let them move through you. Feel them to the innermost depth of your Being. The words, *In the beginning*, do not imply a past. For God knows not of a past, just as He knows not of a future. He but knows only of this Holy Moment. And, this moment is Holy, because He shares it with you. But, what are you sharing with Him?

I.2.22　To understand what you are sharing with Him, you must but *feel* the words contained within the next verse. *And the earth was without form, and void; and darkness was upon the face of the deep. And the Spirit of God moved upon the face of the waters.* This verse does not offer you a glimpse into the past. No! Rather, it is offering you a glimpse into the present, this very moment. For even now, you are but attempting to share darkness. But, darkness cannot be shared, for darkness does not exist in the Mind of God, or His Kingdom. And, you are His Kingdom. For you are His Beloved Child, His Beloved Extension of the Love for which He Is.

I.2.23　Return to the words, which state, *God created the heaven and the earth.* Feel them. Breathe into them. For these words contain the energy signature of a conflicted mind. The word *heaven* has the frequency of unity, while the word *earth* carries with it the energy signature of division and separation. Only to a split mind does the meaning of separateness have any value.

I.2.24　Look at those words again. This time *feel* the unity within them, instead of the division seemingly inherent within each word. Yes! Feel the unity. For when taken as a whole, the words carry an energy field that creates only oneness. To the mind, heaven and earth are distinct, separate places, each different in their states of being. Yet, in Truth, in God, they are but one. They are but whole. For God created both, together in oneness and wholeness.

I.2.25   You are but heaven and earth. They are not separate states of consciousness, nor are they separate and apart from each other. They are one. They are you. For you are both *Heaven* and *Earth*. However, you have come to identify with but one of these. Feel this! For do you not identify yourself as a human being? Of course you do. Yet, within the word *human,* you will but find the truth, which has been hidden from you since the beginning of time. For the word *human*, in the language you call English, was derived from the Latin word *humus*, meaning *earth,* combined with the English word *man*. Thus, you call yourself *human*, which simply means earth-man. Is this not your apparent reality? For do you not believe that you belong to a group of living entities, who collectively refers to itself as man, living on a planet you call earth?

I.2.26   Feel, then, the word *human*. When the mind attempts to make the word stand alone, you can feel the energy of separation. And, it is this energy for which you have become identified with, because you have identified yourself wholly as *human*. In the complete identification with being *human*, you have forgotten that another whole of you exists. This Self, which has been forgotten, is Heaven, which was also created by God.

I.2.27   O Holy Child, feel these next words. Experience their oneness. *You are both divine and human.* They are not separate as the mind would have you believe. For the mind accepts only the *human* part of you, and denies the *divine* you which also exists. You are a *divine-human*. More specifically, you are a *divine-earth man*. You are both wholly *divine* and wholly *human*. This is your True State of Being. And, until you accept this, you will continue to create *only* human experiences, which will reflect nothing but the frequency of separation and division. Only when you rejoin your seeming separate states of being can you create experiences of oneness and unity. In your current state of consciousness, you can only project fear, because you are trying to live a lie. You are trying to be only *human*. When you live in the oneness of your True Nature, as that of a *divine-human*, then you can but extend only Love, which is to create experiences of unity and oneness. And, this is your function, which is to create like the Creator. But, a half-you cannot create. It can only project, because you are not sharing and extending the whole of you: the *divine* as well the *human*.

I.2.28   This is what We refer to as the first-split of the mind. It is the result of asking, *What am I?* This question is still being asked by you. However, the mind cannot answer this question alone. For your mind has sought for this answer for ages; yet, it has never found it. For the mind searches outside itself for an answer that can only be found within. Now, We ask you to turn to your heart once again so that you may *feel* the Truth as it comes forth from deep within you.

I.2.29   Do you not yet *feel* the energy pattern in the question, *What am I?* For the feeling created from this thought is fear. It is terror. The question, which is the cause, created its corresponding feeling, which is fear. Together, through the workings of the Law of Belief, time was born. Yet, let Us go even deeper into the energy field of the question. For in Our *feeling* it, We will see the very energy of the ideas of time and separation.

I.2.30   While the question, *what am I,* appears benign and innocuous, it carries with it the energy signature of *denial.* And, denial is as total as Love is. For as you question what you are, you are denying some part of the Whole Self. Which part of your Self have you denied? By now, it should be obvious. You have denied your Divine Nature. By denying this part of yourself, you have been denying your Eternal Self, the Self of Love. And, from your continued denial of your Eternal Self, time is born with each passing second. In other words, with each tick of the second hand of what you call a clock, you create time.

I.2.31   Therefore, time wasn't created billions of years ago, it is being created by you this very moment. Thus, with your creation of time, you are but denying your Eternal Self. And, by denying what We have referred to as your *Divine Self,* you have become identified with only your human self. Furthermore, with this denial, you have completely forgotten both who and what you are.

I.2.32   Now, We are going to dive deeper into the feeling created by denial. Recognize, that with each second that passes by, you are choosing to deny God, because you are choosing to deny the Whole Self created by Him. And, each moment you deny God, you are choosing not-God. Feel the energy associated with the statement, *not-God.* Feel it deeply to the core of your being. For the energy signature created by the statement is the energy field which creates the experiences of a personal-self. And, this is the great illusion of time. For only in time can there be a personal-self, a self that cannot be shared or extended.

I.2.33   With the identification as a personal-self, you are concurrently identifying as *not-God*. And, through this identification, you can but create conflict, because you are aware on a subconscious level, that you are denying your *Divine Self*. Furthermore, by denying your *Divine Self,* you can but experience creations which are seen as separate, and are therefore fearful.

I.2.34   Yet, the question, *What am I,* while a thought, is more than just a question. For the question is a judgment. And, this is the first judgment made, and is still being made every moment you remain in time. We want you to feel the energy signature of the word *judgment.* And, as you do, let Us take a closer look at the word, so that you can recognize the field of energy around the thoughts which are judgments. Although you believe that some judgments are better than others, all judgments have the same energy pattern, which also means that they have the same effect.

I.2.35   But, how is the question, *What am I,* a judgment? For it is after all, nothing but a question. This is where We must now discuss *intention.* For while words are themselves meaningless, it is the intention that the thought conveys which gives both the thought and its words their power. And, it is from the intention of the thought which determines the energy field of the thought,

45

itself. Therefore, it is the energy of intention behind each thought which ultimately creates what you see and experience. Come then to understand and feel just how powerful intention is.

I.2.36   Intention is everything. And, the intention behind each thought does not come from somewhere outside of yourself, it comes from within you. For your intention, at all times, is completely your responsibility. In Reality, there is only the pure intention of Love. Yet, in your current conscious state, there appears to be another intention, which opposes, or contradicts Love. But nothing can oppose Love. For Love is God. And, in Truth, nothing opposes God.

I.2.37   Like all thoughts, those which are considered judgments, are nothing more than energy in motion. However, while you think judgments are levied against someone or something that has harmed you either physically or emotionally, the energy of a judgment, or more specifically, the energy of the intention, is one that binds the mind. For judgments, like all thoughts, leave not their source. But unlike thoughts of Love, which can be shared, judgments cannot be shared. Instead, judgments and their effects are directed within toward your own mind. In short, the energy field is directed at your own mind.

I.2.38   To ask the question, *What am I,* is therefore a judgment because the energy signature and its vibrational frequency is directed internally. Furthermore, the intention behind the question is that of seeking. And, to seek for anything implies that there is something missing within. In the case of the question, it is the *not-knowing* which is the problem. Since God is All Knowing, to *not-know* what you are, means that you judge yourself as *not-God.*

I.2.39   This too is demonstrated in your Bible, and is found in its second creation story. In the story, the female, Eve, eats of the fruit from the tree of knowledge, because she looked at it as something that would make her wise. Feel what the intention is from this Bible story. See within it the energy pattern of its signature. For in order for Eve to look upon the fruit as something that would give her knowledge means that she questioned what she was. Therefore, she judged herself as *not-having* this knowledge. Furthermore, those Bible verses, which tell the story, are ones which demonstrate that the knowledge of self must be outside of you, and that you must seek for that thing which will provide you with the answer.

I.2.40   Therefore, to continually ask yourself, *What am I,* is to levy the judgment against yourself of being *not-God.* Thus, the energy pattern for any judgment is always the same. For it always carries the energy pattern of being *not-God.* And, to believe that you are *not-Divine,* demonstrates that you have identified wholly as human. This, then, is the error which must be corrected.

I.2.41   Let Us return to the biblical narrative of the second creation story. In it, the woman's name is Eve. Feel the energy pattern associated with that word, that thought. For her name quite literally means *darkness.* Yes! Her name means darkness. The intention, then, is one of judgment. For if God is Light, and We assure you that He is, then darkness implies *not-God.* Therefore, the words *not-God, darkness,* and Eve all carry the same vibrational energy frequency. For they all represent judgment.

I.2.42   In *A Course in Miracles,* it is written, *How does the Son of God awaken. It is a dream of judgment. Judge not. And he will waken.* There is important information given within that text. For the dream is a judgment. And, the original judgment is that of making of yourself *not-God.* And, to be *not-God* means you have to be outside of eternity. And, time is the culprit, or the serpent as mentioned in your Bible.

I.2.43   Remember, in the second creation story, the serpent told Eve that she would not die if she ate the fruit from the tree of knowledge. The serpent symbolizes *time*. And, time is the lie. It is the illusion. For only in *time* does the idea of death seem like a real effect of the judgment.

I.2.44 We ask of you but this: *feel* the first-splitting of the mind. Sense and feel the energy pattern associated with judgment. The energy signature of every judgment made is the same, regardless of the judgment made. And, all judgments that you make reflect but the first judgment made, which is the thought of being *not-God*.

I.2.45 Recall that the energy of a judgment only affects the mind that entertained it. But, how can this be? We shall now share with you the full effect on the mind that the energy pattern of judgments create. Yet, in order to bring this into your awareness, We ask that you allow both your mind and heart to open. Simply observe the energy associated around the word *judgment* as We take you into the energetic effects created by the word.

I.2.46 Remember, the word *judgment*, itself, is meaningless. It is the intention behind the word, given by you, that gives it the power it has. Therefore, We now invite you to join us as We examine the word. *Judgment* is simply the capacity to judge. Your word *judge* came to you from the Latin word *judicare*, which had the meaning *to decide rightly.* Here is where you have not fully understood what making judgments has done to the mind. For within the word *decide* is the energy pattern of what you call *death.*

I.2.47   Feel the energy pattern of the word *decide.* For in it you will *feel* death. This might frighten you at first. For this is the terror which has gripped your mind since the beginning of the nightmare of hell, for which you continue to experience. You are not alone. We are with you in this moment as We have always been and will always be.

I.2.48   Now, focus your awareness on the word *decide.* In your mind, see the word as *de-cide.* Bring your awareness to the ending of the word *-cide.* For the ending of the word *decide* should sound familiar. It is found in other words you use, most notably *homicide, suicide, genocide, pesticide,* and so many others. Your mind already knows the meaning, which is *to kill.* But, how does this fit into the word *decide?*

I.2.49   Again, We ask you to *feel* the energy of the word. Do not try to understand it with the mind. For that is impossible. However, *feel* the intention within the word. For the intention is the creative energy given of the Creator, Himself. You create via intention. In other words, you create via the endless

50

potential contained within the Field of Energy, or that which is God.

I.2.50   The word *decide* quite literally means *to kill*. When this meaning is transposed into the word *judgment*, then the word *judgment* means to kill, or visit *death* upon, rightly. In other words, the energy field of every judgment you make is the energy of death. Is it any wonder that you live in a constant state of terror? Just as *A Course in Miracles* taught you that this experience, the one you are currently having, is *a dream of judgment*, it is then nothing more than *a dream of death*. And, every time you levy a judgment upon anything or anyone, you are levying *death* upon yourself.

I.2.51   When the question, *What am I*, entered your consciousness, it was from having judged yourself as *not-having* the knowledge of *I Am*, which is God. Therefore, the judgment was to decide, as you still do, to be *not-God*. Since *I Am* is Life, to be *not-I Am* is to be death. And, this is the beginning of the reign of terror for which you have visited upon yourself long enough. The end of the reign of terror has come. But, in order to experience the end, We must continue our visitation of the beginning.

I.2.52   The intention, or the energy signature, of *not-God* is death. Thus, when the question, *What am I,* entered into your conscious field of awareness, it is because there was the intention of death upon the *I Am.* For to decide with *not-God,* is to visit death upon the Divine Self. Yet, you cannot *kill* the Divine Self. Even the thought of it is lunacy. It is why We ask that you laugh at such insanity. Together, We will laugh at its meaninglessness.

I.2.53   O Holy Brother, in your deciding to be *not-God,* you believed you killed God. And, in that fateful moment, time was born. With each judgment made, time is born anew. It is for this reason We invite you to relinquish judgment. For the wages of judging is time. And, the wages of time is death. Put another way, *the effect of judgment is time, and the effect of time is death.*

I.2.54   Let Us continue our exploration into the insanity from which the world, the world of the living-dead, where you come to live out that fateful decision of judgment over and over, and yet over again. How many ways are there to die? You have attempted every one of them. For you will not settle for anything less than your own death, since you believe you killed God. Do you yet *feel* the insanity in such a twisted belief? For until you feel the insanity, you cannot free the mind. For the mind holds its belief that it killed God sacrosanct. And, this is where We must shine the Light of Truth. This belief must be released before the reign of terror can be brought to an end.

I.2.55   It is in this most holy moment that We come to share with you the Truth of what is, so that you might release that which never was. We are going to dispel the myths which the mind has conjured in order to hold you captive to its judgment and ensuing terror. What We will share with you will create the experience of disbelief in some, and rage in others. For the mind protects these beliefs with a defense network more powerful than any defenses used by armies and nations of your world. To the mind, its beliefs have become holy. It bows in reverence at the altar erected to worship *not-God.*

I.2.56   We ask you to *feel* what is being revealed. Recognize the energy frequency carried by Our thoughts. For it is the energy of freedom. It is the energy of release. It is the energy of your True Being.

I.2.57   We would like to address the myths around what you call the Book of Revelation, as found in your Bible. The very word *revelation* means *to be revealed.* What was revealed is not of some future time, or even of a past. For neither exist. It reveals the war, what some call the Heavenly War, that rages in this very moment. This war is not in some far off place, it is the war that rages within you. For were you not told, by the man you call Jesus, that *the Kingdom of Heaven is within you?* If Heaven is within you, then you must be Heaven. Thus, the war that rages, is the internal conflict that exists within you this very moment. For if you are not experiencing Peace, you must be experiencing war.

I.2.58   As We begin this portion of Our discussion, We ask that you not attempt to find any meaning to what you are reading. The mind has already twisted the message given by the Awakened Christ, which is but your True Self, the Self that is the Divine Human. Therefore, do not search the mind's memory for what it has learned, for it truly knows not what the revelation is or means. Instead, We invite you to *feel* each word as you read it. Identify each energy signature contained within the words. Then, observe the energy pattern as a whole, for which it is in truth. This is the beginning of the reunification of the personal, human-self with its Divine Self.

I.2.59   Although you will be reading of your descent into madness, if you will allow yourself to *feel* the energetic vibrational frequency associated with the belief into the descent of darkness, you will discover the energy within yourself which must be released. This descent into madness, into the insanity still held in the mind, is the energy that brought forth the world of illusions and dreams, which still keeps the mind entranced. For you are still perpetuating it in this moment.

I.2.60   Now, focus your intention on the words written in the Book of Revelation, *And he causeth all, both small and great, rich and poor, free and bond, to receive a mark in their right hand, or in their foreheads: and that no man shall buy or sell, save he that had the mark, or the name of the beast, or the number of his name. Here is wisdom. Let him that hath understanding count the number of the beast: for it is the number of a man, and his number is six hundred three score and six.*

I.2.61   Those words have caused many a man to tremble. For they seem to point to a future when a man, who some have called the *anti-Christ*, will rise and bring great tribulation into the world. Our question for you is this: *have you not yet experienced tribulation?* The answer to all, who are honest with themselves, is *of course We have.*

I.2.62   This biblical narrative isn't of a time yet to come, it is of a time long since gone. It is of a time that has been overcome. It is of a time which no longer exists. For the verses describe your current state of being, and nothing more. The narrative tells of your descent into madness, otherwise known as an incarnation into the physical realm.

I.2.63 The *he* being referred to in the beginning of the narrative is the self which identified as *not-God*. It is but the self you believe yourself to be. But, what is this mark which seems to be a foretelling of coming events that is mentioned within the story?

I.2.64 *Feel* it as We once again reveal unto you the story of the descent into the realm of hell, itself. For what you are about to be told is considered heresy to the mind. But, what the mind hears as heresy, the heart hears as its release.

I.2.65 You, O Divine One, have already accepted the *mark of the beast*. What is this mark? It is but flesh. It is but the garment for which you refer to as a body. Now, We but ask you to answer a question. Answer it not in thought, but in *feeling*. Allow your heart to answer the question: *without your body would you be able to buy or sell anything?* For isn't the body required to perform these tasks?

I.2.66   Yes! This revelation has created anxiety within the mind. This is what We aim for. We must bring the mind to question everything, so that it will be ready to surrender its madness. For only in its surrender can the mind be released from its madness. The mind must surrender in order for the heart to heal it and restore it to wholeness and unity. As has been stated before, you wage but a war with yourself. And, like all wars, there must be a side willing to surrender, so that Peace might return.

I.2.67   Let's return once again to the biblical narrative, where it is written, *Here is wisdom. Let him that hath understanding count the number of the beast: for it is the number of a man, and his number is Six hundred three score and six.* While in truth, this number, which has come to represent the *anti-Christ,* is meaningless. The wisdom eluded to in the verse cannot be known by the mind, it can only be felt by the heart. For the number, 666, is the number of a man. It is the number of every man who has chosen the mark of the beast – *the flesh of the body.*

I.2.68   The energy, which is contained within the number 666, will be better understood when We share it as *6, 6, 6.* This number is the representation of the carbon atom. Yes! The number, 666, symbolizes the carbon atom. And, all life, as you define it and have come to know it, is made of carbon. For without carbon, the physical realm would not appear as it does. The number 666 represents the fact that carbon has six protons, six electrons, and six neutrons. Furthermore, for a carbon atom to be stable, it must chemically form four bonds. Why is this important?

I.2.69   Carbon requires four electrons in order for its *energetic shield*, known as its electron cloud, to be stable. As with all things within the physical realm, it symbolizes something from the higher realms. In this case, the reason that carbon requires four bonds to be energetically stable is because each bond represents one of the four splits of the mind. For the physical realm cannot be experienced without some aspect of stability. Although it is illusory, the illusion must be stable enough for it to entrance the mind into believability. And, this it has done.

I.2.70   Now, We ask that you focus your awareness on the word *anti-Christ*. We ask you to *feel* its energy. For it is the energy of *not-God*. It is the energy which keeps you entranced. The moment of your freedom is upon you. For it is time for the trance to end – or to *transcend*. The trance ends now. But, you must *feel* the energy and recognize its pattern. Or, you are subject to fall back into the sleep from which you are now awakening.

I.2.71   While the word *anti-Christ* fosters uncertainty and fear, We are with you to shine the Light of Grace upon it, so that it will dissolve back into the nothingness from which it came. Our discussion will again create anxiety and mistrust within the mind, and this is exactly as We, and you, would have it. However, let the heart whisper to you of the Truth it knows.

I.2.72   In your Bible, it is written: *God is spirit, and those who worship him must worship him in spirit and truth.* These words reveal great truth and wisdom. Feel them. Feel their energy. For this is the energy of creation, not projection. It is the energy pattern of your True Self, the Self that is the extension of God.

I.2.73   God is spirit. And, since He is spirit, as His Extension, your True Self is spirit, as well. What does this mean? Simply this: you cannot be a body. You can experience a body, yes! But, you are not a body. In truth, while this will anger the mind, you do not even have a body. For to have a body, would imply that you are a body. And, this would negate the Spiritual Law of Being.

I.2.74   The Law of Being is the Law that defines oneness. This Law can be stated as: *to give, is to have; and, to have is to be.* Again, We ask you to feel the Law. Just like the other Laws We have discussed, this Law maintains the unity of Truth. As such, you cannot *have* a body, because you would then *be* a body. In addition, to *have* a body means you could *give* your body. And, to *give* a body is senseless and meaningless. Why is this?

I.2.75   Because God is spirit, only spirit can be *given*, or extended. To give, or to extend, is to create, which is to share the Self. Since you cannot share your body, you cannot create with or from it. Can you yet *feel* the energy pattern of your body? The energy pattern is the same as the energy of judgment. For it carries the energy signature of *not-God*. It is the energy field of both time and separation, which are themselves meaningless. For they all carry the same energy signature, that of death.

I.2.76   It is in accordance with the Law of Being as to why you were informed in *A Course in Miracles* that the body is neutral. For the body is nothing more than an experience. Yet, the mind believes itself to be a body. And, it is this belief which must be uprooted so that you may once again return to your function as a creator and extend the Love for which you are.

I.2.77   The idea, the thought, the intention of death must be laid down. Yet, while death seems to be all around you, the mind has inverted death by equating it with life, and life with death.

Here, in this moment, We invite you to join Us, the Living. But, to do so, you must come to *feel* the icy grip of death once more. Yet, you have never left it, since the thought, the tiny, mad idea of *time* came to replace eternity within your mind.

I.2.78   Once again, We invite you to feel the words that were given to mankind nearly two millennia ago. These words are also found in your Bible. Feel each word as you read the passage. Feel, too, the wholeness of the passage. For its wholeness but attests to your current state of consciousness.

I.2.79   *And he* (Jesus) *said unto another, Follow me. But he* (the man) *said, 'Suffer me first to go and bury my father. Jesus said unto him, Let the dead bury their dead: but go thou and preach the kingdom of God.*

I.2.80   To the mind, not only are these verses laughable, they have no contextual meaning. But, to the heart, these verses are heard as the call to awaken. Realize, now, in this most Hallowed Moment, the heart hears the call, but the mind has been deafened to it. For the mind hears it not, because it is lost in the maze of illusions, the maze made by its own thoughts.

I.2.81 Look again at the verse, for the man known as Jesus was imparting his inner wisdom. He was simply telling his brother to *let the dead bury their own.* However, there is a much deeper revelation hidden in those verses. It has always been there, but your mind was not yet ready to hear the truth, much less surrender the fight. The message is found in the words spoken by the man to Jesus. For the man says, *Suffer me first to go and bury my father.*

I.2.82 O Holy Brother, it is but your narrative which was spoken. It is the same narrative spoken today. Although the truth may at first sting, it will set you free. Remember, it was the intention, the energy of the judgment, found in the *not-knowing* of what you are, in which you believed you had killed the Father, Our Creator and Source of Life. You believed you murdered Him. But, as laughable as it appears now, it was not the Father you murdered through the intention behind the question, *What am I?* It was but your Self you murdered.

I.2.83 We feel the recoiling taking place in the mind. But, this is necessary in order to dislodge the false belief system which has become so entrenched that its root system has pierced every aspect of your consciousness, as well as your experiences. Yet, how is this possible? How is it that you murdered your Self, but yet you seem to live?

I.2.84　The answer to this question is also found in the Spiritual Laws, specifically the Law of Love. This Law states: *What you give another, you gift but unto yourself.* The Law of Love is the one Law that unifies them all. For this Law is woven through all of the others. And, it is the Law which ensures wholeness is maintained within the Kingdom.

I.2.85　If you will allow yourself to *feel* the Law at work when the judgment was made, and is made in each moment, you will come to see how the energy field responded and continues to respond. For when you thought you murdered the Divine Self by choosing to question it, under the Law, this thought was extended, or *given.* However, the intention, or the energy with its effect was actually gifted but to yourself. Therefore, you are the one who was killed. In other words, it was but you that died. This is why Jesus told the young man, *Let the dead bury their dead.*

I.2.86　Allow the feelings of this statement to pierce your mind. Allow the energy field contained within that statement to bring the mind to its knees. For have you not tasted the bitterness of rotting flesh long enough.

I.2.87   Let Us return to those Bible verses. For there is yet deeper truths buried within them. Recall, this is your narrative. Jesus is speaking to you. But, reread the words spoken by the young man. Hear and feel your own voice in that of the man, when he said, *Suffer me*....Feel those words. For they but reflect your subconscious beliefs, those beliefs hidden within the absolute darkness of the mind.

I.2.88   *Suffer me.* As you will see, the energy of the word *suffer* carries the same energy as the word *death*. They are the same. But, how can this be? The answer is of your creation. For the word *suffer* means *to endure death*. In other words, the intention behind the word *suffer* is the energy field, thus the experience, of *death*. Yet, your creation becomes even more morbid as We share the energy signature of the word *endure* with you.

I.2.89   In order to recognize the energy signature of the word *endure*, you must come to understand what the thought is behind the word. When you think of the word *endure*, you are really stating a wish, or a *not-God* desire, which is *to remain in the same state*. Can you feel the energy pattern? For it is that of separation. Therefore, each time you think of *suffering*, regardless of the reason, is to set the energy in motion of *remaining in the same state of death* that you are currently experiencing. Because, in the state of death, you remain in time and free from that which is eternal. Is there any wonder why you have continued to believe that *suffering* is good for the soul? For the mind believes that suffering is righteous. Yet, the mind understands not what it does or asks for.

CHAPTER 3

The Descent into Darkness: The Belief in Guilt

I.3.1   The judgment, which was the intention behind the question, *What am I,* created the feeling of terror experienced by the mind. As noted in the Law of Belief, a thought and feeling creates a belief. And, the belief creates what is seen and experienced. The belief created by the first, or original judgment, and its associated feeling of energy created what We call *the belief in separation.* For having *believed* that you killed the Divine Aspect of All That Is, time was created, which meant you were no longer experiencing the eternal. For you were in your creation, and this creation is what is referred to as *time.* Time is meaningless because you did not share it with God, that part of your Divine Self. And, because the energy signature is that of *death,* you in essence past from eternity and came into time.

I.3.2   Furthermore, with the original judgment, you exchanged Heaven for hell. But, what is hell? While the thought of hell conjures up differing images depending on your past experiences and upbringing, hell is nevertheless your creation. We invite you to once again *feel* the energy pattern around the idea, the notion, the concept of hell. The energy signature is simply that of separation, of death. For that is its intention, which is but to keep the belief of separation moving from one moment into the next.

I.3.3   Take a moment to *feel* the very definition you have given the word *hell*. Feel the energy of intention contained within it. Hell: *A nether world where the dead continue to exist; a state of misery; and, a state of turmoil and destruction.* The energy pattern associated with the word is merely the same as that of *not-God*. It is the energy signature of *death* and destruction yet again. Are you beginning to see and *feel* a pattern yet?

I.3.4   Hell, just like Heaven is a state of consciousness, a state of awareness. Because you *believe* you have been cut off from Heaven, you can only see and experience hell. But, how did the consciousness come to create such a state for itself? The answer lies in what you call your past. However, in truth, since there is no past, you are deciding upon it this moment, the only one that exists.

I.3.5   We ask you once again to allow yourself to *feel* the energy, the intention, of yet another word. That word is *exist*. As you just read, the word *exist* is contained within the definition of the word *hell*. In the first portion of its definition, the word *hell* is given the meaning, *a nether world where the dead continue to "exist."* And, We just shared with you that this moment is the only one which *exists*. Therefore, the word carries with it a very definitive energy signature. We ask that you *feel* it as We bring this word into your consciousness.

I.3.6   The definition of the word *exist*, as given, is: *to have being in a specified place or with respect to understood limitations or conditions; to live at an inferior level or under adverse circumstances.* Do you feel the energy signature of the word? Do you recognize it yet? For it is but the energy pattern of *the belief in punishment.*

I.3.7   *Punishment* has become one of the central themes of your state of current consciousness. The belief in punishment carries with it sights and experiences for which you have become all too familiar with. The very definition of the word demonstrates the energy pattern contained within the intent behind it. For the word *punishment* means *suffering, pain, or loss that serves as retribution.* And, We have already had you experience the energy field of the word *suffer*.

I.3.8   Therefore, the energy signature of the word *punishment* is the same as the word *suffer*, which is the energy pattern of *death*. For in the belief of hell as a place of punishment is the intention, is the energy, of death. As you are becoming more

68

and more aware of the true nature of intention, or energy patterns, you are beginning to see how all the energy used by your current state of consciousness is to maintain *the belief in death,* which is merely to maintain *the belief in time.*

I.3.9   This is why you were told in *A Course in Miracles* that *death is the central theme of the dream.* But like the mind always does, it interprets death at some future point in time. For the conscious aspect of the mind is completely unaware that it is experiencing death in the moment. Where, then, does this desire to remain in death, this desire to be punished, reside?

I.3.10   It resides deep within your subconscious. It remains hidden in the vast darkness for which the subconscious is. The subconscious is hell, Our Friend. It is where the *separated* mind quakes in absolute terror. For the darkness is so complete that not one ray of the Light of Truth resides there.

I.3.11   As We have already shared with you, hell isn't a place, it is merely a state of consciousness. It is where the dead tremble in terror for what they believe they have done. It is for this very reason that, in your world's ancient mythologies, hell was referred to as the *underworld,* where the dead went to be judged.

I.3.12   The *underworld* is your subconscious mind. It is the condition of death and judgment. For buried deep within the subconscious mind, the *underworld,* is the memory of the original judgment and its associated terror. In other words, the subconscious is the realm of the energy pattern of death and hell. Furthermore, it is that energy pattern of death found within the subconscious mind which penetrates the conscious mind. This energy is then projected in order to maintain the *belief in death.*

I.3.13   Yet, where and how did this twisted belief arise? While none of what We will share with you actually is real, you believe it happened and is happening. And, until the belief is shattered within the subconscious mind, you will continue to create experiences of hell and death, even though Heaven and Life are all around you, because they are within you.

I.3.14   Again, We ask that you allow your mind to open to what the heart has to reveal. For as We share it with you, We join through Our Heart in order to bring an ancient, but current, memory into your conscious awareness. Together, in our unity and joining, We will not fail. For your release and freedom are guaranteed. Therefore, We but ask that you allow the *feeling* brought about by the remembrance to wash through you. For you must *feel it to heal it.*

I.3.15 When the original judgment, which was the intent behind the question, *What am I,* raced through your mind, it created the feeling of terror as We have previously discussed. Together the judgment and feeling created the belief in time as you are well aware of now. This belief in time carried with it an energy signature that triggered the Spiritual Law of Creation. This Law simply states: *what is believed real extends throughout the energy field of potentiality to create the experience to demonstrate its reality unto the believer.*

I.3.16 In accordance with the Law of Creation, the belief in time became a creation within the field of energetic potentiality and possibility, in order for you to experience it. Within that first tick of time, that first passing second, the terror of your creation became unbearable to the mind. As a result, the mind split again. And, a new level, a new dimension, of consciousness was born. We use the term *born* appropriately here, because it came into being in the conscious state of the awareness of time. For the energy of that which is eternal had been denied and forgotten.

I.3.17　With the second splitting of the mind came the division of what you call the Soul and Spirit. We invite you to *feel* the energy signature of these words. For while they are one and united in truth, each word carries its own energy signature. Only in a mind which is entranced in separation does the energy contained within each word appear separate and distinct from each other.

Lesson 3

I.3.18　Now, We approach the third lesson in this Course: *The Joining of Soul with Spirit.* As you did with the previous lesson, write the word *Soul* on a slip of paper, or index card. Then, write the word *Spirit* on a separate piece of paper or index card. Unlike the previous lessons, this one has two parts to it.

I.3.19　First, simply look at the words for one minute each. Do not attempt to define the words. That is not the point of this lesson. Rather, simply *feel* the energy pattern associated with each word. Do this for three of your days. The second phase of this exercise is as simple as the first. On the reverse side of the card labeled *Soul*, write the word *Mind.* On the piece of paper, or index card, that has the word *Spirit* written on it, write the word *Heart* on its reverse side.

I.3.20   Once again, do not attempt to define the words. For that is both pointless and meaningless. Instead, just as you did before, sit with each card for one minute. Become familiar with the energy signature contained within the thought of that word. *Feel* the energy of intention behind each word. You will discover that the energy pattern for the words *Soul* and *Mind* are identical, just are the energy signatures of the words *Spirit* and *Heart*.

I.3.21   Your recognition of these energy patterns will become a part of your awareness as a result of completing this lesson. For these energies must ultimately be reunited in order for you to experience your True Function, which is that of Extending Love, also known as creating. You have been called to fulfill a grand function, the purpose given unto you by Our Creator and Source of Being.

I.3.22   We invite you, now, to return the focus of your awareness on that which We have called the second splitting of the mind. Recall, the terror experienced from the first split of the mind, created the second split. This splitting of the mind is where the separation between the *Mind* and *Heart* occurred. In other words, it is where the *Soul* and *Spirit* separated. This separation had a deleterious effect upon the mind. For it seemed to have made the belief in separation both possible and with real effects.

I.3.23   In your complete identification as a separated one, the *Spirit* within was forgotten. And, the mind trembling in terror once again turned its fear onto the *Spirit*, making it something to be feared and loathed simultaneously. For the mind no longer saw or experienced Love. Therefore, the mind began, and still does see Love as something to be feared. But where did this fear come from?

I.3.24   When the mind believed itself to be separate from eternity, and found itself within time, this experience further strengthened the belief created by the original judgment and its corresponding terror. The mind, having already split again for the second time, had a new thought, one never before had by a Child of God. What was this new thought? It was but guilt.

I.3.25   Just as all thoughts do, this thought of guilt, created a corresponding feeling. That feeling was also fear. Remember, there are but two feelings, Love or fear. What is not Love is fear. But, fear is not real. Yet, because you *believe* it real, as in accordance of the Laws of Belief and Creation, you experience it, making it appear real to you.

74

I.3.26   Recognize, now, the energy pattern created by the thought of guilt and its corresponding fear. *Feel* it. Do not turn away from it and wall yourself off. For this is what you have been doing for eons. And, you are currently doing it. This guilt and its fear have controlled you long enough. You have come to a point in your conscious evolution to stand and look upon your creations. See them for what they are. See their nothingness. For they are nothing, because they were not shared with God, the First Cause of all Creation. Without the Extension of His Energy, nothing you think real is real. It is but a projection, a feeble attempt to create without the Creator. And, this Dear Brother and Sister is your safety. For in it is found your freedom and release of the hell you made to punish but yourself.

I.3.27   Your creations have become your kingdom. But you rule over a kingdom of death and destruction. It is a paltry kingdom at best. For without the Light of God, all of your feeble attempts to create are meaningless and futile. For every creation withers and dies. What else could happen? You who but experience *death* can create nothing but death, for you have forgotten what it means to Live, to be Alive, and to experience only Joy and Peace, as can only be experienced by one who has laid aside his creations for those given by God.

I.3.28   This is only accomplished in oneness. And, this is why this Course is being given to you. But, you must be willing to receive it. *You need do nothing.* For it has been done for you. It is complete. At this point, We but invite you into the *feeling* of oneness. Feel it, so you might begin to enjoy the sweet and gentle experiences that oneness creates.

I.3.29   We will, from time-to-time, remind you of the purpose of this Course, so that you may begin to experience the exhilaration of unity. However, We return to your creation, the one you must finally decide against. Yes! You must consciously decide against it, so that it passes away, so that it *will simply seem to cease to be.* For in its death is your resurrection.

I.3.30   Look then at the beginning. This time, look upon the beginning without trembling in fear. Instead, raise your head as the Love for which you are begins to once again flow through your being. For the time has come to look upon the thought of guilt that arose in your mind. But to do so, We must roll the stone away from your heart. For its Light is the Light that will illuminate the path ahead of us as We descend into the realm of darkness, the realm of the subconscious mind, the realm where the Son of God trembles in terror at what awaits Him.

Fear not O Son of God, We are with you now. Together, We journey into what some refer to as the abyss. But, We recognize it as simply the dreams of a frightened Brother. Take Our Hand.

CHAPTER 4

The Descent into Darkness: Victimhood

I.4.1   Here, We journey into the mind's belief that it should be punished. For it is this singular belief that has crippled the mind to such an extent that it can no longer distinguish fantasy from reality. For what once seemed impossible has become the twisted fantasy of experience for the mind so lost in its contorted beliefs that fantasy is seen as reality, while Reality has been fictionalized.

I.4.2   When the separated mind had the thought of guilt, the energy pattern created the experience of what has become known as the ego. We have yet to use this word, because its energy signature, while that of death, is aggrandized by that same mind. For it feels worthy in its littleness, while boastful of its own creations, namely the kingdom of hell, in which it reigns supreme and with an iron fist clenched in defiance and opposition at the One whom it believes will *take* from it all that it has made and deemed acceptable.

I.4.3   What is the ego? It is nothing. It has no meaning. For it was born in time. It was born in death, in the denial of the

Truth, the Truth for which you are. It is nothing more than the belief that the mind pulled off the impossible: that it separated itself from All That Is. It is merely the belief that it is only human without being or acknowledging its own Divinity.

I.4.4   It is simply the consciousness of *"I."* The ego has been labeled, named, divided into parts, and studied, and studied even yet again. But, those who have done this have done nothing but study that which is their own self. For while the ego has become associated with all that is wrong with the world, you have simply misunderstood what it is. For the word *ego* is but the Latin word for your word *"I."*

I.4.5   We would ask that you feel the energy signature of the ego. Recognize that the egoic mind is the mind that harbors guilt. In *A Course in Miracles,* it is given that *consciousness is correctly identified as the domain of the ego.* But, what does this imply? For within that statement is an energy pattern that seems to give the ego its power. Yet, the power to create has always been yours. For you are an Extension of the Creator. Thus, every desire, whether from the higher realms, or those from the lower ones, are simply the impulse to be what you are – a creator.

I.4.6   Focus, now, your attention to the statement, *consciousness is correctly identified as the domain of the ego.* Feel the energy signature in the whole of the statement. For it is one of opposition. And, it is this opposition which is the impetus for the internal and external conflict you experience. The internal conflict is the Heavenly War We have shared before with you. And, this internal war is projected outward so that you can experience in the physical the war you but have within yourself. It is the reason why war is so prevalent in your world. It is so prevalent that your world has never had one day of True Peace since the moment man took his first step on your planet.

I.4.7   The time has come for the veil of egoic consciousness to be removed. But, for this to happen, We ask that you join us as We bring Awareness to consciousness. And, for the veil to be shown for what it is, you must *feel* what We are sharing with you. The mind has hidden this from you long enough. For without recognition of the energy signature for the word *consciousness*, you will continue along the same path, the path of separation.

I.4.8   To use one of your colloquialisms, here is where the rubber meets the road. For it is here, in this moment, where you choose to remain under the misguided idea of what you are, or

80

you welcome into your energy field the Awareness of Love's Presence, which is but your True State. The mind will begin to shut down in order to protect its secret. Therefore, We join with you so that We may together elevate the heart to its rightful place. This is the first in a series of small, but significant, steps at unifying your separate states of being.

I.4.9   *Feel*, then, the intention, the energy signature, of the word *consciousness.* For unlike other words, it can have two energy patterns depending on the intention behind the word. And, the intention is provided in *con,* the first part of the word. For *con* means either *to oppose* or *join with.* When combined with the Latin root *scio,* which means knowledge, the intention, the energy signature, becomes telling. Because, the energy pattern of the word *consciousness* is that which either reflects the *opposition to knowledge* or is the energy signature of being *joined with knowledge.*

I.4.10   As you have already learned, God is Knowledge. And, to oppose Knowledge is to oppose God. This opposition is the energy of *not-God,* which has the intention, the energy signature of *not-Life,* or what you call *death.* Furthermore, to oppose Knowledge is to *embrace darkness.* Thus, the energy signature of *not-God, death, judgment,* and *guilt* is the same energy as that of *darkness.*

I.4.11   If you will allow for conscious expansion, the energy pattern found in the verse, *And darkness was upon the face of the deep,* in what you call the first biblical day of creation, will begin to be seen and felt. For it is the energy which creates every experience you have while the mind remains captive to the belief in time. Yet, there is another energy pattern behind the word *consciousness* depending on the intention of the belief behind it. What is the energy pattern?

I.4.12   The answer to that question is found within the second meaning of the word *consciousness,* which is to *join with Knowledge.* This is the energy field of your True Self. And, it is the energy signature of creating, rather than simply projecting.

I.4.13   Consciousness is neither good nor bad, right or wrong. Consciousness, like God, just *Is.* It is neutral. Its only meaning is the one you have given it. And, its meaning to you will always be the one you value the most – separation or unity.

I.4.14   The consciousness of guilt was born in time via the belief you had not only separated from the Divine, from the Eternal, but that you believed you had killed God, your Divine Self.

However, there is a Great Truth, which you are asked to feel. What is this Great Truth? It is but this: when the mind, the *Soul*, split from the Heart, the *Spirit* within you, you forgot it.

I.4.15   This *Spirit* is known as the *Holy Spirit*. And, It lives in your heart, not the heart of your body, but the Heart that *Is* the core of your Being. *Feel* the Spirit. *Feel* its energy pattern. For this is also the energy signature which represents your True Self. And, the Spirit within you remembers what you are. It has not become entangled in the mind's, or the Soul's, twisted beliefs. And, this was given you in the curriculum of *A Course in Miracles,* where it is written: *Spirit is in a state of Grace forever. Your reality is only Spirit. Therefore, you are in a state of grace forever.*

I.4.16   *Feel* the power in that passage. *Feel* the hope contained within it. For you are being told that you are in a state of grace forever. And, herein lies your freedom. Here is the Truth that sets you free. And, this freedom is found in the energy signature of the word *grace*. What is Grace? It is but Divine Compassion, or Divine Consciousness. Thus, the energy signature is that of God, of Love, of your True Self. And, this Divine Consciousness resides in your heart. You have not separated from it, you have simply forgotten it.

I.4.17 Now, focus your attention, once again, on the energy pattern in the thought of guilt, which was but born in the belief that you had separated from the Divine Self. And, this guilt created yet more fear within the mind. The belief in guilt spawned yet another thought never before experienced within the mind of the Son of God. That thought was but the belief that the Son would be punished. This thought of punishment created yet more fear, but now the fear wasn't about the mind's current state, it was of something never before experienced – the future, a time yet to come.

I.4.18 This new belief, the belief you would be punished, created even deeper terror in a mind already beleaguered by fear. We have already asked that you feel the energy signature in the belief of *punishment*. Now, We but ask you to put the pieces of the puzzle together. Isn't one of your currently held beliefs that hell is a place that the condemned go to meet their punishment after they die from this plane of existence? O Holy Brother, you are already in that place. Although in Reality there is no such place, to a mind burdened with such beliefs, it seems quite real indeed.

I.4.19 The world you experience is your hell. It is where the dead have come to punish themselves for the crimes of a time they cannot even remember. For they have judged themselves guilty and must be punished for their egregious offenses. What are these offenses in which a loving God would send His Beloved Children to be punished? For if any of this were true, even one speck of it, then God would be cruel. And, there is no cruelty in God. How could there be? He is the Author of Unconditional Love.

I.4.20   Yet, this belief of punishment for separating from the Divine and the terror it wrought, yet created another split in the mind. However, this time, it was in a mind which already believed it had completely separated from God. Therefore, this third split of the mind created dueling aspects of itself. For in total darkness now, the mind knew not that it was warring with itself.

I.4.21   With the third split of the mind, another thought, which you had never had, arose within it. The thought was that the wholly believed self-of-separation could be attacked. Again, like all other thoughts of error entertained in the mind, the thought of being attacked generated a whole new level of fear, which created a whole new level of existence. This level of existence is what We have referred to before as the *subconscious* mind, also known as the *underworld.* It is the condition of the mind which believes it is lost in complete and utter darkness.

I.4.22   While attack in any form is truly impossible, to the mind of a separated-self, it is not only believable, but experienced frequently. *Feel* the energy signature of the word *attack.* For the word *attack* means *the beginning of a destructive act.* Furthermore, the word *destructive* carries the intention of *killing, annihilation, and vanquishment.* Therefore, the energy pattern associated with the thought, or word *attack,* is the same as all the others for which We have spoken. It is the energy signature of *death.*

I.4.23   It should be dawning within the mind that every experience generated by the mind of a separated-self is always of *death,* more *death,* and yet even more *death.* For the mind of one who believes he or she is a separated-self creates experiences to support his or her belief in death. However, the mind has become so distorted that it does not recognize the energy pattern of death. Instead, it has named, labeled, and divided the experiences in such a way that it has become impossible for the mind to recognize anything other than what it chooses to see.

I.4.24   Observe, then, once again the *feeling,* or the energy signature of the word *attack.* For the belief that attack is possible created yet another belief system, one that is the most difficult to release by a mind entrenched in its belief that it is separated and alone. What is this belief and its consequences?

I.4.25   It is the belief that you can be a *victim*. We recognize that this one belief system is the one that the mind of a separated-self cherishes. And, the mind has created a defense network to protect this most unholy belief. We will not ask of you, as of yet, to *feel* the energy signature of the word *victim*. Rather, We invite you to simply become vigilant for the denial that will come from the mind as We take you into exactly how detrimental to the mind's well-being that the belief in *victimhood* is.

I.4.26   When the mind, riddled from guilt and fear, split for the third time, it was a mind already consumed by darkness. The mind no longer had an ally in the heart. For the mind was now capable of seeing the heart, and the Love contained within it, as an enemy. This meant that God had become its enemy, Who was hell-bent on its destruction. Therefore, the mind that had split for the third time began to think, and thus believe, that God was not only vengeful, but murderous in His Intent. This belief spawned a new, more hideous belief system within a mind that was already sickened by fantasies.

I.4.27   This belief system is referred to as the *victim/blame game.* For in order to be a victim, there must be someone or something to blame. And, whoever or whatever you believe to be the guilty party, that person, place, thing, or event becomes the *victimizer.*

I.4.28   The *victim/blame game* is one of the most insidious and destructive beliefs the mind of a separated-self plays. Not only does it keep the mind in the belief of separation, it does so by adding layer upon layer of judgments upon an already fearful and untrusting mind. And, as you certainly recall, it was judgment that created what We refer to as the descent into darkness. For the judgment was simply to condemn yourself as *not-God* by asking the question, *What am I?*

Lesson 4

I.4.29   Before We continue to discuss the role the belief that it is possible to a be victim plays into your daily experiences, We will take this moment and give you the fourth lesson in this Course. While it is akin to the previous lessons, there is a slight difference to it. Again, it will require either two small pieces of paper, or index cards. Something small enough that you can put in a pocket and refer to several times over the time frame given for this lesson.

I.4.30   On one piece of paper, or index card, write the word *victimizer* on the front side, and the word *victim* on the reverse side. Then, on the second piece of paper, or index card, write the word *judgment* on the front side of it, and write the word *blame* on its reverse side. Three times each day, preferably once in the morning, again in the afternoon, and then in the evening, take either piece of paper you choose to start with, and *feel* the energy signature for each word on that piece of paper or index card. Fifteen to thirty seconds is sufficient. Then, repeat the same procedure with the remaining slip of paper or index card. After you have completed this portion of the exercise, hold the slips of paper, or index cards together, and repeat the process. Pay particular attention to the energy field when they are combined. As you perform this lesson, you will begin to *feel* a subtle difference between them. For the card with the word *judgment* written on it will energetically vibrate at a greater or higher frequency than the other one.

I.4.31   Do not become anxious or upset with yourself if it takes a few practice sessions before you can detect the subtle difference. Simply remember, although time is not real, in your mind - the mind that believes it to be a separated-self from everyone and everything including God, it has forgotten the immense power it has available to it because of an ancient judgment made before the first light came forth from the first generation of stars. However, as you practice, the ancient memory of *feeling* subtle energy shifts and changes will return.

Just listen to your heart.

CHAPTER 5

The Descent into Darkness: The Role of Judgment and Victimhood in Your Experiences

I.5.1   As We stated before in Our discussion with you, when the mind split for the third time, your descent into darkness was complete. Not one Ray of Light remained to illuminate the mind. This created the belief that you had been cut off from your Source completely. This belief reverberated in your Soul. Your mind was filled with guilt and terror of the likes never before experienced. And, every experience the mind was creating for itself came from one judgment, and one judgment only – the thought that you were *not-God.*

I.5.2   Every experience the mind has created for itself has arisen from that singular thought. And, the thought of being *not-God* meant that, everything God is, you believed you weren't. This, O Child of God, was the creation in the belief in duality, which meant that, by believing you were *not-God,* you could only create experiences that opposed the very Source of Everything.

I.5.3　　Where there had only been eternity, now there was time. Where there was life, now there was only death. Where there was joy, now there was only misery. Where there had been only peace, now there was conflict. And, where there had only been Love, now there was fear. A fear so haunting that it paralyzed the mind. And, all of this from a single judgment in a form of a question. And, it is the same question you ask yourself in each moment. *What am I?*

I.5.4　　Do you yet *feel* the enormity of this one question? For you still as of yet do not believe what you are in Truth. It is for this one reason We are with you now. We have only spoken to you of your beliefs. For you believe the impossible happened and that it had become real, with everlasting effects. However, none of what you believed happened is with you now. But, this you too must come to believe, or the hell of your own making will continue to be experienced.

I.5.5　　You have asked, *how did the impossible happen?* We are but showing you how darkness came to rule your mind. You have come to believe that darkness is the absence of light. However, where can there be that God's Light, His Love, is absent? Darkness isn't the absence of Light. Darkness is the denial of Light. For denial is as total as is Love. Wherever there is denial, there will always be darkness. And, it is your denial of the Truth of your Being that has brought Us to you. For this discussion, this Course, is being given unto you now in order to break the spell of denial, which has but kept you a prisoner of your own beliefs.

I.5.6   If you will recall, the thought of being *not-God* has as its feeling denial. And, the thought of being *not-God* is the first judgment you levied against yourself. This judgment, like all thoughts, created the belief in time. Yet, here is the undoing of time. For time is a belief created from one judgment, the judgment of being *not-God*. But, you cannot be other than what you are in Truth. Therefore, the judgment was a simple error, but its effects on you have been hell.

I.5.7   While the next phase in Our discussion is one where most minds become closed, We ask that you simply read the words that follow. Rather than have your mind interpret them, allow your heart to *feel* them. Let your heart instruct the mind as to what is being revealed. For the mind will recoil at what it reads, but the heart will simply look past the mind's judgments to the Love that lies beneath them.

I.5.8   Now, We will focus on *victimhood* and the role *judgment* plays within it. You are quite familiar at playing the victim. For everyone on your planet has believed he or she was a victim at some point in his or her life. Of all the beliefs the human mind has created, the belief that you can be *victimized* is the most detrimental to the mind. And, the reason is simple. For in order to be a victim, you must first feel *powerless*.

I.5.9   *Feel* the energy signature for the word *powerless*. It is the energy signature of *defeat* and *hopelessness*. While you think that the words are different with varying meanings depending on how each is used, they are not different energetically. Their energy pattern is the same.

I.5.10   *Powerlessness* is the state or condition held by the mind that has become identified completely as *not-God*. How could it be any different? For God is Power. Thus, *not-God* is power-less. And, as an extension of God, you can only delude yourself with regards to being powerless. For as His Beloved Child, you were not created helpless, hopeless, or powerless. Rather, you have been given all the power under the heavens and in the earth. But, your belief that you could be, or have ever been a *victim,* has clouded the mind so completely that your mind no longer recognizes its immense power.

I.5.11   However, this feeling of powerlessness is only maintained by the judgments you continue to levy against others, yourself, and everything else the mind rejects.

Judgments make you but a victim, not to others or the circumstance you find yourself in, but unto your own self. And, this is but the Law of Love in motion.

I.5.12   Remember, the Law of Love simply states *what you give another, you but gift unto yourself.* In the case of judging against someone or something, you are but gifting the judgment to yourself. This, too, is found in your Bible. For is it not written, *Judge not, lest ye be judged?* It is not some external authority which judges against you for judging another, you but judge against yourself. And, to the degree that you have judged against someone or something is the same degree to which you have judged against yourself.

I.5.13   In *A Course of Love*, you were taught that everything is in relationship with everything else, just as you are in relationship with all that is. As such, *judging* and *victimhood* are in direct relationship. For without judgment, there cannot be a victim. The two are inseparable. They are connected. For judgments are causal agents, and the feeling they create is that of being a victim.

I.5.14   There is a sequencing of events that occurs when you believe that you have been made a victim. Although this sequencing, the causal beliefs and their effects, is rooted in the subconscious, it manifests as your conscious experiences. And, until the root, the causal agents, which are but distorted beliefs buried within the darkness of your subconscious mind, are removed, you will continue to create experiences that lend proof to the belief that you are a separate-self, alone in a world bereft of love. None of this need be. But, until these distortions of truth are corrected, you will continue to believe that what you experience is not created by your mind, but by external events. And, this but further attests to your belief that you are powerless as to what appears to happen to you.

I.5.15   However, the time has come to expose these dark beliefs for what they are. It is time to release them. For they no longer serve you. But, you must be willing to let them go. These dark beliefs are nothing more than the mind creating a story to tell itself. While the mind will certainly want to cling to the belief that it is a separated-self, alone and struggling in a cruel world, the heart rejoices at the return to Truth, which is but the returning of the memory of your True Self, the Self of Love and Joy.

I.5.16   Now that you have completed the lesson on becoming aware of the energy pattern of the word *judgment,* let Us speak to you of what happens to the mind of one who makes a judgment against someone or something. While the word judgment, itself, is meaningless, the *intention* behind the thought of the judgment is not. For it is this intention which but afflicts the mind of the one who judges.

I.5.17   Recall, in *A Course in Miracles,* you were told that *ideas leave not their source.* Thus, a judgment, which is nothing more than an idea, an opinion held in the mind, leaves not the one who makes it. For this, too, is the reason you have been told, *judge not, lest ye be judged.*

I.5.18   The word *judgment* is simply defined in your language as *a proposition stating something believed or asserted to be true.* Furthermore, the word was derived from the Latin word *judicare,* which means simply *to sentence,* or *to condemn.* It is here that the intention of the word *judgment* is truly felt. For to *condemn* is to *pronounce someone or something as guilty.* In addition, once you come to understand the word's deeper implications, you will begin to see and *feel* the energy field called forth from the word's intention.

I.5.19   However, in order to *feel* fully the intention behind the word *condemn,* you must recognize how the word, and its meaning, arose. The word *condemn* was derived from the Latin word *condemnare*, which carries the meanings *to blame, to find guilty, and to damn.* Therefore, when you levy a judgment against someone or something you are *pronouncing that person or thing as guilty,* while laying blame for a perceived grievance on that person, place, or thing. At the same time, you are *damning* that which you are judging against.

I.5.20 It becomes even more of an eye opener once you understand that, when you *judge* against someone or something, you are damning whoever or whatever it is to *hell.* In other words, when you make a *judgment* against someone or something, you are sentencing that person or thing to hell, which means you are sentencing *death* upon him, her, or whatever it is for which you have found fault in. *Feel* this. For this is the intention behind every judgment made. And, it is this intention buried deep within the darkness of your subconscious mind, which creates every experience you have ever had or will ever have until it is released.

I.5.21 It should be crystal clear by now, that with every judgment made, you are maintaining not only the dream, but its central theme, which is but *death.* For every judgment made is but one that continues to support the belief that you are *not-God.* In addition, every judgment made is but a reflection of the first, or original, judgment made in which you believed you were something other than what you are in Truth. Do you yet see that you have condemned yourself to the misery you have but experienced? For although you believe you are condemning another, you but gift the condemnation upon yourself.

I.5.22   The mind has buried this fact so deeply within the subconscious that, unless it is pointed out to you, it is nearly impossible to find by oneself. Yet, there is a deeper implication buried within that same darkness as well. What is this implication, which is so thoroughly ensconced and buried within the darkness of your subconscious, that unless shown to you, you will continue to manifest experiences of pain, misery, and suffering?

I.5.23   It is but the belief that you have been, could be, and are a *victim* to others, the world, or to God, Himself. This is where together We will dive deeply into the bowels of the *underworld* in order to shine the Light of Grace on that which has come to control every aspect of your current state of consciousness. For buried within the abyss of your subconscious mind is your belief that you must sacrifice yourself in order to appease God.

I.5.24   O Holy Brother, once you see this twisted and insane belief harbored within your being, you can laugh with Us as We look upon it with Love rather than condemnation. For to believe that the need to sacrifice anything, much less yourself, is worthy of laughter and nothing more. This is truly a time for rejoicing. The time of terror is gone. The time of redemption from your beliefs has come. Join Us, then, in glad tidings to the One Who is but Love.

I.5.25   We have already mentioned the *victim/blame* game that you employ in order to keep the belief that you are a separated-being to continue unabated within your mind. Now, We will but point to the part of the game that your mind keeps hidden from you. For this is its secret. And, this secret is but this: the mind of the third split, the mind that cowers from the darkness which surrounds it, desires its own sacrifice to end its perceived suffering. It makes of itself a victim to prove to itself that to sacrifice itself is not only necessary to lessen the wrath that it believes God holds in vengeance for its offenses, but to offer itself upon the altar to be slaughtered for what it believes it did. While seemingly contradictory, recall that the mind of the third spit is both the *victim* and the *victimizer.* For it plays both *the god that demands a sacrificial payment* and *the sacrificial victim to be sacrificed on the altar.*

I.5.26   When you see and *feel* the intention behind the word *victim,* you will understand the true insanity that keeps the mind in utter chaos. For behind the intention of the word *victim* is the desire of *sacrifice.* Here, it will be helpful to remember the *four keys to the kingdom* written in *The Way of Mastery.* The keys are: *desire, intention, allowance,* and *surrender.*

I.5.27   Desire, then, is the first key to the kingdom. However, while there is but one Kingdom, the Kingdom of Heaven, you believe that there are two. One governed by a vengeful God, and the other governed by you. Yet, neither of these kingdoms are real. But, to the mind of the third split, they appear both believable and real.

I.5.28   There is only one true Kingdom. And, that is the Kingdom of God. You are His Kingdom, because His Kingdom is you. However, until the kingdom of the separate-self is shown to inhabit worthless, barren lands, then you will continue to toil, all in the hopes of surviving yet just one more day. Aren't you yet tired of sacrificing yourself for things that will pass back into the dust for which they were made?

I.5.29   *Feel* now the energy signature behind the word *victim. Feel* the intention carried within it. For the very meaning of the word is littered with thoughts that are only associated with a mind burdened with dark desires and stuff only nightmares are made of. *Feel,* then, the intention, the energy, called forth each time a thought, in which you believed you have been a *victim,* arises. By its own carried meaning, the meaning given to it by the mind, it is hell, when seen in the Light of Truth. For the word *victim* means *one that is acted adversely upon by a force or agent; one that is injured, destroyed, or sacrificed; one that is subjected to oppression or mistreatment; one that is tricked or duped;* as well as *a living being sacrificed to a deity.*

I.5.30   When looked upon with eyes wide open, can you see the trail of destruction and death left in the wake of such intention? Since the word *victim* and *sacrifice* are coupled to the same energy pattern, is it any wonder that the word *sacrifice* carries with it the meaning of *one who is offered to a deity.* But, who is this deity for which the mind believes it will become the sacrificial offering?

I.5.31   Do you believe that God demands or has ever demanded a sacrificial offering be made to appease His judgment upon you? For many of Our Brothers and Sisters hold this belief sacrosanct. Yet, they do so to the detriment of their own mental well-being.

I.5.32   We turn now, once again, to your Bible. For is it not written in it, *For the Father judges no one, but has given all judgment to the Son, that all may honor the Son, just as they honor the Father.* Therefore, either God will judge against you, or this verse is a lie. And, if you believe that you will be judged at some future time, then you cannot claim to believe the words

102

written within the verse. Nor, can you claim to believe that the man named Jesus is the Christ. For those words are His.

I.5.33   In addition, it is written in your Bible that Jesus said, *You judge by human standards, I judge no man.* Again, you either believe you will be judged by God, or you do not. Yet, ask yourself this question: if God judges you, under the Spiritual Laws, wouldn't He be judging Himself? *Feel* the intention of this question. For in it lies your freedom, because if God could judge against Himself, then He would not be Love. Instead, He would be the harbinger of *death,* rather than the Author and Source of Life.

I.5.34   Look now gently and lovingly upon yourself. For every thought that is a judgment, every thought in which guilt is believed real, behind every thought that you have been made a victim, found within every thought of loss and sacrifice, behind every thought of blame, and every thought of *not-God* you have had or will have is the *energy of death,* the energy of destruction, the very energy of ruin. This, O Child of God, is the kingdom of hell for which you reign over as long you have even one place left in the mind where darkness hides.

I.5.35   O Beloved Brother, look upon these words from *A Course in Miracles* yet again. *A dream of judgment came into the mind that God created as perfect as Himself. And in that dream was Heaven changed to hell, and God made enemy unto His Son. How can God's Son awaken from the dream? It is a dream of judgment. So must he judge not, and he will waken.*

I.5.36   As you read those words, this time let their intention, their energy, their Light pierce the tomb where you lie interred. For the dream of death is over. Fear not the Light. For it is not the thought of Heaven you now fear. It is but the thought that the dream will not end which grips the mind. Yet, whether you fear Heaven or fear the continuation of the dream, fear is fear. And, fear is always the hallmark of a mind which believes itself separated, a mind still playing the game of *not-God*.

I.5.37   It is now time to relinquish judgement. It but serves to keep you separate and alone, guilty and in fear. Yet, We have heard so many of you ask, *How am I to live in the world if I cannot judge?* Our response to that question is simple: *in a world, which is a dream but within a dream, which is itself in yet but another dream, what is there to judge for or against?* For how can you judge one dream aspect or figure more worthy than another, and yet judge against another dream figure believing that one must be the culprit for what you believe is wrong with the world? They are but figures made up in a dream to support the fantasy of the story the mind has concocted to keep you in the belief that fantasy has become reality.

Lesson 5

I.5.38   This brings Us to the fifth lesson in this Course. This lesson will require but the willingness on your part to be honest with yourself, and one index card. On the index card write the following statement:

I choose to awaken from the dream of death by relinquishing this judgment.

I.5.39   Keep the card with you. Every time you recognize that you have judged someone or something, read the words written on the card. This is why We ask that you to be honest with yourself. For you must recognize when you are judging. Now that you have come to *feel* the energy signature of judgment, it will be easier for you to recognize. Continue to repeat the statement you have written on the index card until you truly desire the relinquishment of judgment.

CHAPTER 6

The Descent into Darkness: Guilt and the Fourth Split of the Mind

I.6.1   Thus far, We have covered with you the splitting of the mind three times, each creating corresponding levels of consciousness. However, the judgment and its associated guilt, along with the terror, caused the mind to split yet again. This fourth split is the last level created. And, it is the one you experience daily. For it is the level of physicality.

I.6.2   The very moment of the fourth split is what your science has labeled the Big Bang. It is the moment that your energy pattern became so dense that what you call *matter* formed. While it appears that this occurred billions and billions of years in the past, the truth is: there is *no* past, because time, as you know it, is not real. For all of time is nothing but a series of events placed in a linear manner so that your consciousness can attempt to make sense of the impossible. Yet, time is not linear. Time is fluid. While it appears to move from the past, into the present, then into the future, recognize that time doesn't move at all. It is but your consciousness that moves.

I.6.3　*Feel* the intention behind the statement: *it is but your consciousness that moves.* For the word *moves* has a distinct energy pattern. And, this energy pattern is found in the meaning of the word, which is *to start away from some point, to depart, or to leave.* Furthermore, the word *depart* means *to die.* Thus, the energy signature for the word *move* is the same as all of the rest of the words We have discussed, for it is the energy pattern of *death.*

I.6.4　You already use the word every time you think or say, *the dearly departed,* when you refer to the dead. Yet, there is a deeper implication to the word *departed.* And, it is time for you to recognize it. For the word *separated,* so often used within the curriculum found within *A Course in Miracles, A Course of Love,* and *The Way of Mastery,* carries with it a deeper implication than most students understand. Why is this? It is simply because there are those who believe that the word *separated* means to have *separated physically.* But, this would have to mean that both space and time were real. And, they most assuredly are not.

I.6.5　Allow your heart to speak of the truth in this: that the intention, or the energy signature, found within the word *separated* is *death.* Separation has nothing, absolutely nothing, to do with physicality, but everything to do with death. It is for this reason you have been told time and time again that separation is not real. For separation cannot be real, because death is not real. And, this is why so many students find the curriculum confusing. They do not *feel* or recognize the energy pattern of the word. Instead, they use the meaning of the word as they have used it in their past.

I.6.6   Now, allow your heart to once again speak to you of this truth: *time does not move; your consciousness moves, because your consciousness chooses separation, or death, in the now.* And, this moment is the only *one* there is. Furthermore, you choose *death* until you choose Life. In other words, you choose to *be not-God,* rather than to *be God.*

I.6.7   But, what keeps you from choosing to *be* God right now? It is but *guilt.* Yes! Guilt is what keeps your consciousness moving, because guilt is what binds you to the chains of death. Guilt is the stone that covers your tomb, preventing you from seeing the Light just on the other side. Yet, you do not truly recognize what guilt is. You were taught by teachers, religious leaders, your parents, and others the meaning of guilt by how the world defines it. However, you do not yet understand it, because you have not been taught its hidden intention, which is that of keeping the mind preoccupied on *separation,* or *death.*

I.6.8 The world has taught you that guilt is a feeling. How often have you thought or said, or heard another say, *I feel guilty?* Guilt is not a feeling. Guilt is a thought. And, the intention of the thought is what creates the circumstances of your experiences.

I.6.9 In addition, the world has taught you that *guilt* is assigned to those who have *violated, or broken, the law by committing some egregious offense.* To the mind that is littered with a list of offenses for what it believes it has done, the world's definition of *guilt* makes perfect sense. Yet, to your heart, it doesn't make any sense. For the heart, where your True Self resides, knows that you can neither violate or break the Spiritual Laws. Therefore, it knows only of your innocence. Only in a mind, or *soul,* made mad by *guilt* can it believe that it has broken one or more of the Laws. However, your heart, the spirit within you, knows only of your complete guiltlessness. And, when finally seen in the Light of Truth, you will come to recognize your True State, the state of innocence.

I.6.10 Now, We will expose the intention behind the word *guilt* so that you may once and for all rise above it by releasing it. The word *guilt* comes to you from the Old English word *gylt,* which meant *delinquency.* Here is where the true intention of guilt has been hidden within the dark recesses of your subconscious mind. For the word *delinquent* comes from the Latin word *delinquere*, which means *to fail*. Furthermore, the word *fail* means *lack*.

I.6.11   While it may only yet be a small ray of light piercing the *veil of death* covering the mind, it is enough for you to begin to *feel* the intention, or the energy signature for the word *guilt*, because it is the energy pattern of *lack*. Yet, while you can, in Truth, *lack* nothing, your belief in it creates your experiences that makes *lack* seems real.

I.6.12   But, what is the intention behind the word *lack?* The intention, the energy pattern for the word is also carried in its meaning. For the word *lack* means *a state or condition of being wanting, or delinquent.* Here is where the energy of intention creates the experiences which you have come to believe to be the natural order of things. For the word *wanting* simply means *without.*

I.6.13   *Feel* this now: the energy signature of one who believes he is *lacking* is the energy pattern of *a state of being without or guilty.* O Holy Child, look carefully upon those words. For they but describe your current *state of being.* Do you see it? Can you yet *feel* it?

I.6.14   We have said many times, *Love is your natural state of being.* However, as long as you continue to believe, on any level, that you are *not-God*, then *you are without your natural state of being.* In other words, as long as you believe that you are something other than what you are in Truth, then you are emitting the energy pattern of *lack,* which is but *guilt.* And, what you emit, you will see and experience. For this is the Law of Belief at work.

I.6.15   Furthermore, because you believe deep within your mind that you are *without* Love, you go *seeking* for it in the world, hoping to find it. However, before We continue this discussion with you, We ask that you look lovingly upon what We are communicating with you now. *Feel* it. For to *believe that you are without Love, implies that you are without God, the Source of your Being. Therefore, to believe that you are without God means that you are without Life. And, to believe that you are without Life implies that you are with death.*

I.6.16   Thus, since your Natural State of Being *is* Life, then to be in an unnatural state of being *is* death. O Holy One, because you believe you are without Love, without Life, you carry within you the energy signature of *death.* And, this has *grave* consequences, quite literally. For when a being carries with it

111

the energy pattern of death, that being can but emit, or extend, that energy pattern. Since extension and creation are the same, you can but create experiences which but attests to the validity of *death*. For all you see and experience is nothing more than the energy signature of *death* all around you. And, it is but you who are creating it. For you are the one extending that energy frequency.

I.6.17   This, then, is the true meaning of projection. For projection is nothing but the extension of the energy of death. But, because death is not real, it cannot be extended. Therefore, death cannot be made real by creating it. Yet, when the energy of death is emitted, or projected, it creates within the energy field of potentiality and possibilities the very manifestations and experiences which strengthens your belief in it. And, you will always believe what you see.

I.6.18   Look lovingly upon what We have just communicated with you. Dear Brother and Sister, this need not be. Death is not your natural state. Life is. To exist in death is the very meaning of *hell*. But, hell is not your Home. Heaven is. The world you walk is simply the projection of death. For death, like Life, is all around you, but you see them not. Because, you have given names to the multitude of forms which the energy pattern of death reflects back unto you.

I.6.19   You no longer see death for what it is. Instead, you look upon its manifestations and experiences calling them by the forms which best fit your story, or more notably, your belief narrative. Yet, you look upon nothing that is Real. For you can but look upon but death, claiming it real.

I.6.20   Do you yet see and *feel* how guilt is the glue which holds the universe of physicality together? For without guilt, everything you look upon would simply cease to be. Guilt holds not only the dream of judgment in the mind, but perpetuates its central theme, which is but death.

I.6.21   Now, join Us as We expose the purpose of guilt upon the mind. For here you will discover the deception you but created for yourself. This, then, is another step We take together in dismantling the belief system of hell, so that you may join Us in experiencing the return of Heaven upon the mind.

I.6.22   As We have communicated, the world has but taught you that guilt is determined by the one who has broken a set of laws or commandments. Now, We are inviting you to lay down the false teachings of the world, so that you may see the hidden meaning of the guilt, which lies in the dark corners of your

113

subconscious. For this hidden meaning has its own implications regarding what you refer to as your *life*.

I.6.23   Come to see the ancient truth, buried and forgotten, which but keeps you attached to the energy of time, which is but death. For We walk with you into the catacombs of the underworld. It is here that you will hear the cries of those who are trapped in their distorted beliefs. The cries you hear will be those who suffer needlessly, lamenting in anguish at the grief of having lost what they once believed real. For the time of their release has come. The time to awaken is here. This is the purpose of this Course. We are to bring an end to the suffering and misery that is hell. For the Sons of God have not been created to suffer the torment of the hell they made in their attempt to punish themselves. Rather, We through oneness and unity, are *to be the conduits for the extension of God, Himself.* But, this is only possible when all of the shadows made by the obstacles to hide you from the Light have been forever removed.

I.6.24   In order to do this, We must stand with you and expose the last vestige of guilt. For this vestige is the very symbol of guilt, the belief that you are without Love, in which the mind made to hide the truth from your eyes. Yet, this symbol has come to represent who and what you are. It is but the mind's last attempt at sacrificing itself to the god of time, to the god of death. For this symbol was made but to sacrifice itself on the altar of this god. And, it is this god for which We have come to expose. This god is nothing but a figure within the dream itself. And, you are but the one who plays the part of both the god of death, who is without mercy, as well as the sacrificial offering to be slaughtered on the altar. Both parts are authored but by you.

I.6.25   We have reached the point in the curriculum of this Course where We but laugh with you at the ridiculousness that time could come to usurp eternity. For you will see that the impossible still remains impossible, having neither any accomplishments nor any real effects. We invite your heart to speak to your mind of the freedom that awaits it once it releases every trace of guilt it has harbored. But, for this moment, We must cross the great divide, the last chasm standing between who you think you are and the Reality of what you are. For once this chasm is bridged, the end is in sight.

I.6.26   *Feel* what We are but communicating with you. Recognize the energy signature, once and for all, of a mind gripped by guilt and terror. See the energy pattern of death emanating from it, and hear the cries which come from it as it mourns what it believes it has forever lost. *Feel* it as it longs for the Love for which it believes it is without. Allow True Compassion to answer it as it calls for Love. If you listen carefully, you will recognize its voice. For it is but yours.

I.6.27   Allow the Wellspring of Love at the center of your being to begin flowing again. Look, then, with Love, with understanding, with clarity, and compassion at your creations. Do not pity them, for you will but pity yourself, believing you are a victim still. Instead, take your hand and reach for them. For their hand is but your hand. Let them come unto you and rest. Let them lay their weary heads upon your shoulders. Let them cry if they must. Then, gently brush their tears aside, for the time has come for the sorrows to be wiped away.

I.6.28   Look, then, but at who you believe yourself to be. What is the story you have come to believe about yourself? What are the memories you carry with you? Are they ones of happiness and joy? Or, are they ones which cause emotional pain each time those memories are recalled? All of the beliefs, all of the memories, the story of your childhood, as well as that which you believe to be true about yourself arose but from the fourth split of the mind, a mind which believes itself to be without Love, thus riddled with guilt and fear.

I.6.29   As with most things regarding your world, the truth may sting, but it will set you free if you will allow it. But, it requires that you question every aspect of your current conscious state of being. For not one stone can be left untouched, which would allow even one sliver of doubt or disbelief to remain. There can be no places where guilt can remain safely hidden away.

I.6.30   You carry the symbol of guilt, thus death, with you every where you go. What is this symbol of guilt that you carry with you from the moment you take your first breath until the moment of your last one? It is but the body. Yes! The body is the very symbol of guilt, of lack, and ultimately of death itself. For the body is the final home of a mind which believes it is a separate-self.

I.6.31   To the mind, the body lends proof that it, the mind, is alone and without Love. Yet, like all other things in the world of physicality, the body is nothing more than a projection which can act out the mind's judgments, guilt, fears, and its belief that it is a victim. The body is nothing more than an experience in which the mind can play the game of believing it is *not-God*. But, like all other experiences, the body is neutral. It is neither good nor bad, right or wrong.

I.6.32　Like everything else in the third dimensionality of form, the body is nothing more than an energy signature, albeit a very dense one. The body is simply an avatar for the mind to experience its dark beliefs. We use the word *avatar* with great clarity and understanding. And We would like to share with you now the intention of its meaning and implication regarding the mind.

I.6.33　The word *avatar* is not a word that you would normally apply to yourself. For its implication is such that it would raise suspicion on a conscious level of that which is hidden in the darkness of the subconscious. For the implication of the word *avatar* is such that it would make you question what you believe about yourself and the world. And, this is the reason We but point to it now. For We but invite you to begin to question all of your deeply held beliefs regarding yourself, the world, and the universe of form.

I.6.34　We ask that you *feel* and see the intention behind the meaning of the word *avatar*. The word comes to you by way of an ancient language. And, it is here where the energy of intention was determined. For the word *avatar* comes from the Sanskrit word *avatarati*, which means *he descends*. Furthermore, the word *descend* carries with it the energy pattern of *having fallen.* For the word *descend* means *to lower oneself, or to be changed into a worse state or condition.*

I.6.35   Therefore, the body is the means by which the mind of one who believes he has separated from All That Is, from Love, from God, can live out its dreams of suffering, sacrifice, and death. For the body is the last in a series of descending levels, which simply implies that one's energy field is becoming denser and its frequency slower. The body is not real, it is but a projection of a mind stricken with guilt and fear.

I.6.36   What We will now refer to as a body-mind is the projection, or mis-creation, of a mind that has become lost in complete darkness. For the body-mind is nothing more than the projection of the subconscious mind from the third splitting of the mind. However, when a mind completely identifies itself within a body, or body-mind, it experiences the realm of consciousness created as a result of the mind having split for the fourth time. Once a mind believes itself to be the body, it can but then experience all that would prove to itself that separation is real. For when the mind believes itself to be a body, it will suffer, because that is what it has chosen for itself. It has chosen to become the sacrificial offering by being the victim to a god that demands punishment for having committed offenses which have angered it.

119

I.6.37   This god which demands a sacrifice be made unto it is but you. This god is but that part of your consciousness which resides in the mind of the third split. It is why you willingly commit to suffering and sacrifice. For these are offerings made but unto you. However, the consciousness contained within the body-mind has simply forgotten the part of the mind that harbors the desire for its own destruction.

I.6.38   The time has come but for you to *see* and *feel* the hell you created for yourself. Yet, do not add injury to insult by condemning yourself for this. Simply acknowledge that this has been, and is, but a choice made to experience the dense energy of form. The experience, like every experience you have, is neutral. You have given this experience all the meaning it has had to you. But know, the experience, itself, is neither right nor wrong. It just is.

I.6.39   Recognize, in this most holy, beautiful moment, the power of the mind given unto you by the Creator. Have you yet begun to *feel* this gift? Do you yet see it as a blessing? Or, do you still believe it is a curse?

I.6.40   The power, the very energy, used to create hell and misery is the same power that allows you to simply let go of it. For your creations are but held together by the guilt found within the mind. Release the energy of guilt. Release its energy signature. But, in order to do so requires a willingness to let go of the identity which you created for yourself. Accept, then, your True Identity, the one given unto you as the most precious gift for which it is.

I.6.41   O Child of God, you are not, nor will ever be, a body. It is not your home. Heaven is. The body is nothing more than a device to be used by the mind to sacrifice itself on the altar to the god of death. Yet, what will this sacrifice give you that you don't already have in Truth. It can give you nothing. For the god which demands your sacrifice is not real either. Both the god of vengeance and the body are but ideas held in the mind tormented by guilt.

I.6.42   However, the body can serve a higher purpose than the one assigned to it by the mind. For the body can serve both you and the Creator. It can function within the physical realm as a means by which the Voice for God can speak to those who still believe they are *without Love.* It can serve as the reflection of the Face of Christ, Who is but the Face of Innocence, as well as the Face of the Pure, Perfect Love of God. This the body can do once you release the guilt, the belief that you are without God, without Love.

I.6.43   We now ask you to question which purpose do you choose for the body. For will it serve as a sacrificial offering to the god of death, or will it serve the Kingdom of Love? The choice is yours. And, the choice will be founded on your attachment to guilt.

Lesson 6

I.6.44   Now, We come to lesson six in this Course. This lesson is to bring you one step closer to recognizing your True Identity, to your True Self, the Self created by God, the Self that is the extension of Unconditional Love. For this lesson, write the following statement on an index card:

Love is always with me and is me.

I.6.45   Then, each morning, look at the statement you have written on the card. *Feel* the energy signature behind those words. For that energy signature is you. Continue doing this for at least three to five minutes.

I.6.46   As often as possible throughout the day, silently repeat the statement. Allow your heart to *feel* it. *Feel* the Truth of the statement. The energy that you *feel* is that of your being. Allow it to move through you. Become acquainted with it once again. Welcome it.

I.6.47   Then, just prior to retiring for the night, repeat the same process as was asked of you each morning. Remember to *feel* it. Don't just allow your mind to think of the statement. For it is the Love found within your heart that will heal the mind. Therefore, *feel* it. Allow your heart to share its Love with the mind. For *Love is the energy which heals the mind.*

CHAPTER 7

Seek Not

I.7.1   Only the body-mind of those who believe that they are without something, whether that something is Love, God, or even what is considered basic living necessities, will go in search for it. In other words, they will go *seeking* for it. By the very nature of the word, to *seek* for something is to imply that you are *without* it. Thus, only the mind that believes it is *guilty,* or *lacks,* for what it believes it doesn't have, will go seeking for it.

I.7.2   We now ask that you bring into your conscious awareness the energy pattern of the word *seek.* For its meaning has implications which have been buried by the mind for far too long. Once the energy pattern is recognized, the mind can no longer delude itself, or you.

I.7.3   The world has taught you that *to seek is to find.* Yet, when you have spent a lifetime seeking and have never found that for which you went searching, then the world tells you that you didn't search in the right places, or you didn't search long enough. It will even have you believe that you knew not what you were searching for. However, the time has come for you to finally realize that you will never find what the mind believes it *lacks*. Your entire system is based upon *seek, seek, seek,* but never will you find what you are looking for.

I.7.4   This is found within the meaning that you have given the word. For the word *seek* means *to try and acquire or gain, to attempt.* Yet, the word *seek* also has the meaning of *to be lacking.* And, as We have already shown you, *to be lacking*, is *to be guilty.* It is the energy pattern emitted by one who believes he is *not-God.* Furthermore, the word *seek* and its implication is directly related to the Spiritual Law of Being, which states *that to give is to have; and to have is to be.*

I.7.5   While this may at first appear counterintuitive, *feel* how this Law applies to your experiences. For then you will see how it functions. Look then, again, at the meaning of the word *seek,* which is *to "be" lacking.* When the Law of Being is applied to this statement, the energy pattern of *to seek* can be clearly seen. For to "be" lacking, you must have lack; and to have lack, you must give lack. In other words, to *give lack* simply means that you are emitting the energy signature of lack.

I.7.6   Can you yet see and feel what We are inviting you at this moment to recognize? For it is but this: to *seek* is to emit the energy of *lack,* which is the energy of guilt, or *not having.* Therefore, because you are emitting this energy signature, the energy field of possibility and potentiality can only manifest the experience of *lacking,* and you will continue to seek, because you will continue to see and experience lack.

I.7.7   This is why you will never find that for which you think you seek. For you are emitting the energy of *lack.* This is the hamster wheel the world teaches you to play on. It is meant to keep you running hither and yon, never to find, but always to seek, seek, seek.

I.7.8   However, there is a deeper, more insidious implication regarding the word *seek.* And, the time has come to expose it as well. For the implication keeps what you call the future just like the past, which but ensures the continuity and perpetuation of the experience of the original judgment made.

I.7.9   Remember, the original judgment you levied against yourself was that you must be *not-God,* when you asked *What am I?* This judgment, like all judgments made, creates the belief that you are *guilty,* which is the belief in *lack.* Yet, when you look upon it as *being without God,* the implication becomes strikingly clear. For the mind interprets it as: *I am a Being without God.* And, whatever the mind believes it is without, it will go and search for in the hopes that it will find it and satisfy its *without-ness.*

I.7.10   Look carefully upon this. For to be a *without-ness being,* implies that you are *external* to God. And, if you are external to God, then you are external to everything. And, this is exactly what the mind has projected, or mis-created, for itself. It has created what appears as an external universe, an external world, so that it can seek for everything it believes it is lacking.

I.7.11   Do you yet see the utter madness in this? For in order for God to be external from you, then God would be separate. This, O Holy Brother, is the great deception. This is the deception the mind plays with itself. For to believe God is external is to believe that you are *not-God.*

I.7.12   Therefore, the mind still clings to its first, or original, judgment – that it is *not-God.* And, the mind has created a whole story, a narrative, for you to play in an attempt to prove this is true. *Feel,* then, the energy of *seeking.* For it is nothing more than the mind's attempt to prove itself right and God wrong.

I.7.13   This is the mind's purpose of time. It is the purpose of hell. It is to demonstrate, at all costs, that you were right all along. But, there is a much deeper, hidden, intention behind this attempt to be right. And, the intention, the energy signature is found in the meaning of the word *right*. For within its energy field is what the mind believes to be its salvation.

I.7.14   The word *right* carries the meaning of *real*, which simply means to *"be" genuine*. In other words, it is the intention *to "be" true*, or not *illusory*. And, it is this intention for which the mind strives. It wants its belief that it is *not-God* to be true, to be real. For in the *denial* of Truth was the mind's *desire* for what it wanted truth *"to be."*

I.7.15   This takes Us into the dark intention behind the desire to be *real*, to be right. And, you can find this in your Bible, as well. For in your Bible, is it not written, *And God said, Let us make man in our image, after our likeness?* We invite you now to just sit for a moment with the energy of that verse. For within its intention is either your freedom or your damnation. And, that is determined directly by who and what you identify with.

I.7.16   Recognize that this particular Bible verse has caused much consternation in mankind for many millennia. For the confusion created by and within the mind comes in the intention of the word *image*. And, it is the energy signature of the word *image* which either creates experiences of Heaven or hell.

I.7.17   Your word *image* has an archaic, or what you consider to be outdated, meaning. What did the word once mean? It simply meant *an illusory form*. Let the meaning, then, come both into your mind and heart. For the intention, the energy signature, of the word *image* is fear. *Feel* it. See it. For the energy pattern is the same for all fear, regardless of the form the fear may present itself as. Look closely, once more, at the meaning of *image*. For although it may appear archaic in the history of your language, it is still quite pertinent in its intention. *Image: an illusory form.*

I.7.18   Can you yet see and *feel* the energy behind the word? For it is implying that the form of man, which is the body, is *illusory,* which means *something not "true" or "real."* And, this one thought strikes *terror* into the mind of man, because of the mind's identification as a body. Why? Simply because it means you are *not-right,* which the mind interprets and perceives as *wrong.*

I.7.19   It is here, within the interpretation of the mind as perceiving itself as *wrong,* which created the belief that you are *without God,* or *not-God.* For the intention, the energy signature, is also found within the meaning of the word *wrong*, which is *the state of "being" guilty*. In other words, your *beingness* is that of *guilt, of lack,* or *being with-out,* or that which is *external*.

I.7.20   Although We have discussed the first thought that you could be a *victim,* it is here that We ask that you *feel* it. Follow the energy pattern. Recognize the energy signature is resonating within you. For this one Bible verse is given you so that you may recognize the birth of your belief that you were or could be a *victim*. However, on a more fundamental level, it is pointing you to the *guilt* that is held within in the mind.

I.7.21   Yet, it is here that We ask you to *feel* what We are telling you. For this Bible verse also points to where the belief that *guilt* and *being wrong* merged and became what it has. And, hidden within it is also the creation in the belief in *sin,* the one belief that keeps the mind cowering in terror within the darkness which blankets it. Recognize, then, just how deep the rabbit hole goes.

I.7.22   The belief in *sin,* which is nothing more than the belief that you are guilty, is itself the belief that you have broken or transgressed the Laws. More specifically, it is the belief that you usurped the Law of Being. For the mind believes it judged itself when it asked the question, *What am I?* This judgment created the guilt for believing it had transgressed the Law of Being.

I.7.23   Do you see it? Can you yet *feel* the terror created by the thought of having usurped the Law? For in the mind the logical conclusion was that to *be not-God* usurped *being God.* And, this is the guilt and the terror which still plagues the mind. Realize, this guilt and terror isn't held in the consciousness of the body-mind. Rather, it is held in the subconscious mind, which is that portion of the mind that projects the *avatar,* or the you that you have identified with.

I.7.24   We have already stated that the Laws of God can neither be broken or usurped. Yet, this you must come to accept. For how can you have broken or usurped God's Law? For if you had, then your being would forever be that of *not-God.* But, your belief that you are *not-God* is only found in time, not eternity. For only in time can you believe that you are *not-God.* However, in the Eternal, that which is God, you have always been, are now, and forever will be an Extension of Pure, Perfect Love. You have not *separated* from Truth. You only believe you have.

I.7.25　Look again at the Bible verse, where it is written, *And God said, Let us make man in our image, after our likeness.* Feel it. But, this time, *feel* the salvation it offers if you will but accept it. What is this salvation for which it brings? The answer is found in the same word that created the belief in sin and guilt. It is but the word *image* and its meaning, *an illusory form.* Rather than *feel* the terror within it, *feel* its salvation. For the verse is offering you the Truth: *that the form, the body, and all of its sufferings, is not real.* What does this mean? Quite simply, O Holy Child, it means that you are without guilt, because the Law of Belief was not broken.

I.7.26　Laugh with Us at the ridiculousness of it all. Yes! Laugh. For in your laughter is your release from having taken it seriously.

Lesson 7

I.7.27　This brings Us to the seventh lesson of this Course. As with all the other exercises, you will need an index card. On it, write the statement: *I am an Extension of Pure, Perfect Love, who is guiltless and free to return Home.* For this exercise, We invite you to look upon the statement as often as possible. *Feel* it. Own it. Be certain in it. Silently repeat this statement throughout your day. When any thoughts of guilt, or *not-God,* arise, repeat the statement. For contained within the statement is the energy signature of your True Identity, your True Self.

CHAPTER 8

What is Death?
Lesson 8A

I.8.1 We begin by inviting you to complete the first of two lessons that will be a part of this discussion. Consider this lesson 8A. For this lesson, you will need a piece of paper. Label the top of the page with the word *Death.* Then, underneath the word *Death*, write as many beliefs you have regarding what *death* means to you. This lesson isn't one meant to be depressing. Instead, its purpose is to demonstrate to you how your beliefs shape your experiences.

I.8.2 Yet, recognize that your beliefs will only be those for which you are consciously aware. They will not demonstrate the beliefs regarding death found within your subconscious. For that is Our purpose for this moment in time with you. We are with you at this time to bring the Light of Truth to that which has been with you since time began.

I.8.3 Death, as you think of it, is not Real. Period. Case closed. But, what is death, if it is not what you think it is? To the body-mind, the answer will not be understood. But, to the heart, the answer is one that is welcomed. For the answer is but a simple reminder of what it has always known.

I.8.4   Like everything else, the world has taught you what it believes death to be: that death is simply *the cessation of life.* It even teaches that death is natural. Yet, every teaching around death that the world offers involves the passing of form. This description, given by the world, even uses the word *death* when describing the end of a star's life.

I.8.5   As We have already stated, *everything that enters time must exit time.* And, this exit of time is referred to as *death,* just as the entering into time is referred to as birth. Regardless, the world's definition of *death* has nothing to do with the intention of the word. For the energy signature of *death* is so much more than what the world believes.

I.8.6   Like the energy signatures of other words that We have pointed to, the energy pattern of *death* is bound to its meaning. Although you believe that the meaning of *death* is that of *the cessation of life,* the word *death* really carries the meaning of *a cause of ruin.* Remember that the Law of Cause and Effect, simply states, *For every cause, there is a simultaneous effect created.*

I.8.7   Therefore, *death* is the cause, and *ruin* is the effect. But, what is the energy signature of *ruin*. It too is found in its meaning. For the word *ruin* means *a falling down*. Here is where the intention has been buried deep within the subconscious, and is unknown on the conscious level, the level experienced in physicality. For the word *ruin* is what is being described in what is referred to as *the fall of man*. Furthermore, the word *fall* is where the deeper implication is hidden.

I.8.8   The word *fall* means to *stray,* or *detour.* In *A Course in Miracles,* it is written, *these related distortions* (the splitting of the mind) *represent a picture of what actually occurred in the separation, or the "detour into fear."* Thus, the intention, or the energy signature, of *ruin,* is fear.

I.8.9   Recall, thoughts are the causal agents, feelings are their effects. Therefore, the thought of *death* creates the feeling of *fear.* In other words, *death* is the *detour into fear.* Recognize, the energy signature of *death* is *fear.* Thus, the thought of *death,* and its associated *fear,* creates within the mind the belief that it is *not-God.* And, this belief is the energy emitted by the mind, which serves but to create experiences that strengthens the mind's belief that it is *not-God.*

I.8.10   The time has come for you to recognize the havoc that the belief of *not-God* has created. And, this havoc is the conflict you experience both internally and externally. Come, now, to see and *feel* what the belief of *not-God* really is. What is *not-God* in the easiest terms for which the mind can accept?

I.8.11   It is but this: *not-God* is a *state of being*. And, since the belief that you are *not-God* is created from a thought of *death* and its feeling, which is but *fear,* then you can also see that *death/fear* is a *state of being* as well. And, the mind can only perceive and experience what it believes to be its *state of being*. This, then, is what you would call the take home message. For as long as you continue to believe that *not-God* is your *state of being,* then under the Laws of God, you will continue to experience the *state of being not-God*.

I.8.12   When it finally dawns within your mind that the *state of being not-God* is nothing but denial and resistance against your True State of Being, then the Light will have finally returned, because it has been welcomed once again. Therefore, the belief that you are in a *state of being not-God* is nothing more than the opposition towards your *True State of Being,* which is God. This opposition, or resistance to Truth, results in what is called *duality*. And, duality is the gift you have given yourself in the belief that your *state of being* is *not-God*.

137

I.8.13   Conflict is the gift, the experience, created by the belief in duality. And, this belief arose when it seemed possible, within the mind that believed itself to be *not-God,* that God could have an opposite. Yet, your heart knows not of duality, or opposites. It only knows Truth: that only God is Real. But, to the mind, opposites seem to exist, always offering a choice between two things. The heart recognizes there are no choices to make. For the heart knows only of Love.

I.8.14   Now is the time to recognize that the experiences you have are the gifts you but give yourself. Not only is this in accordance with the Spiritual Law of Love, it is also in accordance with the Spiritual Law of Giving and Receiving. For these two Laws work hand-in hand. Where the Law of Love states, *Whatever you give another, you but gift unto yourself,* the Law of Giving and Receiving simply states, *What is given is received, and is increased unto he that gives.*

I.8.15   *Feel* these Laws. For they do not work against you, but with you. They only appear to work against the mind held sway by its belief that it is *not-God.* Once you remember the Laws, and their function within creation, you will have gratitude for them, the gratitude that you have always had. But, how exactly do these Laws determine your experiences?

I.8.16   In order for this part of Our discussion to be fully understood, recall that the Law of Being states, *To give is to have; and, to have is to be.* Therefore, to believe that your current *state of being* is *not-God* is to *be not-God.* And, to *be not-God*, is to *have* the belief that you are *not-God.* In accordance with the Law of Being, to *have* the belief that you are *not-God* means that you can only *give not-God.* As a result of *giving not-God*, in accordance with the Law of Giving and Receiving, you can only *receive not-God* in return. The *receiving* of *not-God* is what you call your experiences. In other words, your experiences are the gifts you *receive* as the result of *giving not-God.*

I.8.17   To a mind in rebellion, this is utter nonsense. However, it is the way it works. But, in order for there to be healing within a mind beset with false ideas regarding itself, this discussion must be *felt*, while no *thought* is given to it. For *thinking* is what brought you here. Yet, it is *feeling,* instead of thinking, that will allow you to experience your freedom.

I.8.18   We have used the term *not-God* frequently in Our discussion with you. But, what does *not-God* mean? For by *feeling* what *not-God* is, only then will you be able to choose again. And, from your choice to remember what you are in

139

Truth, you will be able to create experiences that reflect Heaven, rather than hell.

I.8.19   While it may seem that *not-God* is as all encompassing as God is, *not-God* is not eternal, infinite, or without limitations. For the kingdom of *not-God* is a kingdom rife with war and conflict, plagued by scarcity and lack, and beleaguered by suffering, misery, loss, and death. This is the kingdom you created and fight daily to save. But, why do you fight so hard to save that which is the antithesis of Heaven? The answer lies in your belief of who and what you are.

I.8.20   We have stated that you believe that you are *not-God*. Therefore, *not-God* is what you believe is your *state of being*. However, the implication of this belief runs even deeper than what you might think or *feel*. For it is found in every experience you have ever had.

I.8.21   Your belief in your state of being has become one that you never question. You have accepted it completely, and you have become thoroughly identified with it. There is no shred of doubt left in your mind about your identity with regards to your current *state of being*. In fact, you are proud of it. Why is this? Because, in your belief system, this *state of beingness* is viewed as the pinnacle of evolutionary development.

I.8.22   Do you yet recognize the energy signature with regards to your believed current *state of being*? For it is the energy signature, the energy pattern, associated with one who believes that he is a *human being*. Yes! You believe that you are a *human being*. Therefore, your current *state of being* is a *human being*. This, then, is why every experience you have ever had reflects, or mirrors back unto you, that you are a *human being,* fraught with all the pitfalls that has plagued humanity since its inception.

I.8.23   *Feel* the implication of what We are relating to you. *Feel* it to the depth of your being. For to believe that you are a *human being* means that you are a *not-God being*. O Child of God, you are so much more than what you currently believe you are. For in your denial of your Divine Self, you could only identify as *not-God*, or as that of being completely human. And, to identify completely as a *human being* is to identify completely with *death* and *fear*. They are the same. While your mind sees them differently, the energy signature is the same. For it is the energy signature of a being who believes he is *not-God*. Recognize that with your complete identification as a *human being* you are bound by time and all of its effects. Furthermore, in accordance with the Law of Belief, because you have become completely identified with the belief that you are a *human being*, you can but see and experience being

141

human. And, everything you see and experience does nothing but strengthen this belief, making it more difficult to release.

I.8.24   This is the underlying belief for which all other beliefs hinge. There are many students who have studied the curriculum and thought that it was in the complete identification with and as a body which created the suffering experienced. While the body is the final act in the mis-identification of yourself, the underlying belief in *being human* is the one which allows for the identification as a body.

I.8.25   There are those, who will read this discussion, and promptly determine that what they are reading is both arrogant and blasphemous. To those who believe as such, We but ask *which is more arrogant, to believe that you are what you have told yourself, or that you are as God created you to be?* For only one is deceptive, while the other one is Truth. And, We also ask, *which is blasphemous, to tell God what you are, or to believe in that which He has revealed unto you of your True Nature?*

I.8.26   To the naysayers, We but point to another biblical passage. It is written in your Bible, that the man called Jesus said, *I and my Father are one. Then the Jews took up stones again to stone him. Jesus answered them, Many good works have I shown you of my Father, for which of those works do ye stone me? The Jews answered him, saying, For a good work We stone thee not; but for blasphemy; and because that thou, being a man, makes thyself God. Jesus answered them, Is it not written in your law, I said, Ye are gods? If he called them gods, unto whom the word of God came, and the scripture cannot be broken.*

I.8.27   There it is written for all to see, *feel,* and experience, but doubt clouds the minds of those who are tormented by *guilt* and *fear* to such an extent that they cannot look upon the Truth, save they be struck down. For they believe themselves to have committed such egregious offenses that to believe such a thing is blasphemous, indeed.

I.8.28   Do you not yet recognize that you, nearly two thousand years after the recording of this event, still have the same conversation with yourself. And, the conversation has not changed, one iota: *that you, being a man, make yourself God.* Herein lies the crux of the problem. And, it is found in the words, *you, being a man.*

I.8.29   Although you have been told, even by the Christ, Himself, that *you are gods*, you still cling to the belief that you are just human. And, then you wonder why nothing truly seems

143

to change in your life no matter how hard you try, no matter how hard you struggle. For it always appears that you are one step behind where you would like to be. But, this need not be.

I.8.30   We ask of you now, *Why do you continue to cling to a belief regarding yourself that isn't true?* What does this belief offer you that Heaven, Itself, seems not to have? Are you so attached to the idea of being a *human being* that the truth of your divinity has no value? These are questions you must ask yourself. They are ones you must answer. However, while it appears that three questions were asked of you, they really are the same. For they but ask, *Are you ready to return to your Natural State of Being?*

I.8.31   Death is not as the world has taught. For it isn't the cessation of life. Death is merely the belief, as well as the experiences created by the belief, that you are not what you are in Truth. It is nothing more than believing that you are *not-God.* It is the long held belief that you are a human being and nothing more. Yet, with this one belief, born of the original judgment levied against yourself, you have made of Heaven, hell. And, the war between what you are and what you are not continues to rage within the mind.

I.8.32   O Holy Brothers and Sisters, the war is over! Your rebirth into Truth is upon you. Your Divine Self but awaits your awakening. Do not cling to *death* one moment longer. Why experience hell, when but Heaven calls you Home? Always remember, while hell is of your making, Heaven is your birthright, given to you by the Author of Love.

Lesson 8B

I.8.33   This brings us to the next lesson. Let's call it 8B. We ask that you take the paper from lesson 8A, and look at it. Read what you wrote regarding your belief as to what death was. Mark a huge "X" through it. Then, at the bottom of the page, write the following statement: *I accept my True State of Being, and I accept my Divine Self.*

I.8.34   Any time that you are ever tempted to believing in the world's teaching of death, or you're tempted to believing that you are only human, repeat that statement silently to yourself. Continue to repeat the statement until you *feel* your True State of Being settle back in. At first, this may seem childish to you, and that is just fine. Play with this exercise. Don't become overly serious with it. Repeat the statement as if you were a small child saying it. *Feel* the incredible joy it offers. And, if the desire to laugh at yourself arises, laugh! Yes, laugh at yourself and with your Self. For this is the beginning of letting go of the seriousness of a belief that has kept you in chains.

CHAPTER 9

Fear: The Gift Which Takes Everything and Gives Nothing

I.9.1   We begin this discussion with you by reminding you of several passages contained within the *Introduction* to *A Course in Miracles*, where it is written, *The opposite of love is fear, but what is all-encompassing can have no opposite. This course can therefore be summed up this way:* **Nothing real can be threatened. Nothing unreal exists.** *Herein lies the peace of God.*

I.9.2   Then, within *A Course of Love,* you were told that there are only two emotions: love or fear. Recognize, then, that every feeling you have ever had, whether it was anger, sadness, or joy, arises but from either love, or its opposite – *fear.* However, only one of them is real.

I.9.3   Although *fear* appears real, and *feels* real, when it is being experienced, the Truth, which will forever be true, is: *fear* is an illusion. It is nothing but the effect of judgment and guilt, both of which are only found in *time.* For *time* is the foundational illusion upon which all other illusions rest. Without *time,* there can be no *fear.*

I.9.4   There is a beautiful truth contained in two of your bible verses. These two verses expose the intentionality of *fear.* And, once exposed to the Light of Truth, *fear* will always evaporate. It will simply cease to seem to be. Furthermore, those two bible verses contain the remedy for releasing *fear.* However, it is important to recognize that, for *fear* to be released for all time, the causes of fear, which are thoughts of judgment and guilt, must be released as well. For without their undoing, fear will continue to haunt the mind.

I.9.5   Look, now, upon the bible verses which expose *fear* for what it is. In the two verses, it is written, *There is "no" fear in love; but perfect love casteth out fear, because fear hath torment. He that fears is not made perfect in love.* Read those two statements once again. This time allow the intention contained within those verses to bypass the mind. *Feel* the energy pattern contained within them. For it is the energy of Truth, the energy of Love.

I.9.6   What is this grand truth which was revealed to man so long ago? First, come to realize that the energy signature of a word is always found in the meaning of that word. Second, recognize that it is the assigned meaning which creates the intentionality. And, it is the word's intention which creates the manifestation that you experience. For the intention behind a word is what arises within the energy field of possibility and potentiality.

I.9.7   Therefore, We invite you to explore with Us the meaning of the word *fear*, so that you may recognize its energy pattern and its effect on the mind which emits it. For hidden within the meaning of the word *fear* is the singular, most destructive energy found within the human psyche. And, *fear's* intention is buried deep within the subconscious, where it remains both *out of sight* and *out of mind.*

I.9.8   Your word *fear* has its beginnings in the Latin word *periculum*, which itself means *attempt*. Furthermore, the word *attempt* is where your word *temptation* came from. However, there is an archaic meaning for the word *attempt*, which is where the energy signature for *fear* arose. What is the archaic meaning, then, of the word *attempt*? It is but this: *to try to take by force - attack.*

I.9.9   Look, then, upon the meaning of *fear*. For it carries the energy signature of *attack,* which is but the energy pattern found in one who *takes*. This should raise an eyebrow or two.

Do you yet see the implication for the mind? For the mind that *fears* is consumed with the thought that it will be attacked. In other words, *fear* is the *feeling* created in the mind by the thought that something will be *taken* from it. Therefore, the implication is that of *loss*.

I.9.10   Now, We will expose the underbelly of the beast. For it lies on the unholy ground of *loss*. When you understand that the intention of *loss* is that of *ruin*, then it should become strikingly clear as to what the energy pattern of *fear* is. It is simply that of your current *state of being*, which is, as We have already shared with you, the *state of being not-God*.

I.9.11   Let, then, those whose eyes have opened see the Truth. Let those whose heart have opened *feel* the Truth. For in the intentionality of *fear* lies your current *state of being* - your humanness. This, O Child of God, is Love's opposite.

I.9.12   Just as it is said that *love is giving; fear is taking.* Hear us O Holy One, Love *gives,* fear *takes.* Since God is Love, by default *not-God* is fear. God *gives; not-God takes.* Can it be any simpler than this? For herein lies the peace of God. Do you yet *feel* it?

I.9.13 As found in the introductory words of *A Course in Miracles*, what is all-encompassing can have no opposite. How could it? For there is no *loss* in Love, because Love *gives*. And, under the Law, *what is given is received*. Therefore, Love knows not of the idea or concept of *taking;* thus, it has no *fear* within it. And, this is Peace.

I.9.14 Look yet again upon the intention of the words found within the bible verse We discussed earlier. *Perfect Love casts out fear,* For Love does not recognize *fear,* because It does not recognize *attack.* It does not recognize *taking.* And, It does not recognize *loss.*

I.9.15 Hear Us, O Brothers and Sisters, *Love only recognizes Itself.* Therefore, Love does not recognize its opposite. As such, God does not know, or recognize, *not-God.* This is Our salvation. For if God recognized, even for one moment, *not-God,* then *not-God* would be made real, and hell would be permanently affixed within the mind.

I.9.16 *Feel,* then, the Love, which is God. *Feel* it. Breathe it. Experience it. Release the notion that God could *take* anything. For what needs does He have? Only those who currently believe that they are *not-God* have needs. Therefore, they will *take* in order to meet their perceived needs. This is *fear:* it is the gift you have given yourself for believing that you are something other than what you are in truth.

I.9.17   Commit this to memory: *Fear is the gift that has taken Everything from you, but has given you Nothing in return.* In other words, fear has *taken* the God within you, and has given you nothing (*not-God*) in return. Know, in this most Holy Instant, this need not be. For what is *fear?* It is *NOTHING!*

Lesson 9

I.9.18   We come now to the ninth lesson found in this curriculum. It is a lesson designed to restore Truth to a mind still held sway by illusions. For this lesson, you will need three index cards. Write only one statement on each of the three cards. Then, hold one card at a time and read the words you have written on each. As you read the words, *feel* the intention of the statement those words are declaring. *Feel* the power within each statement. The power you will *feel* is your power. It is the power of God. It is His Peace. It is His Truth. It is your Peace. It is your Truth.

I.9.19   The statements are:

Only God is Real.

Only Love is Real.

I am only Love.

CHAPTER 10

The Reign of Terror

I.10.1   In Our last discussion with you, We exposed *fear* for what it is. Now, We will expose the deeper side of *fear*. For the intention of *fear* is the complete darkness associated with the subconscious. This intention is not only well hidden, it is protected by a series of defense mechanisms, whose sole purpose is to defend itself, at all costs, against what it perceives as a coordinated attack upon its existence. These defense mechanisms must be exposed so that Light can once again penetrate the mind.

I.10.2   What is required of you to recognize these defense shields? Nothing more than a little bit of willingness is required. In other words, you need but the desire to *Let there be light.*

I.10.3   When We last spoke with you, We pointed to two bible verses, which were given mankind in order to deliberately expose the intentionality of *fear*. We ask that you recall, now, those verses. For they also demonstrate that *fear* has a twin. And, it is this twin, with which the subconscious has hidden so thoroughly, that it has never seen the light of day.

I.10.4   The verses simply read, *There is no fear in love; but perfect love casts out fear: fear hath torment. He that fears is not made perfect in love.* Read these words again: *fear hath torment.*

I.10.5   Let's look at the intentionality of the word *torment.* For it is within it that you will discover *fear's* twin. What is the name of this twin? It is but *terror.* And, it is but *terror* which has *torment.* What, then, is the effect, or the energy pattern, of *torment*? It is but this: *anguish of the mind.* However, if *torment* is the effect on the mind, then what is its cause?

I.10.6   The cause is *terror,* which is itself *distorted beliefs* held as truth within a mind that accepts separation as real. And, the intentionality of *terror*, thus *torment*, is found in the meaning of the word *distort*, which is *to misshape.* Here is where the energy signature of *terror* is found. For the word *misshape* means to *mis-create.*

I.10.7   Therefore, it is its own *mis-creations* which creates the mental anguish, or the *torment,* found in a mind that believes itself to be separated from God. The *distortions,* the *mis-creations,* were detailed thoroughly for you within *A Course in*

154

Miracles. What are these *distortions*? They are but the splits of the mind.

I.10.8   Look now upon what the subconscious has hidden deep within the darkness. It is the third distortion, as given in *A Course in Miracles,* which has created the *reign of terror* for which you experience. What is the third distortion? It is: *you believe you can distort the creations of God, including yourself.* And, this *distortion* is what We are exposing as the *mis-creation.*

I.10.9   In other words, the mind believes it can *mis-create* God's Holy Creations. But, what does this mean? For it is the implication of the mind's *mis-creation*, which remains not only hidden, but upon the altar of worship found within the unholy temple of the twisted labyrinth of the subconscious. And, this temple, with its altar, is protected by *terror*, itself.

I.10.10 However, to fully recognize the effects of your *mis-creations,* you must come to recognize its energy signature. Although it remains hidden and carefully guarded within the subconscious, the effects created the world you perceive and experience. The energy signature, like all other words, is contained within its meaning. And, the meaning is found in the prefix *mis.* For *mis* means *opposite.* Thus, *to mis-create* is to create the opposite of God. In other words, where True Creation is the extension of Love, *mis-creation* is the extension of *fear*. It is for this reason that everything you create is fearful, because it is the opposite of Love. It is the opposite of God, which is - as you are becoming more conscious of – *not-God*.

I.10.11   Now, We invite you to look at the larger picture that We are showing you. Allow your consciousness to expand beyond the tiny, narrow focus that you have for so long had. In other words, We are asking that you step back and look upon all that these *distortions* entail. *Feel* them. For this is what *denial* has wrought.

I.10.12   Recall that *denial* of your True Self is where the descent into hell began. For as We have already stated, *denial is as total as is Love.* Just like Love, *denial* is all-encompassing. Although your denial encompasses *nothing,* your belief that you have denied *Everything* means that you believe it to be true.

I.10.13   Come to *feel* the implication behind *denial.* For *denial* of Truth results in *mis-creation*, or the projections of *not-God.* And, since *denial* results in *mis-creation*, it also means *denial* results in *terror.* The time has come for you to become familiar with the energy pattern behind the intention of *denial.* For *denial* is the energy for which *time*, itself, arose. And, it is *time* which supports your *mis-creations*. However, *time* rests upon *denial*. For without *denial* of Truth, *time* would simply cease to be.

I.10.14 Therefore, the energy signature of *denial* supports the terror which you encounter each moment you choose to entertain the original judgment that you levied against yourself. When you understand the energy pattern contained within the word, its effect will become crystal clear. And, the energy signature, like everything else, is contained within the intention behind the word.

I.10.15 The meaning for the word *denial* is simply this: *to negate*. Can you *feel* the energy of *negation*? For it too has an implication. And, it is this implication which lies upon the unholy altar of the subconscious mind. Furthermore, this implication rests within the meaning of *negation*, which is: *something that is the absence of something actual – nonentity*. In other words, it is the *negation of being*.

I.10.16 O Holy Child, can you see and *feel* the energy pattern of *negation*, which is that of *denial*? For it is the *state of being nonexistent*. This is the energy pattern of *not-God*. What, then, is the implication? It is but this: *it is the absence of existence*.

In addition, it is the state of *lack*. In this sense, it is the *state of lacking Everything*. Or, the *state of lacking God* – the *state of lacking Love*.

I.10.17   This is the *state of being not-God*. It is the *state of being human*. And, it is your *humanness* which lies on the unholy altar of the subconscious. Recognize, it is your *humanness* that your subconscious hides within its dark recesses. And, your subconscious has created defenses to keep you from looking upon its unreality.

I.10.18   *Feel*, in this most wonderful moment, what We are sharing with you. Your *humanness* can only exist in the dark. For it can only exist within that which itself doesn't exist. It is why it has never seen the Light of Truth. How could it? For when Light is present, you will see that there is nothing upon the altar. Only in darkness, does the altar remain unholy. For when the Light shines upon it, you will see that the altar has remained untouched. It remains just as Holy as it has always been.

I.10.19   In truth, you cannot change, or *distort,* that which God created like Himself. For to do so would imply that the opposite of God exists: that the opposite of Love exists. This, then, is what your subconscious hides from you, so that it can play its game. And, *you are its game piece.* You are the *avatar.*

I.10.20 The subconscious has buried its untruth in darkness and cloaked it with fear, with terror. For the subconscious relies on two things. Its defensive network keeps you from discovering the truth of yourself. These are its defenses: terror and distraction. Its defenses are but games of a mind bent on proving its existence.

I.10.21 O Dear Brothers and Sisters, the subconscious mind wants you dead. *Feel* what We are saying. Do not allow the mind to interpret it. For the mind is what is in need of healing. Therefore, *feel* that which We now speak to you of. *The subconscious wants you dead.* It doesn't want you dead in some future time to come. It wants you dead in this moment. For in your death, *not-God* lives.

I.10.22 *Feel,* then, the implication of that statement. Feel its energy signature. For it is the energy pattern of *not-God.* And, as long as you play in the *state of being not-God,* the *state of being human*, you are *dead* to your True *State of Being,* which is an Extension of the One. The subconscious keeps this hidden safely out of your conscious mind. And, it uses every weapon within its arsenal to keep you from discovering the Truth: that you are a Divine Being.

I.10.23 In our discussion, thus far, it may seem as if We are describing something external to you, which controls you. But, this couldn't be farther from the truth. The subconscious is not an external entity controlling and manipulating you. Rather, it is but a part of you, albeit a part of you that you have hidden from your own self. For the subconscious lies hidden to what you consider to be your consciousness. The subconscious remains hidden and forgotten. But, how can this be?

I.10.24 The answer, while quite simple, seems improbable. Yet, it is nevertheless fact. And, it is here that We will lay it out for you. Your mind will recoil as it reads these words. However, let the words you read bypass the mental constructs you have created. Rather, allow your heart to whisper to you of its *feeling* as your eyes read each word. You will recognize the *feeling*. For it is the *feeling* of Truth. It is the *feeling* of Love. *It is the feeling of your True Self.*

I.10.25 When you asked the question, *What am I,* you had already levied a judgment against yourself. And, the feeling of that judgment was denial. Thus, you *denied* your Divine Self. In this *denial*, which is as complete as is Love, you forgot your

Divine Self. As We have already discussed with you, this was the first split of the mind.

I.10.26   As a result of this first split of the mind, you thought you had separated from God. Having believed you had broken the Law of Being, a thought of *guilt* crept into your mind. And, with the *guilt*, came the feeling of *fear*. This created the second split of the mind. By identifying with the guilt and *fear,* you forgot both the cause and effect from the first split.

I.10.27   The *guilt* and *fear* from the second split created the belief that you would be *punished*. And, this belief created the third split. Just like the previous splits, you forgot the *guilt* and *fear* of the second split when you identified with being a *victim.* This was the creation of the third level, or that of the subconscious. Thus, the belief that you were *not-God* was complete.

I.10.28   Yet, the mind split once again, because of the belief you could be a victim and the associated feeling of *terror* it created. And, it is this fourth split with which you now identify with. For you now fully identify as a human being. However, in your complete identification as a human being, you forgot the mind of the subconscious, the mind that believes it is *not-God.*

I.10.29 Do you not believe you are human? Of course you believe that you are human. And, because you have identified so thoroughly and completely as human, you have no memory of your Divine Self, as well as the splits within your mind which brought you to this current *state of being*. But, do you yet understand what this implication means? Do you *feel it?*

I.10.30 The implication is this: because you have no memory of your True Self, your Divine Self, the Self which is one with God, you can only have experiences which validate and prove your humanness. And, these experiences further fuel the subconscious belief that you are *not-God*. Know, now, that this is what We are here to help you see. We are here to help you open your eyes to your current state, so that you can change your mind by changing your beliefs.

Lesson 10

I.10.31 In order to help you with this, We come now to the tenth lesson in this Course. This lesson is quite simple. On a single index card, write the following statement:

My beliefs create what I see and experience.

I.10.32 As often as possible, silently repeat this statement to yourself throughout your day. While going about your daily tasks and experiences, begin to ask yourself, *What beliefs do I have which created this experience?* You are not asked to change any belief at this time. You are only being asked to experience identifying your beliefs.

CHAPTER 11

Distractions as a Defense

I.11.1   The world you see and experience is a reflection of the darkness which lies within the subconscious mind. Its primary purpose to that mind is to act as a distraction to keep Truth hidden from you. It is the first line of defense used by the subconscious. For it has created a network of distractions which serves to entertain and delight your conscious mind. The world glitters and shimmers with trinkets which seem to call to you to come to them and play. And, you have senselessly moved from one to another hoping to find something from each one that would satisfy your belief that they will provide comfort.

I.11.2   You move from one shining object to the next always with the hope that, if you can just attain it, you will have found the magic elixir that will heal the parts of you that you believe are lacking. Yet, every time you acquired that thing for which your mind desired, it never really gave you the peace or joy for which you had so hoped. Thus, your mind went looking for another glittery, or shiny object hoping yet again that, once it had it in its grasp, the need it believes it has would be silenced and filled.

164

I.11.3   This, then, is the purpose given the world by you. It is simply meant to keep you distracted externally so that you won't go seeking internally. And, to this means, the world has fulfilled its purpose. For it is but a game of *distraction*.

I.11.4   Like all other words We have shared with you, the word *distraction* carries with it an energy signature that has devastating consequences for your mind. And, We mean this quite literally. For the implication carried within the word's meaning is the insanity experienced by the mind of one who believes himself separate and alone.

I.11.5   While archaic, the original meaning of the word *distract* is *insane, mad,* which as you are aware simply means *a disordered state of mind.* Furthermore, the implication goes deeper. For the word *disordered* simply means *to breach* or *break.* It becomes very telling once you recognize that the word *break* carries the meaning *to divide*, which carries with it the meaning *to be separated.*

I.11.6   Therefore, the intentionality, or the energy signature of the word *distraction* is *a mind in a separated state.* When seen in this light, is there any wonder as to why the world is a

165

playground of *distractions.* For the world can only reflect the current *state of mind,* which believes it is *distracted* or separated.

I.11.7   We ask you now to allow the intentionality of the word *distract* to be *felt.* Yes! *Feel* it. For the energy signature is that of a mind that believes it to be *not-God.* And, to demonstrate the intention of the word *distract* yet again, We but remind you that its current meaning is *that which diverts.* Your word *divert* came to you via the Latin word *divertere,* which literally meant *to separate.*

I.11.8   We shall borrow an old phrase still in use by your culture today, in order to help you clearly see and understand what you are reading. The old phrase is: *all roads lead to Rome.* In the cases regarding the intentionality of the words We have shared with you, *all words lead to the belief in separation.* In other words, *the energy patterns all lead to not-God.*

I.11.9   O Child of God, what other intention could the belief in *not-God* create? Like everything else, *distractions* provide the energy to create experiences which but allow the altar of *not-God* to remain hidden in darkness. For you have heard people say of others, *they are out of their minds!* Recognize, then, that the statement applies to every one residing on your planet.

Until the Light is allowed to shine upon the altar dedicated to darkness, then darkness can but continue to consume the mind.

I.11.10   Now, We will paint for you the clearest picture yet of the games played by the mind that resides in total darkness. It is a picture of death and despair. The picture is one that will offer you the opportunity to recognize the energy signature that is emitted by all those who believe that they are separated from their True Self. We ask you to read the words slowly and deliberately. *Feel* what the words are describing. Recognize that the mind will naturally want you to become *distracted* by something, so it will search for anything and everything it can find to keep you from *feeling* what you are reading. For the mind has not yet been made perfect in Love. Therefore, it can but fear the words it reads. Recognize, then, that what you will be reading is the reflection of an insane thought system predicated on maintaining its darkness.

I.11.11   As We have stated before, the subconscious mind is that of darkness. Recall, *darkness isn't the absence of Light, it is the denial of it.* And, found at the center of that darkness is the unholy altar erected to the *god of denial.* That god is what We have thus far simply called *not-God.* Behind the unholy altar is a throne. This is the throne upon which the *god of denial* sits. It is where he controls and manipulates his dark kingdom.

I.11.12 Upon the unholy altar in front of him lies his sacrificial victim. The one offered up in order to meet his unholy and dark demands. Yet, this sacrifice remains completely unaware of where it is or what is happening to it. For it is fascinated with what it believes to be the sights and sounds around it. Thus, it remains distracted and unaware of its true state.

I.11.13 The sacrificial offering is caught up by the forms which but dance around it with their colorful, exotic outfits displayed in what looks like magnificent glory. It is further held sway to the cacophony of sounds which serve to keep its mind mesmerized at the dance occurring all around it. To it, this surely must be heaven. For this must be what it means to be alive.

I.11.14 Although this sacrificial offering knows that it will ultimately meet its end, this little fragment of time spent surrounded by such sights and sounds are worth its death. It accepts death without question just so it can experience the thrill of form. For this form has given it sensation. The sacrifice upon the altar has experienced the warmth of sun upon its face, the beauty of a rose, and the sting of tears from heartache. Yet, these sensations are worth the ultimate price that it is making – that of its own death.

I.11.15   Besides death, there are other prices paid in order to play in the world of form. The price is a burdensome one. Guilt, shame, conflict, sickness, lack, worry, fear, and judgments are but the hefty price for the experience. Yet, once in the trance of form, the sacrificial offering who but lays upon the unholy altar quickly realizes that what was once Heaven, has become hell. It is here that the games and vengeance that the *god of darkness* creates are experienced by its *avatar*, who is but the unsuspecting pawn in the *dark lord's* creations, the *mis-creations* of a mind lost in the agony of guilt and fear.

I.11.16   You, who are but the *avatars* in a *game of make-believe*, know not what you look upon. For your eyes were made but to see in artificial light. This artificial light, too, is but a part of the game. Even the sun, with its warmth and glow, is but artificial light. The sun but sheds light during what you call day, so that form may be seen on full display. Yet, upon the fall of nighttime, you turn on creations of your own making, to provide just enough light for your eyes to see what lies around you.

I.11.17   Do you not yet recognize that, without this artificial light, darkness would but surround you. Yet, this is your *current state of being*. You but exist in a state of darkness, a *state of denial,* the denial of True Light, where you have but made artificial light to allow you to see and experience your own dark creations. Yet, you protect yourself from the Light of Truth for fear that what you have made will be taken from you.

I.11.18 O Holy One, how can that which doesn't exist in the Light be taken from you? The *mis-creations* you have made can only exist in darkness. For once the Light of Truth enters, the dark creations are no longer there. They aren't taken from you. Rather, you will simply know of their unreality. And, you will laugh at ever having believed they were real.

I.11.19 Yet, the *god of darkness* and its *avatar* must be shown for who they are. For until they are exposed, the *dark lord* will continue his *reign of terror*, and you will continue to experience hell. Open your eyes, O Sleeping Child, for it is but you. It is but you who have been playing a game of *make-believe*. For you are but the *god of denial* and its avatar. You are both the victim and victimizer. You are but the *dark lord* who reigns over a blood bath, as well as the one whose blood is spilled.

I.11.20 Is this a pretty picture? No. However, it is one that lays before you the darkness of the subconscious. Is any of this real? Of course not. Yet, to the mind that clings to the belief that it is *not-God,* it can but create experiences that reflect its own inner darkness. And, this inner darkness is what We are here to expose. For until you recognize it as yours, you will continue to believe that you are a victim to outside forces that you have no control over.

I.11.21 We are but here to expose the *game of make-believe* for which you have been playing. While it is but a game that is without real meaning or consequence, you have become so thoroughly identified with the role of *not-God,* of being human, that you have forgotten you but play a game. You have allowed the game to frighten you. And now this fear has become so overwhelming that it has become that which controls you.

I.11.22 Recognize, in this most holy moment, that it is but your own mind that has created both the game and its players. Recognize, too, the power of thought. For your thoughts have created the manifestations and experiences you have had. And, until you change your thoughts, you will continue to experience hell.

I.11.23 Look, then, upon your world. Look upon your experiences. For they are but the reflections of what you *believe* to be true about yourself. And, the belief that you are only human reflects back to you in the world you see and experience. You see lack, war, conflict, poverty, hunger, homelessness, disease, and greed. These do not just live in the world. They live because you allow them to live within you. For you cannot see war unless thoughts of war live within your mind. You cannot see lack, unless you believe you have needs of your own. And, you cannot experience conflict, unless you believe you can be attacked. You see and experience these things because they live within your mind.

I.11.24 These beliefs do not reside in your current state of consciousness. They live in the darkness of the subconscious. And, it is for this reason you see things in the world for which you believe to be external to you. Yet, nothing is external to you. Nothing! Absolutely nothing.

I.11.25 The time has come for you to understand that everything you experience was first birthed within your mind. For nothing happens by mere chance. However, until the subconscious is purged of its darkness, the *reign of terror* it creates will continue. But, within you is all of the Power under Heaven and Earth to change your experiences. For within you is the Power to experience the beauty, the peace, and the joy that is Heaven.

I.11.26 You are Heaven, O Child of God. For what else did God create? And, He endowed His Creations with the same Power for which He has. God did not leave you powerless. Yet, in your belief that you are only human, you but deny the Power within you that would restore your mind to its Holy state.

I.11.27   We cannot take from you your *mis-creations*. But, We can point to the Truth that is forever true: that you are the Light. Darkness cannot hide from the Truth you carry within your heart. Yet, in order to know this Truth again, you must be willing to surrender the *game of make-believe*. You must take off the mask and costume you have been wearing. For they are but the mask and costume of *not-God*. Beneath them, you are clothed in righteousness and glory. These are the garments given to the Holy Child by Its Loving Father.

I.11.28   Where you have adorned yourself with a crown of thorns, We but hold out the *Crown of Glory* that is your birthright. Remove, then, from your head the crown that but symbolizes guilt and suffering. The crown worn by one who believes he is *not-God*. It is but a crown of one who plays *make-believe*. It is not befitting of the Holy Extension of the One. Accept the *crown of glory*. Place it upon your head. Let this simple act bring the *reign of terror* to its end.

I.11.29   We offer to you, now, the eleventh lesson in this course. This lesson is one filled with great hope and joy. For the Light of Truth comes. This lesson will aid you in releasing those beliefs that no longer serve you. Play with this lesson. For it is one of joy. *Feel* its energy. Become one with it. See yourself in it.

Lesson 11

I.11.30 On an index card, write the following statements:

The Light has come.

I am that Light!

I.11.31 For five minutes each morning, as well as five minutes prior to going to bed each night, sit quietly and silently repeat these statements to yourself. Don't just repeat them within the mind. Rather, allow your heart to *feel* them. Allow your heart to experience them. Let your heart repeat them. *Feel* the Power the statements hold. *Feel* their energy. *Feel* their intention. For the statements but represent the Truth of your Natural State of Awareness. If you *feel* like smiling as you silently repeat them to yourself, by all means, allow yourself to do so. For the smile but represents that you are *feeling* the joy for which you are. Experience, then, the joy as it flows through you once again. This, O Holy One, is but the joy that you are. It is but your inheritance.

Rejoice! For the Light has come!

And you are that Light!

CHAPTER 12

The Trance of Time

I.12.1   Just as *darkness is not the absence of Light, but its denial,* time is not the absence of eternity, it is but its denial. Time arose from the denial of Truth. Time provides the scaffolding that allows all of your *mis-creations* to be experienced. Without time, none of what you believe you see could be seen or experienced. It is for this reason that We have already stated that you look upon time as *Father Time.* For time, it would seem, is that entity that gave birth to all that exists in the realm of physicality.

I.12.2   Of all of your *mis-creations*, you fear time more than any other. While you have sought to tame and manipulate most of what you see and experience, time is such that it *feels* to be completely out of your control. Like most of what has arisen within the physical realm, time seems to be governed by its own set of laws. Not only do you fear the laws of time, but you also believe that they are working against you. Time, then, is never seen as a friend, but always as an enemy. One that is silent in its approach, but deadly when it strikes. For in the mind that believes itself to be separate from Everything, *time both giveth and taketh away.*

I.12.3   Time weighs heavily on your mind. With regards to time, you have more aphorisms for it than anything else: *time heals all wounds; there's no time like the present; time is money; time goes by faster when you're having fun; time takes time; spend your time wisely; time and tide wait for no man;* and, many more that you think and say. Is it any wonder that, of all of your *mis-creations*, time consumes more of your daily thoughts than anything else? And, this makes sense, because time is the *first-born* of *denial.* Yet, what you yet fail to realize is: with each moment you spend in denying your True Self, time is birthed anew. For each second is born from the moment-to-moment *denial of eternity* made by you.

I.12.4   Although you believe time is linear, moving from what you perceive as the past, through the present, then into the future, as We have already stated, *time doesn't move, consciousness moves.* The belief that time moves is the great deception. And, it is but yourself you have deceived. You have considered the movement of time as something for which you cannot control. Therefore, you fear it, because you seem to be under its control, rather than time being under your control. Yet, what is this *mis-creation* for which you fear so greatly?

I.12.5   When you recognize what time is, then you can truly laugh it away. For it will no longer be seen as something external to you. Instead, you will see that it is nothing more than a mental construct, a construct which allowed form to take shape. Recognize, now, that form is just energy, which has slowed and become dense.

I.12.6   We will begin our discussion on time by stating that the fear resulting in the belief that time is real comes from the first three words found in your bible. The words, *In the beginning*, signify the moment time was imagined. For only time, and that which is within it, can have a *beginning*. And, since time and everything within it has a *beginning*, it must naturally have an *ending*. For everything that has a beginning has an ending. And, this is the mental construct from which all form has arisen. Thus, all form has its beginning and will therefore have its ending, just as you believe you will.

I.12.7   Let's examine what the word *beginning* implies. For it has a much deeper implication than you think. And, it is this implication which keeps the mind entranced within the matrix of time. As with all words We have discussed so far, the energy signature is contained within the word's intention. And, the intention is buried within its meaning.

I.12.8   The word *begin* means *to start* As you are familiar with. Yet, it is within the word *start* where the implication for the word *begin* is uncovered. For the word *start* means *to alarm*, which itself is defined as *to disturb*. It is here where the implication is *felt*. For the word *disturb* carries with it the meaning *to destroy the tranquility of.* And, the word *destroy* means to *ruin,* which We have already discussed with you. *Feel*, then, the implication of the word *beginning*. For the implication is the *destruction of Peace.* It is the destruction of your birthright as a Child of God.

I.12.9   Recall, the word *ruin* means *to fall*, or *descend*. Therefore, the intention of the word *begin* is the energy of *ruin,* which is simply that of *one who descends*. When you learn of the meaning of the word *time*, you will discover the true implication behind *time.*

I.12.10   Your word *time* came to you via the Old English word *tīd*, which means *tide.* The energy signature for *time* is found within the word *tide,* which means *to befall*, or *fall.* Again, the implication behind *fall* is *to descend*. However, like every word that We have discussed with you, they all involve your *state of being.* And, the word *fall* is no different. For the word *fall* carries with it the meaning *to pass suddenly and passively into a state of body or mind or a new state or condition.*

I.12.11   Do you yet see the implication of *time?* Do you *feel* it? For *time* is your current *state of being.* Hear Us, O Divine Child, your current *state of being IS time*, because you believe yourself to *be a fallen, or separated, one.* More specifically, your current *state of being* is that of a *body-mind*, which is the meaning implied behind *a fallen one, or one who has descended.*

I.12.12   Let your heart speak to you now of the intentionality of *time.* For *time* and *form* are synonymous. You cannot have one without the other, just as you cannot have a cause without an effect. In this case, *time* is the cause, form is its *effect.* Furthermore, *time* is the cause, the *body-mind* is its effect.

I.12.13   Now, We ask that you *feel* the energy pattern of *time* and its effect, For it is the very energy of *denial,* whose effect is *not-God.* Time was born of denial, as surely as the *body-mind* was born in the mind of one who believes he is *not-God.* As such, *time* was born in your mind the moment you levied the original judgment against yourself when you asked the question – *What am I?*

I.12.14 Open your eyes and look upon what you have made of yourself. Just as cause and effect cannot be separated, neither can time be separated from its form. Therefore, in your current *state of being,* you are both *time* and *form.* This is why the word *beginning* strikes fear within the mind. For just as time will end, so too will its form.

I.12.15 Come to understand, then, the reasoning behind the statement that *time doesn't move, consciousness moves.* For time seems to only move when form moves. And, this has been shown to be true by your scientists. It is one of the reasons as to why time seems to move more slowly when you are sitting still. However, time does not ever seem to fully stop because your consciousness never stops. Recognize the greater implication here: that *you are time in form.* In other words, *you are time in the flesh.* For how else could you experience your creation?

I.12.16 You have been told that *this is a dream of judgment.* Yet, if *time* and *form* are the effects of the original judgment levied against yourself, then what is meant by the statement, *this is a dream of judgment?* Remember, like words, statements carry an energy signature as well. Therefore, what is the energy signature of this statement?

I.12.17   In the statement, *this is a dream of judgment*, the intention is actually found in the word *dream*. Therefore, the word *dream* carries with it a specific energy pattern, and that pattern creates what you see, what you hear, and what you experience. And, like all other words, its energy is found within its meaning. However, as you are now aware, the meaning of most words are hidden within multiple levels and layers meant to keep you from recognizing the word's intention.

I.12.18   The word *dream* is defined as *something that fully satisfies a wish: an ideal*. Furthermore, the word *ideal* means *relating to or constituting mental images, conceptions, or ideas*. This is where the intention of the word *dream* lies hidden. For your word *idea* came to you via the Greek word *idein,* which means *to see.*

I.12.19   Again, you should be raising an eyebrow right about now. For while you understand that the meaning of the word *see* is *to perceive by the eye*, it also carries the meaning *to judge.* Therefore, to *dream* is *to perceive* and *to judge.* Thus, the statement, *this is a dream of judgment*, quite literally means that *this is a judgment of judgment,* as well as *this is a perception of judgment.* Can you *feel* the energy pattern, then, for the statement? For it is the energy pattern of *judging*. And, you will *see* what you have judged.

I.12.20 What is the implication of *judging?* It is always guilt. Remember, a thought of judgment creates the feeling of fear. And, the judgment with its fear creates the belief that one is guilty. Since the words *to dream* and *to judge* carry with them the same intention, meaning they carry the same energy pattern, let's take a moment in time to look at how emitting this energy creates your experiences.

I.12.21 Recall that the word *dream* runs through the word *see,* which means to perceive with the eyes. And, as you have already learned, *projection leads to perception.* Therefore, *projection* leads to that which you *see.* And, like all other words, the word *projection,* or *to project,* carries with it a distinctive energy pattern. When you *see* what the word projection implies, you will *feel* it within you. For it will stir old emotions buried within the darkness of the subconscious, causing them to rise back to the level of your conscious awareness.

I.12.22 The word *projection* means *the externalization of blame, guilt, or responsibility as a defense against anxiety, and placing them on other people or objects.* This just simply means that you *project*, or *cast away* from you, blame, guilt, and responsibility on others, because of fear held within your mind. Furthermore, the word *project* is defined as *idea,* as well as *to cast forward*, or *cast off.*

I.12.23   Earlier in this discussion, you learned that the word *idea* means *to see*. And, We have spoken before of *casting off*, when We discussed with you the bible verses, *There is no fear in love; but perfect love casts out fear: because fear hath torment. He that fears is not made perfect in love.*

I.12.24   Now, the *time*, which is really you, has come for you to open your eyes. We are not speaking of the body's eyes, but the eyes of your heart: the eyes that allow you to know Truth. Let, then, your heart look upon what your body's eyes are going to read. For your heart is ready to be free again.

I.12.25   *There is no fear in love.* Read that statement again. *Feel* it. For it is Absolute Truth. There is no *fear* in love, because love has no opposite.

I.12.26   Look carefully upon the next section of the bible verse, *perfect love casts out fear.* For here you will discover the Truth, which will set you free, if you will but *feel* it. Do you yet *see* it? For it is contained in the very words being used. Here it is: in order for perfect love to cast out fear, then that perfect love must have first recognized and felt fear. Yet, *love knows not fear*. What, then, is meant by *perfect love casts out fear*?

I.12.27   It will help you to *see* it more clearly when you read it as *perfect love projects fear*. Yet, how can perfect love project fear? The answer, O Holy One, requires your heart to read these words, and not your mind. Always remember, it is your mind that created hell, not your heart.

I.12.28   O Holy One, you are *Perfect Love*. Period. But, to know this, you must come to understand what is being implied behind the words *Perfect Love*. In order to understand what the implication is, you must come to know what the word *perfect* means. The word is simply defined as *pure* and that which *lacks no essential part of the whole: complete*. In addition, *pure* means *to be free from guilt*. Therefore, *Perfect Love* is Love which is *free from guilt* and *lacks nothing*.

I.12.29   YOU ARE PERFECT LOVE. This is your Truth. This is your *True State of Being*. You are free from guilt. And, you do not lack anything. You are, in this very moment, whole and complete.

I.12.30   However, since you believe that you are *guilty* for having separated from God, you, who are *Perfect Love,* project fear. Why? Because *fear has torment.* Therefore, when you denied Love upon the original judgment, your mind felt anguish. Wanting to save itself from this anguish, your mind projected, or *cast out*, its fear. *Remember always, that there is only Love or fear. What is not Love, whether it is anguish, torment, or anger, can only be fear. And, it is never justified.*

I.12.31   Realize, in this holy instant, that projection is nothing more than a defense mechanism the mind uses in order to free itself from its fear. Yet, projection does not free the mind. It only creates sights and experiences that further creates more fear within the mind. Here is where *time* and *projection* intersect. For in each moment that you deny Love, you simultaneously project the mental anguish created from your denial of Truth.

I.12.32   Therefore, you have the sense that time moved forward. However, time didn't move forward, you projected it forward by projecting externally the mind's torment. Never forget, you cannot separate cause and effect. They occur simultaneously.

185

I.12.33 *Feel* what you are reading. For *anguish of the mind* is the meaning of torment, which is also that of the word *disturb,* or *to mis-create.* Recognize, that because of judgment, you *project* fear. And, *projection is the misappropriate use of extension,* which is synonymous with *mis-creating.*

I.12.34 Follow the reasoning. For Love is not illogical. Since a thought of judgment creates the feeling of fear, then *time* creates *form.* Hence, *time* is the cause and the *body-mind* is its effect. Here, then, is the implication: *time* is the symbol of the original judgment, just as the *body-mind* is the symbol of its effect.

I.12.35 In addition, the time has come to bring into your awareness Truth by pulling back the veil of guilt. For the *time* has come for you to *be made Perfect in Love.* But, you must first come to recognize how guilt is created. Once understood, then you will recognize that you have the power to change your beliefs, thus experiences, by changing your thoughts.

I.12.36 Allow what you are about to read to settle within your mind. You are not asked to change anything as of yet. You are simply being invited to allow this information to enter into your mind without interpreting it. Simply *feel* it. Everything you will read is in accordance with the workings of the Spiritual Laws. And, this your heart knows.

I.12.37   Judgment creates fear, and these create the belief of guilt, which creates more fear. This guilt and fear creates the belief that one will be punished, which creates even more fear. The belief that one will be punished creates the belief that one can be a victim. And, the cycle merely repeats itself, because once you believe that someone or something has made you a victim, a new judgment is birthed.

I.12.38   Look, then, upon this cycle. For it is the hamster wheel that keeps you in the trance that is time. This is the energy pattern that creates your experiences. It is for this reason that nothing seems to change in your life. Why? Because you have not broken the cycle. And, breaking this cycle is the purpose for this Course. For until the cycle of judgment is broken, you can but create more experiences in time. More importantly, until you break the *cycle of judgment*, you will continue to *project* time. And, you will have no choice but to continue to experience time.

I.12.39   Since God is eternal, then *not-God* is time. Since God is Love, then *not-God* is fear. Therefore, by identifying as *not-God,* you are identifying with time and fear. These are your *mis-creations.* And, this is what you have made of yourself. In order to exit the realm of time and form, the realm of time and the body-mind, the realm of physicality and its experiences, you must release your identity as *not-God.* There is nothing more asked of you.

I.12.40 The *trance of time* is nothing more than the continued *denial of your True State of Being,* which is but the fear of time. O Child of God, to fear *time* is but to fear your creation. More importantly, to fear *time* is but to fear yourself. Is it any wonder why you create the experience of *time?* How can you but create experiences in *time?* The answer should be obvious now. You continue to experience *time,* because you project *time.*

I.12.41 Just as God can only create that which is like Himself, you can only do the same. However, because you believe that your current *state of being* is *not-God,* which is *time,* you can only create, or *mis-create,* time. *Feel* these next words: *you create time by the subconscious denial of God in this moment and every moment which is.* It is for this reason, that time appears to move. For in this moment, as you continue to deny your True State of Being, you create a moment of time. As the next moment comes and you once again deny your True Self, the previous moment becomes your past. And, the past continues to expand, making it appear real. Furthermore, your

188

belief in time, thus your belief that you are *not-God,* is strengthened.

I.12.42   To help you break the *trance of time,* We invite you, now, to complete the twelfth lesson of this curriculum. This lesson will help you discover some of your beliefs in time, so that you can release them. When you are free from these beliefs, you will begin to create experiences of oneness and unity, rather than those of separation and time.

Lesson 12

I.12.43   For this lesson, you will need a sheet of paper. At the top of the paper, write: *the beliefs that bind me to time.* Then, underneath the header, write every saying you can remember regarding time, just as We did earlier. For example, *time is money.* Write all that come into your mind. Do not attempt to complete this lesson in one sitting. Rather, allow yourself several days to *think* about time. Continue to record every saying, every belief, regarding time that comes into your field of consciousness.

I.12.44   When you *feel* that there aren't any other beliefs, or sayings, that you can recall, then sit quietly and read them to yourself. Then, mark an "X" across them. Beneath the "X," write this statement:

I release these false beliefs.

I.12.45 After writing that statement, sit some place that you find quiet and comfortable. And, simply repeat this statement to yourself for approximately five minutes. Do this for three days or nights, whichever works best for you. On the fourth day, take another sheet of paper and write the following statements. Over the next seven days, again, sit quietly and repeat these statements for approximately ten minutes. It matters not whether you do this in the morning or evening. Simply provide the willingness to complete this lesson. The statements are:

The trance of time ends.

I am now ready to transcend.

CHAPTER 13

The Heavenly War: The Cycle of Conflict

I.13.1   You, Child of God, are Heaven. For what else did God create? Your *True State of Being* is *Heaven.* It is Love. It is Joy. And, it is Peace. They are your treasures. Yet, with each moment that you *deny* your *Divine Self,* you are not experiencing what you are. Until you experience Oneness with All That Is, you can but experience conflict. And, this conflict is the *Heavenly War.* But, what is *conflict?* What is its energy pattern? And, how is internal conflict externalized to create your experiences?

I.13.2   Just as *darkness is not the absence of light, but its denial; conflict is not the absence of peace, but its denial.* It is for this reason that the world cannot know peace. Why? Simply because it believes peace is the absence of conflict. In other words, the world defines peace as it relates to conflict. And, as long as there is a comparison made between two seemingly opposing ideas, then there can be but conflict.

I.13.3   When you recognize what the implication of the word *conflict* is, you will understand why peace has nothing to do with conflict. And, like other words, the intention of the word *conflict* is found within its meaning, which is: *the mental struggle resulting from incompatible or opposing needs, drives, wishes, or external or internal demands.* Recognize that the implication arises from the word *incompatible* as found in the meaning of *conflict.* Therefore, the energy signature of the word is found there as well.

I.13.4   The word *incompatible* simply means *not both true.* Thus, conflict arises within your mind because you are trying to make *an opposing wish true.* What is this opposing wish? It is but this: *to make of yourself what you desire.*

I.13.5   Here then We expose the deeper implication of conflict. For the energy pattern associated with conflict is that of a *wish.* We ask you, once again, to allow what you are going to read to bypass the defenses of your mind by letting your heart interpret the words. For within the following words, lies the power used by the subconscious to maintain its stranglehold over your conscious field of awareness and experiences.

I.13.6   What, then, is a *wish?* It is but this: *the desire to give FORM to something or someone.* In addition, the word *wish* also implies *a want or need for something so desired.* Thus, the energy signature of *conflict* is the energy of *desire; more specifically,* the *desire to give FORM to something.* For the *body-mind*, while created from the denial of truth, arose from the mind that had *the desire to be something other than what it is in Truth.*

I.13.7   This, O Divine One, is what We call *wishery*. And, *wishery*, is always associated with *wishcraft,* which is nothing more than using the power of the mind for its *dark desires,* rather than using the mind for its created purpose – to extend Love. For the subconscious knows the power of the mind. It knows that every thought you think gives form to its desire: *the desire to create as it WISHES.*

I.13.8   Yet, *wishery* can but create *conflict*. For internal conflict is born each moment that you *desire* to *deny Truth.* As We have previously discussed, with each creation of a new moment of *time*, the mind is tormented. For *time* is *conflict,* because *time* opposes eternity, just as *form* opposes Spirit. This opposition, which is between the *Divine Realm* and those of the lower ones, is the *Heavenly War.* This war is not waged on a battlefield. Rather, this war rages within your own mind. And, until you surrender the *wish* to be something other than what you are in Truth, the war and its conflict will continue. For you cannot know Peace as long as there is conflict and war raging each moment within your mind.

I.13.9   Furthermore, in the attempt to assuage the mind, you *project*, or try to cast off, the conflict. Again, this is not done on the conscious level, but at the subconscious level. It is for this reason that you see and experience some *form* of conflict almost daily. It is also the reason as to the wars which seem so prevalent on your planet. When you understand the nature of energy patterns upon the *grand field of possibility and potentiality*, you will immediately see how the *intention* of a thought, a word, affects the *grand field*, thereby creating what you *see* and experience.

I.13.10   Now, We ask you to *feel* the words you are going to read. Allow your *feelings* to wash through your being. Let your *feelings* soothe your mind, so that it can become still. In the stillness, your mind will comprehend what your heart is sharing with it.

I.13.11   Recognize, in this sacred moment that We share with you, that God is Peace. Therefore, *not-God* is conflict. Although God knows not of conflict or war, you do. Why? Because of your identification as *not-God*. As long as you continue to identify with that which you are not, you will continue to see and experience conflict, because you will continue to *project* it to that which you believe lies external to you. And, the conflict, which is *projected* externally, becomes the very distractions that the subconscious uses to keep you consciously focused on the world and your experiences so that you won't turn within and discover the Truth: that you are a Divine Being.

I.13.12   Look, now, upon the greatest, deceptive game perpetrated upon you by your own subconscious mind. For the energy pattern of conflict is tightly wrapped within the *victim/blame* game. Although We brought this to you in an earlier discussion, We will take this opportunity to expose the con job being played between two levels of your conscious being, namely your subconscious and conscious states of mind. For it takes a willing partnership between the two, in order to have the game appear real.

I.13.13   Recall that the belief that you could be a victim occurred as a result of the third split of the mind. This belief rests upon another belief, one that distracts the mind more than any other, save the belief in time. What is that belief? It is but the belief that *attack* is both possible and real. Without the firm, almost unshakable, belief that you risk being *attacked,* the *victim/blame game* could not be played. For you would have walked off the playing field long ago.

I.13.14 Because of the belief that you can be attacked, you remain hyper vigilant for any threats against you, whether emotional or physical. This hyper vigilance keeps your mind in a defensive posture, always looking for where it believes the next attack will come from. In addition, this seemingly innocuous act keeps you focused outward. And, this outward focus is just another distraction created from the fear and torment simmering within the subconscious mind.

I.13.15 As We did before, We are going to paint a vivid portrait of how the *victim/blame* game keeps you embroiled in *conflict*, while strengthening your belief that *attack* is both possible and real. This, too, is likely to create turmoil within an already conflicted mind. Therefore, We invite you to simply read the words. Do not interpret or judge what you will be reading. Just allow the string of words to flow into your conscious awareness. We do ask, however, that you *feel* the totality of the picture being painted for your eyes. For your *feelings* will later serve as the catalyst to create the change of thinking required to create experiences of Unity with the All of Everything.

I.13.16 In order to be a victim, you had to experience something happening where you *BELIEVED* you were attacked, whether it was verbal, or one perpetrated against your physical being. Yet, allow this to settle into your mind: *in accordance with the*

Law of Belief, you can only see and experience what you believe to be true about yourself, another, or the world around you. Therefore, in order to *perceive* that you had been *attacked,* and were therefore a *victim,* you have to maintain, as a part of your belief system, a belief that you can experience attack and be made a victim. Read these next words slowly and with an open mind: *you CAN NOT SEE or EXPERIENCE anything for which you do not believe is possible.* And, like all beliefs, they are created from a thought and feeling.

I.13.17   However, here is where the game goes unchallenged by all who play it: in order to believe you were a victim to another's words or actions, you had to have *judged the offender guilty of an offense against you.* That means: *you judged that person guilty of attacking you.* Yet, even before you could levy the judgment against the other person, you had to have first judged either the words or actions as hurtful. And, in that fateful moment, a grievance was born.

I.13.18   With the birth of the grievance and a judgment of guilt levied against the offending party, you are now officially a *victim.* What does this mean? Quite simply, you believe you were attacked, harmed in some manner, passed judgment against the offender, and demanded some form of recompense, which can be anything from an apology or something harsher depending on the severity of the perceived form of the attack. With this belief that you were a victim, a *resentment* has been created within your mind. And, every chance your mind has, it will replay the circumstance of the attack over and over, and yet over again.

I.13.19 Like all games played by the subconscious mind, there is a dark desire hidden within its intention. And, this dark desire goes unnoticed by you. For with each act where you believe you were a victim, there is also a corresponding increase in your level of distrust for others. This increase in your distrust of others is used by the subconscious mind to fortify your defense shield and goad you into being more alert and hyper vigilant for the next attack that you are sure awaits you just over the horizon.

I.13.20 It is here where We expose the final act in the game of conflict played out by the subconscious mind. This final act is where its darkest intention lies buried beneath layer upon layer of judgments, hurts, and resentments. For the subconscious ever so quietly whispers to you, *how can a loving God have allowed this to happen to me?* And, with that thought, your distrust of God widens, which only strengthens your identification as *not-God.*

I.13.21   O Divine Child, look carefully upon what you have just read. For not only did We describe the game of conflict, but We described how your mind remains *entranced by time*. For just like the finest watch made with its internal, intricate gears perfectly synchronized so that the hands displayed externally will reflect the precise movement of time, so too does your subconscious use its internal world to precisely shape and form what you believe to be your external experiences.

I.13.22   As long as you identify, even if it is on a subconscious level, with *not-God*, you can but create experiences of conflict, because of the inner conflict playing out within your mind. The aim of this Course isn't to teach you what oneness is, but to help your mind unify itself. Although, in Truth, you are whole and complete in this very moment, your mind still believes that it is bound to *time*. And, this belief must be undone before you can experience True Unity within your Self.

I.13.23   Only in True Unity, True Oneness with your Self and All That Is, will you know Peace. Until now, you have only *felt* this Peace for fleeting moments. Yet, those moments were long enough for your heart to yearn for its return. However, to know the Peace which passes all understanding, you must first release your belief as to what Peace is. For the world knows it not and has taught you erroneously.

I.13.24   The world defines peace as: *tranquility resulting from an agreement to end conflict.* Thus, according to the world's teachings, peace is defined in terms of *conflict*, rather than Love. This means that peace cannot ever be permanent within your world, because conflict is its determiner.

I.13.25   *True Peace knows not conflict.* For True Peace only recognizes Love. It knows not of an opposite, because True Peace has no fear within it. True Peace knows not of attack, simply because it *sees* Itself in all things. To know True Peace once again, you must give up the belief in attack for all time and forevermore.

I.13.26   The belief that you can be *attacked* is insidious indeed. And, the belief that it is *right* and *justifiable* to return *attack* for *attack* is the one belief which must be undone first. Recognize, then, that all conflict experienced, whether internal and external, is predicated on the belief that attack is not only possible but expected.

I.13.27   Like all other words We have discussed with you, the word *attack* has an energy pattern that affects the *grand field of possibility and potentiality*, as well. You know that the word *attack* carries with it the meaning *to assail, or assault, with physical force or unfriendly words, as well as the beginning of some destructive action.* However, the intentionality of *attack* is found within its hidden meaning, which is *descend.*

I.13.28 You are aware by now that the intention behind *descent* is *to fall,* which carries with it the energy signature of *death.* Remember, *death* is not the cessation of life. *It is its denial.* Therefore, the energy signature of *attack* is that of *not-God.* This means that thoughts of attack, or their actions, always create experiences of *conflict,* both internally and externally.

I.13.29 It is helpful to remember that only a body can attack another body, whether verbally or physically. The mind, however, can only attack itself. Yet, in an attempt to free itself from the internal conflict that rages within it, a mind will project onto its body, or other bodies, the conflict it feels. When a mind projects the inner conflict upon the perceived body-mind of itself, the body will experience disease and illness. When the mind projects its internal conflict onto another, then it will experience what it perceives as an attack from which it must defend itself. Yet, where did this belief in attack arise? For in understanding how the belief in attack arose will you find its undoing.

I.13.30 The belief of attack came into the mind in the exact moment that the belief in time arose. Recall that time is the moment-to-moment creation of a mind denying eternity. It is the moment-to-moment denial of your Divine Self. This denial is an attack against yourself. And, this denial, this attack, is perpetuated with each moment that you choose to identify as a body-mind. This is the reason that the mind stays conflicted.

I.13.31 However, there is a much broader implication here. For your mind believes that it is attacking God in its denial of Truth. Now, recall into your consciousness the Law of Love that We have shared with you. Once again, the Law simply states, *that which you give another, is but gifted unto yourself.* Look carefully upon this Law. *Feel* it. Understand it. For as We have shared before, *the Laws do not harm you; rather, they protect you.*

I.13.32 What does this mean? Quite simply and literally, you cannot attack God, or your Divine Self. For your Divine Self *being* an Extension of the One, is that One. Do you yet see and *feel* the insanity of the belief that you could perpetrate an attack on or against God? The Laws prohibit it. And, regardless as to what you might have previously thought, or were taught, you can neither break nor usurp the Laws.

I.13.33 Furthermore, this is the reason why *defense* against attack is nothing more than attack hiding in sheep's clothing. In order to believe you need to defend yourself, whether the defense is erected for a perceived future attack, or one that you believe is happening within the moment, is to believe that attack is real. And, what you perceive as a defense against attack is nothing more than an attack against yourself. Yet, how can this be?

I.13.34 When you defend yourself, not only have you strengthened within you the belief that attack is real, and that you can be attacked, you further strengthen the belief that you are a separate body-mind moving amongst other separate body-minds. And, because you believe deep within your subconscious that you could attack someone or something if necessary, you have a certain level of distrust for everyone including yourself. Never forget this: *THAT WHICH YOU DISTRUST, YOU FEAR.*

I.13.35 Here, then, is the intention for both *attack* and *defense*. For the intention lies in *distrust.* Therefore, the underlying energy pattern emitted by holding the false belief that attack is real is that of *distrust.* And, the energy of *distrust* creates many of the experiences which seem to occupy your *time.* For *distrust* is but another *distraction* the subconscious mind uses to keep you from seeking within yourself for the Truth of your Reality.

Lesson 13

I.13.36 This brings us to the thirteenth exercise in this Course. This exercise is different than those you have completed thus far, for you will not be asked to write anything. You are only being invited to observe your thoughts and, when necessary, generate a new thought pattern. Thus, this exercise is to help you recognize thoughts that involve *attack* or *defense* of yourself, as well as the perception that you have been or are experiencing attack.

I.13.37 As you go about your day, maintain a constant vigilance as to the thoughts that arise within your field of consciousness. Look for any thoughts which signal that a trigger has been pulled where you believe you are either being attacked or that you are attacking another. Until you become better equipped at recognizing thoughts as they arise, or even before they do, allow your *feelings* to act as your alert mechanism.

I.13.38 For instance, if you *feel* anger or hurt within your consciousness, rest assured you have already entertained and accepted a thought of having been attacked in some form. *Do NOT judge yourself for this.* For that does nothing but add another judgment to the judgments which have already been made within the mind. Instead, upon the moment that you recognize anger or hurt, say to yourself:

I see this for what it is.

This experience has arisen from my belief that attack is real.

I.13.39 Then, come to recognize that you *have a choice* in what you experience, because you have a choice in the thoughts you entertain. Let your *feelings* be your guide. Allow your *feelings* to show you which path you are on. For there are only two paths: Peace or conflict. If you are *feeling* anger, then you are on the path of conflict. And, you are emitting the energy pattern that will create more experiences of conflict, both internal and external. However, if you are feeling Peace, then know that you are consciously moving in Love.

CHAPTER 14

Distrust

I.14.1   Of all the energy signatures that We have discussed with you so far, the energy pattern of *distrust* is likened unto a thread interwoven throughout each of the energy signatures that you project. The energy of distrust is by far the one in which the mind clings to the most vehemently. Where the intentionality of other energies remain hidden within the subconscious, *distrust* is an energy found in both your conscious awareness, as well as your subconscious.

I.14.2   As you are well aware by now, under the Law of Cause and Effect, thoughts are causal agents, feelings are their effects. In the statement, *that which you distrust, you fear*, distrust is the thought, fear is the feeling. However, on the energetic level, what does this mean?

I.14.3   O Holy One, it simply means that *distrust* is the thread which holds the veil of dreams together. Think of time as the scaffolding that keeps the veil in place and *distrust* as the thread binding each illusion to the next, creating what appears as a solid veil standing between you and Truth. Now, We will expose the deception that is created by the energy of *distrust* that is held within your mind. For until the depth of *distrust* is seen by you, its energy will continue to quietly create experiences that strengthen your belief that not only is attack possible, but that you can be attacked. Furthermore, *distrust* leads to the belief that conflict is just a normal aspect of human life. And, this belief must be dissolved before new experiences can be created.

I.14.4   In order to understand and recognize what *distrust* really is and how it affects everything you create, let's examine the word and uncover its intentionality so that We can expose its energy signature. Then, once recognized, you will see how it affects the *grand field of potentiality and possibility.* And, you will also see how your experiences of attack and conflict manifest.

I.14.5   The word *distrust* is defined as *to have no trust.* But, if *distrust* is *to have no trust*, what does *trust* mean? To discover its true meaning, you must recognize that your word *trust* was derived from the word *true.* And, it is within the meaning of the word *true,* which means both *truth* and *reality,* where the intention of the word *distrust* is found.

I.14.6   *Feel*, then, the intention, or the energy signature, of the word *distrust.* Come to understand what its implication really is; because within its implication, you will *perceive* how it affects the well-being of your mind. In addition, *feel* how the implication behind *distrust* has shaped every experience you have ever had. And, We mean that quite literally.

I.14.7   Since God is Truth, then *not-God* is *not-Truth*. Yet, it goes much, much deeper. And, it is here that your mind will attempt to control what it is ingesting. Why? Because what you are about to read is what creates the terror and all of the conflict the mind experiences. Allow then your heart to read these words. For your heart already knows this truth: only God is Real. Thus, *not-God* is *not-real*.

I.14.8   O Child of God, do you yet *see* the implication behind *distrust*. For it is simply this: *that which you distrust, you fear, because of the unreality created.* Do you understand this? For it is implying that, in Truth, there is *nothing real, or true, found in that which is unreal.* This quite simply means that *not-God does not exist.* Therefore, neither does any of its mis-creations. For everything that you believe real - is not. None of it exists in Truth. None of it exists in Reality. And, there is no amount of *wishcraft* that will make it Real.

I.14.9   This, then, is the terror born of the original judgment you levied against yourself. For the mind to know that everything it has made, including time, is not real breeds a terror so profound that the mind split four times from it, and it still hides in the dark trembling. Thus, the greatest deception played by the mind is the one in which it believes everything it sees and experiences is real. And, it is this deception which creates the distrust that is then projected onto God, as well as everyone and everything within the world, including yourself.

I.14.10   Yet, herein lies your freedom if you will but *feel* it. You have for so long carried the *fear of loss* with you that it has become like a family member. Although you would like the *fear* to be removed, you also don't want to give it up, because of what you perceive will be lost by doing so. But, We ask you now, *Is it truly possible to lose what never existed in reality?*

I.14.11   Allow yourself to *feel* the energy behind that question. For in *feeling* it, you will come to finally understand these words: *Nothing real can be threatened. Nothing unreal exists. Herein lies the peace of God.* Look gently and lovingly upon those words once again and you will *feel* your freedom. And, from this freedom, you will finally taste True Peace.

I.14.12   *Nothing real can be threatened.* Yes! *Feel* the energy of the statement. For it is the energy of Truth. It is the energy of hope. And, it is the energy of true, everlasting freedom. For in this statement lies the dismantling in your belief that *attack* is possible and that *defense* of yourself is not only warranted, but necessary.

I.14.13 Recognize, then, what that statement *IS* implying. For its implication is not just that of eternity, but also of your safety. *Feel* the energy of that statement yet again. For in it is found the only defense you ever need remember. And, it is the *defense* provided by Truth.

I.14.14 What is this Truth? It is but this: you are Love. You are spirit. You are Holy. And, you do not lack for anything, for everything has been given you.

I.14.15 Furthermore, your safety rests but upon this Truth: your spirit is in a state of grace forever. This spirit is the Spirit of God. And, spirit is eternal. Therefore, you are eternal. Your spirit cannot be threatened, harmed, attacked, or destroyed. Your spirit cannot and will never pass away. For your spirit is not bound by *time.* And, because it isn't, neither are you.

I.14.16 However, here is where the consternation and fear is found: *nothing unreal exists.* O Holy Child, this simply means that *fear* and all of its manifestations, time, death, disease, illness, grief, loss, lack, loneliness, depression, conflict, attack, anger, and rage *do not exist.* Is the body included in those? *Oh, yes!* For the body is but the symbol of every conceivable manifestation of fear created by the mind. Yet, more specifically, the body is the ultimate representation of *distrust,* because it is the ultimate symbol of *not-God.*

I.14.17 What good reason, then, do you have for *wishing* to maintain these things that are *not real?* Do they bring you Joy? Do they offer you Peace? Are these really the things that you value and treasure? If they aren't, then *rejoice* in this most glorious moment. Why maintain the belief in hell, when your Self but awaits your laying aside your identification with things that are not real? It is but a choice you make each moment. One choice offers you freedom, the other can but offer pain and bondage. Yet, your decision rests but on your willingness to *TRUST* your Father, thus your Self, once again.

I.14.18 Know, in this moment, that those things that are real will never be taken from you. What are those things? They are but the gifts given to you by God. They are your real treasure. And, each time you extend your treasure, you extend your Self, thereby increasing the Kingdom. Fear not, O Holy Brothers and Sisters. For every loving thought you have ever had, or will ever have, awaits you. They are not taken from you by some thief in the night. For every loving thought is of you and is you. Each one blesses the whole of creation. And, they bless you.

I.14.19 Yet, to a mind entranced by *time,* there is a thief, which stands in the shadows, who but waits for the moment to strike you down. And, it is the fear of this thief and his attack that prevents you from fully trusting God. Who is this thief? What is his name?

I.14.20 He is *Father Time.* And, it is but he, whom you distrust. For it is but he who will come, hiding behind the cloak of darkness, to take from you all that you treasure. O Child of God, do not fear this stranger. For *time* is but your creation. And, when he comes calling, gladly give him all those things he comes for. Do so with the knowledge that you but give him nothing. Therefore, he can but take nothing. For no longer do you treasure those things which once bound you to both *time* and hell. Instead, you know where your true treasures lie. They lie within you, where they have always been – safe from the insanity wrought by the mind.

Lesson 14

I.14.21 We now bring you the fourteenth lesson in this Course. Here We will focus on rebuilding trust. For once trust comes to replace distrust, you will trust that your experiences are exactly what is required for you to purge the beliefs which have kept you in hell. In addition, this exercise is to bring into your consciousness the power of choice. For trust is as much a choice as is distrust. And, each moment you identify with that which is unreal, then you have chosen conflict over Peace, and hell over Heaven.

I.14.22   For this exercise, you will need one index card. Write the following statements on it. Then, each morning and each evening for ten days, silently repeat the statements to yourself for five minutes. Where you choose to complete this lesson is completely your choice. However, a place where you can sit that is quiet is often the most beneficial. As you silently repeat the statements, allow yourself to *feel* them. *Feel* their power. *Feel* their Truth. *Feel* the energy behind each one. Come to *feel* how the power resides within you and radiates to the world around you. Recognize this power comes from your True Self.

I.14.23   The statements to write on the index cards are:

There is only Truth. There are no half-truths.

God is my Truth. I trust Him.

And, I trust my Self.

In this trust lies my freedom.

213

CHAPTER 15

Projection Leads to Deception

I.15.1   As We begin this discussion, We invite you to take a few deep breaths. Allow the body to relax. Let the mind still. And, allow the heart to read the words We are sharing with you. *Feel* that you are a part of this discussion. For We are listening, just as you are. And, We are communicating through *feeling*. Therefore, let your heart *feel* this discussion. We ask this of you, because We are going to pull the veil back and expose the darkness within the subconscious mind. We are not doing this without your wholehearted consent. For you are with us at this moment because you heard the call to return to oneness and responded. Remember, everything you have ever experienced brought you to this moment.

I.15.2   We come to you now to share with you the deceit being perpetrated by your mind. This does not mean you have done, or are doing, anything wrong. For that would imply duality. Rather, We are revealing how *fear,* which is but your creation, has tricked your mind into believing it is what it is *not.*

I.15.3   Although We have previously shared the Spiritual Law of Belief with you, We will look at it once again. For the deception in which you have come to believe real rests upon this Law. Recall, the Law of Belief simply states: *Thoughts and feelings create beliefs, and beliefs create what is seen and experienced.* In addition, you will always believe what you see and experience, because they further strengthen the belief from which they arose.

I.15.4   What is this great *deception* which you have perpetrated against yourself? The implication of this deception is found in the very word itself. As you are well aware, the meaning of the word *deception* is: *the act of causing someone to accept as true that which is false; something that deceives.* Look once again upon its meaning. For the implication of the word deception is found within it.

I.15.5   Since *deception* is the *act* of causing someone to accept as true that which is false, then what is the *act* that creates the *deception*? Quite simply, the *act* is that of projection. And, *projection makes perception,* just as you were taught in *A Course in Miracles.* Remember, it is the subconscious mind which projects, into what it considers the external, its beliefs and fears in order to free itself from the terror of its own darkness.

I.15.6   Therefore, the *deception* is: *it is but yourself whom you deceive*. And, it is in the word *deceive* where the intention, the energy signature, arises. When you understand the intention of the deception, then the veil of illusions will have been rent, so that the Light of Truth can illuminate what has become lost in darkness.

I.15.7   The intention behind the word *deceive* is found in its meaning, like all the others We have exposed to you. Your word *deceive* comes to you via the Latin word *decipere*, which carries with it the meaning *to evade*. This is where the intention of *deceiving* yourself has been hidden. For *to evade* means *to defy*. Now, the time has come for Us to expose the hidden intention of the *deception*.

I.15.8   While your word *defy* carries with it the meaning *to resist*, or *to oppose,* the intention is found much deeper. And, this deeper meaning is hidden within how the word *defy* arose. The word *defy* also came to you via Latin, from the word *de-fides,* which literally means to *oppose trust,* or *to not-trust.* Therefore, the intention, or the energy signature of *deception* is *to have no-trust.* And, this is the *distrust* for which We have previously discussed.

I.15.9   Look, then, upon the intention through the lens of the Law of Being. Once again, the Law simply states: *to give is to have; and, to have is to be.* Thus, *to have no-trust* means that you not only *give no-trust, you "be" no-trust.* Although this is what you consider bad grammar, it nevertheless states the intention.

I.15.10   Yet, what does this mean? Simply this: when you have no-trust, you can only give no-trust. And, what you give, you receive. In other words, you but gift no-trust to yourself. Furthermore, since *to deceive* is *to have no-trust*, and you give yourself *no-trust*, then you *deceive* yourself. *Feel*, then, what you are reading; because only by *feeling* the intention, can the Light come to replace the darkness.

I.15.11   *Feel* these next words: if you have *deceit,* and you give *deceit,* then you are *(be) deceit.* This, O Holy One, is the great *deception.* What is this great deception? It is but this – you *deceive* yourself, because you *have no-trust* in yourself, which means you have *not-God* in yourself. However, the *deception* goes even deeper than you as of yet know.

I.15.12   In *A Course In Miracles*, it is written that *projection makes perception.* And, this is undoubtedly the case. For what is projected is perceived, or seen, by the body's eyes.

Therefore, you are *deceived* by what you *perceive.* Yet, both the perception and deception arise from the beliefs that the mind projects.

I.15.13   In addition to what We have shared thus far, We ask that you take note of this: the word *deception* and *perception* have the same root. And, it is the root which gets to the heart of the intention. What is this root which literally causes the hell you experience? The root is but -*cept,* which means *to take.* And, it is this root which must be pulled out of your mind.

I.15.14   Remember, *fear takes.* And, the word *take* has the energy signature that creates the *deception.* For the word *take* carries with it the meaning *to remove.* Again, We ask you to *feel* what We are sharing with you, because everything you have ever seen and experienced comes from the energy pattern emitted by the belief that you *took* something that did not belong to you. And, it is this belief, hidden so deeply within the subconscious, that you have completely forgotten its memory. What, then, is this belief? What do you believe you *took* from God? For it is here where the seed of terror is found which continuously rubs the mind, ever reminding it of its *perceived* wrong doing.

I.15.15 *Feel* this, O Holy Child. For you believe, deep within all of your states of being, that you *removed* yourself from the Love and Truth that is God. In other words, you believe you *took* yourself from God. *THIS IS THE BELIEF IN SEPARATION*. And, it has paralyzed the mind since the thought was first entertained. Furthermore, you believe you *threw away* everything that was worthy and holy about yourself, and replaced it with those things you consider unholy and unworthy. This, then, is the great deception you but perpetrate upon yourself: *you believe you took yourself away from God.* And, this is the cause for the fear which has plagued the mind since the beginning of *time.*

I.15.16 Now, We return Our discussion to *projection.* In *The Way of Mastery,* it was given you that *projection is an act in which you physically try to throw out of your ownership everything you have judged as being despicable and unworthy of you – something you do not want.* O Child of God, *feel* the intentionality of *projection.* For in your attempt to save yourself from the consequences of the original judgment and fear, as well as those beliefs that sprung up around the one where you think you *took* yourself away from God, you have been perpetrating nothing but a con-job with yourself. For how can you throw out what you do not want? Does this make good sense to you?

I.15.17   To the mind lost in the maze of darkness, it makes perfect sense. But to the heart, it is seen as folly. For the heart knows the truth: that *you remain just as God created you.* We ask you now, *do you really believe that you could remove yourself from God? Do you truly believe that you could separate from All That Is? Do you yet find it insane to believe that what is eternally One could be shattered into tiny pieces?*

I.15.18   Yet, this is what your subconscious believes. Keep those questions in the forethought of your mind as We further expose the madness that has consumed the mind. For the true insanity lies yet deeper in the subconscious mind. And, the lord of the underworld, the subconscious mind, guards this unholy secret with all its dark intentions. These intentions are the energy patterns emitted in order to *deceive* your consciousness. For nothing can be projected without the unholy allegiance to this closely guarded secret.

I.15.19   Everything, and We mean *everything*, projected upon others, as well as the world you appear to inhabit, is done so from fear. Yet, this fear, like all other feelings, arises from a thought. And, it is this one thought for which the subconscious mind guards with its very existence. For once exposed, the subconscious, and its labyrinth of dark *wishes* and *beliefs,* will simply cease to be. Can you, therefore, *feel* the terror building as We approach the entrance where this dark, ancient secret is held?

I.15.20   The secret that is guarded by the subconscious involves the dark intention behind the word *take*. Although We have already shared with you that the word *take* has the meaning *to remove*, the dark intention is found in an almost hidden meaning of the word. For this dark intention is the energy behind EVERY sight, sound, and experience you have had. Yes! This intention, this energy, is what has created everything you see and experience.

I.15.21   What, then, is this meaning of the word *take* which has literally made the hell you consider to be your home? Before We reveal it, We ask that you recall something that We have already shared with you. And, it is: *God gives; fear takes.* For the dark intention rests here. But, how can this be?

I.15.22   The answer, while appearing convoluted, is really quite simple to understand once the dross has been cleared. And, this intentionality has literally been hiding in plain sight. For the word *take* also carries the meaning *to accept as true: BELIEVE.* Here, then, is the depth of *deception* for which has been kept hidden from your conscious awareness.

I.15.23 Although you have been taught that the words *give* and *take* have opposite meanings, they are more similar than you might think. Before We share the implication behind the word *give,* We invite you to open your mind. It is ready to experience the Light of Truth. It yearns for the remembrance of its Divine Self, the Self that the heart has always known you to be before madness came to rule the mind.

I.15.24 The word *give* has as one of its many meanings *to bear.* Furthermore, the word *bear* simply means *to accept.* Now, We expose the oneness between the words *give* and *take.* For the word *accept*, just as the word *take,* has as one of its many meanings *to accept as true: BELIEVE.* Yes! You read that correctly. As you can see, both words, *give* and *take*, have the same meaning. Thus, they are one. And, it is from the misappropriate use of this oneness which creates the *deception.*

I.15.25 Let's look, then, upon the word *believe.* For here is where the subconscious has twisted the intention to meet its own dark *wishes.* The word *believe* has the meaning *to accept the word.* Allow this meaning to settle throughout the mind. For here is darkness exposed to the Light.

I.15.26   In your bible, it is written: *In the beginning was the Word, and the Word was with God, and the Word was God. The same was in the beginning with God. All things were made by him; and without him was not any thing made that was made. In him was life, and the life was the light of men. And the light shineth in darkness; and the darkness comprehended it not.*

I.15.27   O Holy One, the Light shineth now in the darkness. Time is not real. This statement isn't about a past that you cannot recall. This statement is for *YOU* in this moment. If you look upon it through the lens of *time,* then you will not comprehend it. *Feel* it NOW. *Feel* it in this moment, the only moment that is Real, the only moment that exists.

I.15.28   O Dear Brothers and Sisters, the mind cannot comprehend it. For the mind is *darkness.* But, your heart can *feel* the implication behind the statement. It can *feel* the intention carried within it. *Feel* it. For in *feeling* it you will comprehend the energy, the Glorious Energy, that the statement *IS.*

I.15.29   The Energy is Life. The Energy is God. The Energy is your Divine Self. *Feel* God. *Feel* your Self. *Feel* Life.

I.15.30 O Beloved One, God is the Word. You are the Word. Look, now, upon Truth. *Feel*, now, the Truth as it dawns in the mind. *Let there be Light.* Hear Us Divine Child, *It has always been about BELIEF.* And, it always will be.

I.15.31 The very word BELIEF carries with it Love. And you are that Love. Rejoice in awakening. See the Truth as it unfolds before your eyes. For the word *belief,* just like the word *relief,* have a common root. And, this is what remained hidden from you. The root *-lief* is from what you call Old English in its origin. It comes from the Old English word *lēof,* which simply means *LOVE.* Therefore, to *BELIEVE* is to *BE-LOVE.*

I.15.32 This is why the Spiritual Law of Belief creates everything you see and experience. For it is in a sense the Spiritual Law of Love. It is you. It is God. It is Everything.

I.15.33 Can you now see the *deception?* For the *deception,* like everything experienced, rests in *belief.* And, as long as you *believe* you are *not-God,* you can but experience darkness. *Believe* that you and God are One, and you will experience Light. You will experience Life. You will experience Freedom. And, you will experience your Self.

I.15.34 You but need look no farther than the Brother you call Jesus. He *accepted the Word*. He *accepted the Truth*. He accepted His *Self*. And, even within your bible it is written of Jesus, *Who, being in the form of God, thought it not robbery to be equal with God.*

I.15.35 If Jesus thought of himself as not robbing God by *being* equal with God, then you must come to *believe* the same. The only thing that prevents this is FEAR. Yes! It is but FEAR. Decree this very moment O Son of God, *Let there be Light*. Let there be truth. Let it radiate from your heart and fill your mind. For it is but a choice you must make. The choice is between Heaven and hell. One is Light. One is darkness. One is Real. One is not-real. One is God. One is not-God.

I.15.36 Let not then the great *deception* rob you of the Truth any longer. Let not your *deception* keep you in darkness, when the Light is within your heart, waiting to Light your mind. The *deception* is finished. Therefore, in the immortal Words of Our Brother, We proclaim, *IT IS FINISHED.*

Lesson 15

I.15.37 If you are ready to comprehend the Light, then join Us as We enter into the fifteenth lesson of this Course. Unlike the previous exercises, We ask of you but this: *REJOICE*! As often as you will, *feel* the intention as you decree:

I Believe the Word.

I Be-Love the Word.

CHAPTER 16

Dimensions and the Levels of Consciousness

I.16.1   We have shared with you what We have called *levels of consciousness* throughout Our discussion. Now, We would like to share with you what this means and how it has affected your experiences. For We are with you in order to assist you in unifying the different levels in which you believe yourself to exist. Recognize that, in Truth, you are whole and complete. However, your mind has split to such an extent that you are no longer conscious of the varying aspects of yourself. With each split of the mind, you forgot the realm above. Therefore, We are with you at this time so that you can begin to *feel* the different energy patterns of consciousness. As you *feel* the energy associated with each level and become familiar with them once again, you will then be able to heal the many rifts within the mind, thereby remembering your True Self.

I.16.2   This is where the Love within your heart simply shines Its Light into the mind, providing the gentle healing that restores your mind to its original function, which is *extending Love* rather than *projecting fear.* And, it is your heart that carries with it the Love, which can illuminate the mind, setting the mind free.

I.16.3   Only Love can truly heal. However, in order for this healing to take place, you must first make peace with your heart. For your mind and heart have been in a state of conflict since the beginning of time. And, until peace returns between what you still see as separate and different, healing cannot occur. Therefore, you must come to trust your heart. For *distrust* has given you nothing but hell. And We mean that quite literally.

I.16.4   Again, the heart We speak of is not the heart of the body. Your *Real Heart* is the center of your Being. It is what you are in Truth. Is it difficult to trust your *Heart?* Of course it isn't. In fact, it is the most natural thing that there is.

I.16.5   We have used the word heart at great length in this ongoing discussion. Yet, We have not invited you to *feel* the *Heart*. Like every word We have shared with you, the word *heart* has a definite energy signature. Before We continue Our discussion, We would like to share with you what the *Heart* is. It will help if We begin with the word, itself. For the meaning gives the best description. It is one that will aid you in coming to trust your *Heart* again.

I.16.6   Your word *heart* comes to you via Latin like many of your words have. The Latin word *cordis,* besides carrying the meaning of *heart,* has a much deeper implication. For *cordis* also carries the meaning *soul/spirit.* Look, then, carefully at the implication of the word *heart.* Can you see and *feel* it? For the implication is that of *unity,* of *oneness.* It is the energy pattern of wholeness, of completion. It is the energy signature of your True Self. *It is but the energy of your Self.* Become reacquainted with this energy. For everything you have so long desired is found within it.

I.16.7   Therefore, your *Heart* is *Everything.* It is your soul and spirit in wholeness. But, how can you be whole if your mind is split on so many different levels? The answer, while seemingly difficult for the mind to grasp, is simply this: *BELIEF.* For while you are whole and complete in this moment, your mind *believes* it is separated from everyone and everything, including God.

I.16.8   Your mind believes it to be what We have already termed the *body-mind.* Thus, you *believe* that you are a *personal-self,* set apart from everyone you meet and from everything you lay your eyes upon. Furthermore, you believe you inhabit a planet, separated from other planets by space and time, orbiting a separate star, located in a separate solar system, found within a galaxy that also appears to be separated from the one hundred billion other galaxies that you know of within the universe that have been shown to exist. Is there any wonder why the *belief* in separation is so entrenched within your mind? For everything you *believe* you see and experience but points to separation. To the mind, nothing seems connected. This is why the mind, as you know it, is incapable of knowing oneness and unity. For the mind cannot comprehend its own expansiveness and boundless nature, because it has fully accepted and *believes* it is but the *body*. It has settled for its version of truth, which is: it is housed in a limiting and fragile casing of flesh.

I.16.9   We ask you now to *feel* the energy pattern for which the mind has come to accept as its temporary home. And, this energy pattern is found within the very word used to describe itself – *incarnation*. While there are many myths and stories which swirl about the word, its implication, its energy signature, is attached to the word's origin. As most of the words We have invited you to *feel*, the word *incarnation* also has its origin in Latin. The Latin word is *incarnatus*, which carries the meaning *make into flesh, carnal.* And, it is in the meaning of the word *flesh* where the implication leads to the energy pattern for the word *incarnation.* For although the word *flesh* carries the meaning of *the parts of the body comprised of muscle and skin*, it has a much, much deeper meaning. And, it is here that you will *feel* the intention of the word.

I.16.10 In addition to the meaning you read, the word *flesh* carries with it the meaning *human being*. Therefore, the energy pattern of *incarnation* is that of your current *state of being*, as believed by your mind. In your bible, it is written, *For they that are after the flesh do mind the things of the flesh, but they that are after the Spirit the things of the Spirit. For to be carnally minded is death, but to be spiritually minded is life and peace.*

I.16.11 *Feel* the intention behind those verses. For they describe things as they appear to exist. Let's look deeper into them, so that the implication can be exposed, in order for the mind to be set free. But in order for the mind to be freed, it will take the *Heart* to reveal the energy pattern stored within those verses.

I.16.12 You now know that the word *flesh* is referring to the *belief of being only human.* The word *after* simply carries with it the meaning *in the form of.* Therefore, the intention contained within those bible verses can be more easily understood when read as: *For they that are in the human form do mind the things of the human form, but they that are in the form of the Spirit the things of the Spirit. For to be human minded is death, but to be spiritually minded is life and peace.*

I.16.13 Yet, let's take those verses even deeper. For their true intention lies in their depth. Since you already know that God is Spirit, as well as now having the knowledge of the Law of Being, those verses can be read as: *For they that believe their state of being is a human body judge the things of the body, but they that believe themselves God the things of God. For to be HUMAN MINDED is to be NOT-GOD, but to be GOD MINDED is to be GOD.*

I.16.14 Seen in this Light, it becomes strikingly clear as to the intention contained within those verses. For the intention is that of *states of being*. For you either believe you are human, which is to believe that you are *not-God,* or you believe you are a Divine Being, which is to believe you are *God.* These are the only two *states of being*. One is deception, while the other is but Truth. And, your *state of being* is determined by what you *believe* yourself to *BE.*

I.16.15 Besides demonstrating *states of being*, those bible verses also point to what We have called the lower realms and the Divine Realm. While the lower realms do not exist in Reality, because your mind is attached, thus bound, to them, your *Heart* must guide you out. And it does so gently and lovingly. It does this by always pointing you towards Truth, towards God, towards your Self.

232

I.16.16   Many on your world refer to the realms as *dimensions*. And, the implication of *dimensions* is even referenced in your bible. It is found in the verse where it is written that the man named Jesus said, *In my Father's House are many mansions: if it were not so, I would have told you.* Look again at the words, *my Father's House.* For Our Father's House is given in the singular. What is the implication here? It is but this: there is but *One Divine Realm,* which contains many mansions. But, what is meant by the word *mansions?* For it does not mean what you might think it does upon the first read.

I.16.17   When you think of a mansion, you believe it to be a large home, or house. However, the word *mansion* has a much more profound meaning. And, it is within its deeper meaning that the implication and intention rests.

I.16.18   The word *mansion* also comes to you from Latin. Your word *mansion* comes from the Latin word *manere,* which means *continuance.* Therefore, when Jesus spoke of His Father's House having many *mansions,* he was referring to *continuances.* And, it is in your word *continue* where the implication for the bible verse is found.

I.16.19   Just as in other words where We have exposed the hidden intention, the hidden energy, We shall do the same for the word *continuance*. While you believe the word *continuance* means *to carry on with what you were doing*, its hidden implication, thus intention, is found in the origin of the word, which came to you via the Latin word *continuari*. Again, here is where the meaning and its intention lie. For the Latin word *continuari* means *uniting oneself with*. Therefore, the bible verse is stating that Our Father's House has many aspects where We *unite with Our Self.*

I.16.20   Now, We invite you to discover the true meaning, the true implication of the word *House,* found in the phrase *My Father's House*, as it is being used in the bible verse. For once Truth has illuminated your mind, the Love that is Truth will begin healing it. In the case of the word *house*, it too has a meaning that has remained hidden from your consciousness. Join, then, with Us as We pull the veil of deceit that has severed your mind from your *Heart* since time began.

I.16.21   As you are already aware, the word *house* means *home, or domicile.* However, your word *domicile* came to you from the Old French word *dôme*, which means *throne, head.* And, it is from the meaning of the word *head,* where the Glorious Truth resides. For the word *head* simply means *mind.*

Therefore, the phrase *Our Father's House* quite literally means *Our Father's Mind*. In other words, it is referring to the *Mind of God*. Thus, the implication and the intention of the bible verse is as follows: *The Mind of God has many aspects where We unite with Our Self.*

I.16.22 These aspects are the *levels of consciousness* of which We have spoken. And these levels of consciousness are also referred to as *dimensions*. But, what is a dimension? Although most who inhabit your planet believe that a *dimension* is a place defined by space/time, much like what you refer to as your *third dimensional* reality, the word has a much broader implication. For the word *dimension* carries with it the meaning, *a level of existence or consciousness*.

I.16.23 Recognize, in Truth, there are *NO levels*. For *levels* imply states of inequality. And, in the Kingdom of God, there is only perfect equality. Therefore, come to understand that *levels of consciousness* are really *states of consciousness*. This is a more reasonable descriptor. For it doesn't imply inequality.

I.16.24 Yet, what is meant by the phrase *states of consciousness?* The answer will be one that will be reasonably accepted by the mind. For it will not see it as a threat. Rather, the answer will give the mind pause. And, this is the pause, the silence, needed by the *Heart,* so that it can speak to the mind with the gentleness of Love, such that it can begin to heal and know of true rest. For your mind has grown weary and is in need of the loving care that only the *Heart* can provide.

I.16.25 The energy signature of the phrase *state of consciousness* resonates at the same frequency as the phrase *state of being.* This is because they are the same. For your *state of consciousness* determines your *state of being.* And, the energy pattern of both is found in the implication of the word *state.*

I.16.26 The word *state* carries the meaning *a condition of mind.* Furthermore, the word *condition* has an archaic meaning, which is where the implication has been hiding. The archaic definition for the word *condition* is *temper of mind.* Although you normally associate the word temper with *anger,* the word *temper* carries with it the meaning *calmness, or tranquility, of mind.* Thus, your *state of consciousness* is directly proportional to the peace you allow to be expressed within your mind.

I.16.27 Let's return briefly to the biblical passage where We have revealed as: *The Mind of God has many aspects where We unite with Our Self.* Having a better understanding of *dimensions,* the passage can be stated as: *the Mind of God has many dimensions where We unite with Our Self.* In addition, it can also be stated as: *the Mind of God has many states of consciousness where We unite with Our Self.*

I.16.28 Come now to recognize that there is only the *Mind of God.* Nothing exists outside the *Mind of God.* Everything, and We literally mean EVERYTHING, exists within His Most Holy Mind. It is for this reason that to believe you could be separated from God is laughable. Furthermore, can you see how it is *impossible* for *time* to have circumvented *eternity*? It is not only impossible, it is insane to believe otherwise.

I.16.29 You exist in the *Mind of God* in this moment, just as you always have. You are perfectly safe, perfectly whole, and perfectly loved. However, while you remain in a perfect *state of being* within His Holy Mind, your mind, which is one with His, believes itself to be separate from All That Is. And, your mind, having split four times, is lost in a d*imensional maze.* Although you are perfectly complete, your mind created *levels,* or *dimensions.* And, with each split, not only did your mind create a new level of existence, which it believes it inhabits, it forgot the *dimension* above it.

I.16.30 As a result of fragmenting so many times, your mind has become so thoroughly convinced that it is separate and alone, that re-unification would be impossible without the Love found within your *Heart.* While your *Heart* retains the memory of your Self, your mind only recognizes the personal-self for which it *believes* it is. Therefore, your *Heart* must now speak to you of your True Self, a Self that is truly one with everything and everyone, including God. Yet, in order for your mind to accept this Truth, it must first be willing to trust your *Heart.* For it still perceives your *Heart* to be an existential threat to its beingness.

I.16.31 It is here that We simply invite you to allow your mind to begin to trust. For as you are now aware, *distrust* is at the root of all of your current beliefs and experiences. This *distrust* must be undone. In *A Course in Miracles,* it is written, *for all mistakes,* which are but false beliefs held in the mind, *must be corrected on the level on which they occur.* And, in order to understand the levels, or *dimensions,* unto which the errors occurred, you must allow your mind to listen to the *Heart.* For only then will you come to *feel* the fragmentation held within your darkened mind, so that Love can heal it.

I.16.32 We will share with you, now, the dimensions for which your states of consciousness of mind seem to exist. As We share this with you, always remember that, in Truth, in Reality, none of this exists. It only appears to do so to a mind which still believes itself to be alone, isolated, and separate. Yet, it is through this recognition that We, united in Love, can laugh at the game your mind has been playing.

I.16.33 Again, We take your hand and look back at a time that never was. We simply look back at a beginning, which you believe real, but is not there. The Light of Love found in your *Heart* will simply shine upon it. And, you will come to see and *feel* its unreality. Yet, to the mind, the *unreal* is believed *real*, while that which is Truth continues to be denied.

I.16.34 We now present you with a picture of how torn and fragmented your mind appears to be. We simply ask that you allow the words you are going to read to draw a mental picture, while your *Heart* gently holds your mind in a loving embrace. Although the mind may *feel* overwhelmed, perplexed, and frightened, allow your *Heart* to sing to you of Heaven's Song. For it is one of Peace, Joy, and Comfort. Let, then, your mind find rest and refuge in the sweet sound that is the *Song of Oneness*.

I.16.35 In addition, come to realize that *time is NOT real.* Thus, speaking in terms of a past is meaningless. Yet, the mind is so entrenched in the *belief in time* that it will attempt to reconcile what it reads as *something* that occurred in a distant, ancient past. Yet, there is NO past. To the mind, this is incomprehensible. But, to the *Heart,* it is merely a statement of Truth. How, then, can the truth be revealed in a meaningful way such that healing can occur within the mind?

I.16.36 Although the wording of the picture being given you will be that of what reads as past tense, recognize, in this most Holy Moment, when We speak of creation, it is a process that wasn't simply done and has long since been over. For this would be to speak of creation in terms of *time,* rather than that which is eternal. Creation, like eternity, is not static. However, neither does it change. Creation, like God, just *is.* It has always been and will always be. And, it is this Truth that the mind resists. For the mind seeks answers in terms that it considers concrete and absolute. Yet, creation, just like eternity, just like God, just like your True Self, is neither concrete nor absolute. It is wholly in the realm of the abstract.

I.16.37 As We begin to lay out the picture before you, We would like to re-introduce you to *abstractia.* We ask that you *feel* the energy of the word *abstract.* For the energy found in the word is that of creation, itself. While the word *abstract* literally means *difficult to comprehend,* there is an ease to its *feeling.* The *Heart* recognizes the *feeling* as Itself. For it has known nothing else.

I.16.38   The word *abstract* is more readily understood and *felt* when viewed in the terms by which the word came to you. Therefore, look upon the word *abstract* as a uniting of the two seemingly separate words, *abs* and *tract.* For only when seen in the Light of True Unity will you remember the *feeling* which is *creation.*

I.16.39   *Abs* is what you consider a prefix. And it simply carries with it the meaning *from.* However, the intention, the energy field, is found in the second half of the word, which is *tract.* Like many of your words, the implication is found in its origin. Your word tract came to you via the Latin word *tractus,* which means *to extend.* Therefore, the word *abstract* quite literally implies *from extension.*

I.16.40   O Holy One, *creation* is *from extending.* As is written in *A Course in Miracles, Truth is beyond your ability to destroy, but entirely within your ability to accept. It belongs to you because, as an extension of God, you created it with Him. It is yours because it is a part of you, just as you are a part of God, because He created you.*

I.16.41   Truth has never left you, nor you it. You have but denied it. And, in denying it, you but denied your Self, since you and Truth are one. Therefore, Truth, being an extension of you and

God, is *creation*. Furthermore, Truth is Love. They are inseparable. Thus, the energy field, the energy pattern, of that which is *abstract* is merely that of *extension*, or *creation*. It is the energy pattern of your Holy Self.

I.16.42 It is said that *God Extended Himself in Creation*; and, that you are His Holy Extension. To the mind, this is utterly meaningless. But, to the *Heart* it is but Its Truth. In order to bring healing to the mind, the time has come for you to understand what is meant by *God Extended Himself in Creation*. For this is the purpose given you by the Source of All That Is. It is your Holy Function to extend, just as God has, does, and forever will be extending Himself.

I.16.43 In order to understand what extension is, you must come to *feel* it. For in *feeling* it, your mind will begin to see *what it is in Truth*. And, in order to *feel* it, We will reveal to you now the implication and the intention behind the word *extend*. Among the many meanings of the word *extend* is found the intention of creation. For *to extend* carries the meaning *advance*, which simply means *to raise*. And, the energy pattern of the word *extension* is found in the implication of the word *raise*. O Holy Child, here is the energy signature of *the Christ*, which is your Holy Self.

I.16.44   Look lovingly, then, upon the meaning of the word *raise*. *Feel* it as We share with you its meaning. For your freedom from the hell of your making rests upon it. The word *raise* means *to awaken*. In addition, *raise* means to *ascend*. Therefore, your function, your purpose is *to awaken, to ascend*.

I.16.45   Now, *feel* these next words. *Feel* them within your Being. *You, O Holy One, are an extension of God. You are an awakening of God. And, you are an ascension of God.* This is *WHAT YOU ARE!*

I.16.46   Furthermore, this is the intention of *creation*, this is its energy. For the time has come for you to know what *creation* is, because it is not what you *believe* it to be. And, it is your *belief* in what *creation* is which has kept your mind in the dark. In Truth, you are *creation*.

I.16.47   Again, We ask you to *feel* the energy signature for the word *create* as We pull back the veil of darkness which has shrouded the mind for far too long. For this shroud is the first which blanketed your mind. Therefore, it will be the last to be removed. This, too, was given you in your scriptures. For does the scriptures not state that the man named Jesus said, *So the last shall be first, and the first last*? This, then, is the meaning:

for the last veil to cover the mind is the first to be removed, just as the first veil will be the last one to be pulled back.

I.16.48   The reason for this is simple: it is God's Will. It is but His Desire that you awaken gently. For to pull the first veil back would be to expose a mind, which is in deep sleep, to Light. Thus, the Light would be seen as fearful, rather than the blessing and gift for which It is.

I.16.49   Join Us as We expose what the first veil has hidden from you. Again, We ask you to *feel* this most Glorious, Holy Truth. For this is what your *Heart* has for so long yearned. *Feel* then the energy, the power, the Truth, of what you are.

I.16.50   Like so many other words in your language, which were born from Latin, so too was your word *create*. Your word *create* comes from the Latin word *creatus,* which carries with it the meaning *begotten by,* or *child. Feel* this O Holy Child. This is Truth. For you are *the Holy Child of God.* You are His Begotten. Although you have heard this Truth before, you have never *believed* it. Now the time has come for you to *feel* it. Yes! *Feel* it. This is the intention of *creation.* For you are God's Desire and His Intention. And, it is this Truth for which you have *denied* and continue to *deny.*

I.16.51   You cannot just *think* it. You must *feel* it. For the healing of your mind starts with this simple correction to it.

I.16.52   Take our hand once again as We further expose the mind to the Truth. In addition to the word *create* meaning *child,* there is an even deeper meaning to the word. And, it too is found in Latin. For the Latin word *creatus* arose from an earlier Latin word. That word was *crescere,* which carries with it the meaning *arise.* Yes! In addition to meaning *child,* the word *creation* means to *arise.*

I.16.53   At this point in the discussion, it should be apparent that the intentionality of the word *arise* is that of *awaken,* or *ascend.* Therefore, recognize the words *create, extend, awake,* and *ascend* are one. They are the same. For their implication, their intention, their energy pattern is identical.

I.16.54   When you asked the question, *What am I,* you did so from *not-Knowing.* This *not-Knowing* is simply the first reference of the *belief* that you were, and still are, *not-God.* And, this *belief* is *death*, as We have already discussed with you. Furthermore, the effect from this belief was the making of *time.* And, for each moment of *time* that seems to pass is nothing more than the continuation of *denying* but the Truth of your Reality.

I.16.55 We have but given you the first brush stroke of the picture We are painting in order for your mind to accept the healing that your *Heart* so eagerly desires. This desire is but God's Desire for you, His Holy Child. It is the desire to *awaken*, the desire to *ascend*, in the firm knowledge that you are the Holy Child of the Most High. And, as Jesus is recorded in scripture as having said, *Did I not say, "Ye are but gods?"* For what else could God have? To *believe* otherwise is but *denial* of the Truth of your Being.

The Divine Realm: The Highest Dimension

I.16.56 Although *dimensions* do not exist in Truth, We will use the word as We continue painting the picture of how your *belief* in separation and fragmented *states of consciousness* have kept your True Nature hidden. No one hid this Truth from you. For you are not a *victim*. Rather, you have been a most willing participant in the *game of deceit* – the ultimate *game of make-believe*.

I.16.57 *In the beginning, God created the heaven and the earth.* This is the first verse given within your bible. And, this biblical passage has a much deeper implication than you have yet come to grasp. At first appearance, it would seem to denote a level of separation. For does it not appear that the earth is separated from heaven? To the mind bereft of Light, this certainly seems to be the case. However, upon closer inspection, We ask that you take note of the word *and*. For it simply denotes a connection, or a joining of like things.

I.16.58 In the case of this biblical passage, the like *things* that are joined, that are one with each other, are God and you, His Holy Child. This verse is simply a reminder that *In the beginning, God awakened the divine and the human.* Although you have been taught that to be divine and to be human are separate, thus different, the verse clearly demonstrates their unity, their oneness. And, it is this oneness for which your *Heart* seeks to remind you.

I.16.59 Look once again at the verse as written: *God awakened the divine and the human.* The wholeness, the completion, written into those words is known as *the Christ*, the Child of God. And, because you are a Child of God, in your wholeness, you are the Christ. When We speak to you of your completion in this moment, We are referring to *the Christ* in you. For you are *the Christ*. You are, in truth, a Divine Human.

I.16.60 To the mind, that statement is seen as *heresy*. For the mind knows not of Truth, much less of what it is. The mind only recognizes its humanness, and does not accept, or allow, any thought be given to its divinity. And, herein lies its fear. For the mind *believes* that, if it even entertains the possibility of it being divine, it will be struck down. Yet, the mind knows not what *heresy* is.

I.16.61 Your word *heresy* came from the Ancient Greek word *hairein*, which carries the meaning and implication of *to take*. Recall, the word *take*, while meaning *remove* or *to separate,* also means *to accept as true: belief.* Thus, the mind *takes* its humanness quite seriously. In other words, it believes that it is only human and nothing more. This is the *great deception* for which We have already communicated with you. And, it was in *denying* its divinity in which gave rise to the *beliefs* of *time* and *fear* within the mind.

I.16.62 Recognize, here, that We have just drawn the picture of what is referred to as the *Divine Realm,* or *Heavenly Realm.* Although numbers themselves are meaningless, this is what is referred to as the *seventh dimension.* You have heard it called *seventh heaven.* In either case, it simply denotes the Realm of *the Christ,* the Holy Child of God. In addition, this is the Kingdom of God.

I.16.63 Does the *seventh dimension* lie outside of you? Certainly not. For the *Kingdom of God is within you.* And, it *IS* you.

However, because of the many veils that blanket the mind, the mind knows this not. For when the mind asked the question, *What am I,* the first, or original, judgment was made. And, remember, that judgment was a declaration in which you denied your Self, which is *the Christ.* Until you *accept the Christ* as one with you, then you continue to *deny* your Holy Self, which is your True State of Being.

I.16.64 Now that the intention of the word *state* has been re-introduced to you, it should be both clear and obvious that, what is referred to as *seventh heaven,* the Divine Realm, is that of a mind which experiences nothing but Peace. For the mind does not experience any conflict, because *It Knows What It Is.* It is where the mind is one with Itself, which means it is one with *the Christ.* And, *the Christ* is one with God, since *the Christ* is the Holy Extension, the Holy Creation. the Holy Child of God.

I.16.65 The Divine Realm is the only Realm which exists in Truth, within the Mind of God, Himself. And, you dwell within this Realm. This too was given you in your bible. For it unequivocally states: *For in Him, we live, we move, and have our being; as certain also of your own poets have said, "For we are also His offspring."*

I.16.66 Yet, in this moment, you are completely without awareness of it. Why is this? Quite simply, you have, as of yet, not allowed your *Heart* to correct the original judgment you levied against yourself. Even in this moment, your mind still is in opposition, in conflict, with the Truth of What It Is. For your mind still identifies as *not-God*.

I.16.67 The *seventh dimension* is the only one that is eternal in nature. For it is the only Realm that is Real. All other dimensions, or realms, are either *transitional*, or *temporal*, in their nature. It is for this reason that they do not actually exit. But, because the mind *believes* they exist, the mind wanders aimlessly within the *dimensional matrix* of the lower realms. And only your *Heart* can provide the Light that can guide your mind out of the dark labyrinth of the matrix and return it to the Peace that is its *Home*.

I.16.68 We will now direct your focus on the word *awareness*. For God is *Awareness*, just as you, *the Christ*, are. The energy of *Awareness* is that of *IS, or Isness*. To the mind as it believes it exists now, this is truly meaningless. However, to the *Heart*, it but knows that only *Awareness* is True. Since *Awareness* and God are one, then *Awareness* is only found in the Divine Realm. The mind, as you conceive it to be, is only capable of *states of consciousness*.

I.16.69   Although people in your world use the terms *awareness* and *consciousness* interchangeably, the time has come for you to recognize Truth. For they are not the same. They are opposites. Yet, only one is True.

I.16.70   Remember, as you have already learned, *consciousness is correctly identified as the domain of not-God.* Therefore, *consciousness* is found only in the lower realms of the mind. What, then, is *awareness* if it is not *consciousness?*

I.16.71   The intentionality of *Awareness,* like many words, is found in its deeper, hidden meaning. Although the word carries with it the meaning of *awake,* the implication is found in the origin of the word, which came to you from the Old English word *gewær.* It is here that the energy signature is *felt* and experienced. For the word *gewær* was a word combined from two sources, *ge,* which in your time has become the prefix *a,* meaning *not* or *without,* and *wær* which has the meaning *wary.* Furthermore, your word *wary* comes to you via the Latin word *vereri,* which means *fear.* Thus, the implication, the energy pattern associated with *awareness* is literally that of *being without fear.*

I.16.72 *Feel,* in this moment, the energy associated with *awareness.* For to *be without fear* is to be Love. Do you see it? Can you *feel* it? It is God. Thus, the energy of *Awareness* is the energy of God. And, as We have discussed before with you: *THERE IS NO FEAR IN LOVE.*

I.16.73 It is for this reason that *awareness* and *consciousness* are not the same. For *consciousness* carries with it the energy of *fear.* And, where there is *fear,* there is always the identification with *not-God.*

The Transitional Realms

I.16.74 When the thought of *being not-God* entered the mind and was taken seriously, it caused the first split within the mind. This split created the first of the lower realms. It is what is referred to as the sixth dimension. And, it is neither wholly eternal nor wholly temporal. Therefore, it is considered *transitional.* It does, however, have what can be seen as properties of both *states of beingness.*

I.16.75 The term *transitional* is rightly applied here, because the word denotes a slowing of the frequency of the energy field of potentiality and possibility. And, this is found directly within the meaning of the word *transitional,* which is: *abrupt change in an energy state or level usually accompanied by the loss or gain of a single quantum of energy.* Furthermore, the energy signature of this definition is found within the implication of the word *quantum.*

I.16.76   As with other words, your word *quantum* came to you via the Latin word *quantus*, which carries the meaning *how much worth or worthiness.* Thus, the word *transitional* carries the implication of the *state of worthiness.* This is useful only in Our description of how the *levels or dimensions of consciousness* arose. Look, then, lovingly upon the energy pattern of that which is considered *transitional.* For it directly implies a loss of the *belief* in *worthiness* upon the descent into hell, just as it carries with it an increase in the *belief* in *worthiness* upon the ascent into the Divine Realm.

I.16.77   Yes! You are *feeling* it. You now recognize that your *states of consciousness* directly depend on *how worthy* you *feel* and *believe* yourself to be. It is for this reason that you remain in a *transitional state of consciousness* most of the *time.* And, this is but logical and reasonable. For the degree or level of Peace found in your mind changes from one experience to the next. Therefore, the tranquility of your mind, in its conscious *state of being,* is said to be *transitional.* Because, in one moment you can be in the depths of despair and misery, in other words – you can be experiencing hell - and in the next moment you can feel like you're walking on cloud nine. This abrupt change in your mind's energy state is determined by *how worthy you feel* in every moment. If you feel *worthy*, then you are ascending into Love and Peace. However, if you feel *unworthy*, then you are descending into the hellish, lower realms of consciousness.

I.16.78 The time for you to come to recognize the energy of *worth* is now upon you. For without this recognition, you will continue the dance between dimensions, believing that your experiences are just the natural order of things. Realize that the intentionality of the *feeling* of *worthiness* goes so much deeper than your mind currently comprehends.

I.16.79 In your world, *worth* is bound to the idea of riches or wealth. However, this is not the true implication or intention regarding the *worthiness* of which We now speak. For true *worth* is devoid of anything found in or associated with your world. Yet, just as the world defines *worth* as an accumulation of worldly treasure, your true *worth* is bound to your Real Treasure, the Treasures of your *Heart*.

I.16.80 The intention of the meaning of your true *worth* has been buried deep within what is referred to as an archaic meaning of the word. And, it is in this archaic meaning where the intention lies. In what you would consider an ancient past, the word *worth* had the meaning *become,* which is a uniting of the words *be* and *come.* Here is where the implication is found. For among the many definitions for the word *come* is the meaning *extend.* And, you now recognize that the intention, the energy behind the word *extend* is *awaken.* Therefore, your true *worth* is that of *being awake*, which is *being aware.*

I.16.81   *Feel*, then, your *worth.* For your worth is your Divinity. It is your True Self. And, your Divinity is without question. However, because you still doubt your Divinity, your consciousness remains *transitional.* Furthermore, the energy of consciousness is always affecting the *quantum energy field of potentiality and possibility.*

I.16.82   O Holy One, *feel* these next words: *the energy emitted by your consciousness is always affecting the Divine Energy Field of Potentiality and Possibility.* It might be helpful to think of the Divine Energy Field as the ocean and your consciousness like that of a wave. For just like the wave cannot be separated from the ocean and still be a wave, the energy of your consciousness cannot be separated from the Divine Energy Field beneath it. In addition, the Divine Energy Field of Potentiality and Possibility always responds to any *quantum* shift within your consciousness. And, the response by the

Divine Energy Field is what you have called forth to experience.

I.16.83 The sixth dimension is where consciousness was born. But, in order to understand the *conscious realms* as they pertain to the splitting of the mind, it is necessary to come to realize that there are three *states of consciousness*. They are simply known as the *supra-conscious,* the *conscious,* and the *subconscious*. These states do not exist outside of your mind. Rather, they exist together and act to shape the experiences you have.

I.16.84 The *state of consciousness* associated with the sixth dimension is known as the supra-conscious. You have most often simply heard it referred to as the *Higher Self.* Remember, the *Heart* is where your soul and spirit remain united. Herein lies the reason as to why the sixth dimension is *transitional.* For your spirit remains in a *state of grace* forever. This simply means that your spirit remains in eternity. However, your mind, that part referred to as your soul, only recognizes time.

I.16.85 The term *supra-consciousness* aptly describes this *state of consciousness.* And, the reason is found in the first part of the word – *supra,* which simply carries the meaning *above.* In addition, the word *above* means *Heaven.* And, it should be apparent that the energy signature for the *supra-conscious* lies within the intention found behind the word *Heaven.* For your *supra-conscious* is that of your *Heavenly Consciousness*.

I.16.86　When We speak to you of receiving messages from above, We are referring to messages received in your conscious mind from your *Heavenly Consciousness* or your *Higher Self.* This is the *state of consciousness* from which your *Heart* speaks to you. But, in order for your mind to hear your *Heart*, the mind must be still. While your *Heavenly Consciousness* is always speaking to you, you very rarely listen to it. Why? The answer is really quite simple. For your conscious mind is preoccupied with the *distractions* coming from below of which We have already spoken.

I.16.87　This now brings Our discussion with you to that of the fifth dimension. While you believe that your conscious mind resides in what you call the third dimension of space-time, it doesn't. Your conscious mind is *asleep* in the fifth dimension dreaming of a third dimensional space-time experience. And, this too is found in your bible, where it is written, *And the Lord God caused a deep sleep to fall upon Adam, and he slept.*

I.16.88　Take note that, in the passage, God and Adam appear as separate entities. This is simply there to demonstrate that the mind, the consciousness, already *believed* it had separated from All That Is. For the mind now completely identified with being only human, or *not-God*. And this meant that the conscious mind no longer identified with or remembered its divinity. At this level, or that of the fifth dimension, the veil of separation completely blanketed the mind.

I.16.89   This biblical narrative occurs in a place referred to as the *Garden of Eden* or *Paradise*. It is for this reason that in your bible it is written that the man named Jesus, before drawing His final breath in the realm of physicality, answered the man hanging from a cross beside Him with these words, *Verily I say unto thee, today shalt thou be in paradise with me.* The implication here is that Jesus was referring to that of the fifth dimension, where the conscious mind sleeps.

I.16.90   Furthermore, it is helpful to come to understand that the fifth dimension is what is termed the *Real World* in *A Course in Miracles*. It is also the reason that, written within that curriculum, you are told, *the Real World lies just outside Heaven's gate.* Yet, We now remind you that Heaven's gate, the gateway to the sixth dimension or the *supra-consciousness*, is forgiveness. For only through complete forgiveness within the conscious mind does Heaven's gate open, thereby allowing the conscious mind to re-unite with that of the *supra-consciousness* ending the needless *cycle of time.*

I.16.91 Although the experiences of the Real World *feel* more real than those you currently have is because the fifth dimensional conscious mind is no longer in a deep sleep. It is no longer *entranced by time.* Yet, the Real World of the fifth dimension is still a dream. And, dreaming only comes from one thing – sleep. However, the mind is no longer focused on nothing but physical existence. Yet, although the mind is more consciously aware of unity in its fifth dimensional state, there is still the *belief,* the sense, that a personal-self exists apart from God. Why is this? The answer lies in the *guilt* that the mind still harbors within itself. For until the *guilt* is laid aside, the mind will continue to dream of separation.

I.16.92 O Child of God, come to know, in this most Holy Moment, that nothing in your world, the world found only in deep sleep, can hurt or harm you. For your body-mind is simply a dream figure, an *avatar,* in a *game of make-believe.* Your mind, therefore your very *soul,* is safe and perfectly protected – always. And, We mean - ALWAYS!

I.16.93 As We have spoken before to you regarding *guilt* and *fear,* come to see and *feel* that your freedom lies but within the release of these. Know that it is but *guilt* and *fear* which keeps your mind sleeping and dreaming of experiences of suffering, of pain, of misery, of loneliness, thus of hell, itself. None of these lies outside your own mind. They are but *projections* meant to keep your mind in the hell of its own making. Yet, this need not be. But, in order to awaken from the nightmare, you must *feel* the Love that but awaits you just beyond Heaven's gate. The Love for which you *feel* is real. It is the nightmare that is but part of the *game of make-believe.*

I.16.94 You always have a choice. You can either hear and answer the callings from above, or those from below. Answering the one from above will but lead you *Home*, while answering the other can but lead you deeper into the darkness of the lower realms. The decision is yours, just as it has always been. Know, in this most Hallowed Moment, lies the very gate which leads but to your freedom. You need but *extend* your hand to open it. You need but *extend* Love.

The Temporal Realms

I.16.95 The realm of the *underworld,* ruled by the *lord of darkness*, is that of the fourth dimension. This realm, this dimension, is also found solely within your mind. It is the area of your mind where you have hidden your *guilt* and *fear*, as well as all other things for which you dislike about yourself.

This is the realm where your mind languishes in agony over what it has perceived as its wrong-doings. As We have mentioned before, it is completely devoid of Light. For this area of your mind is where terror hides.

I.16.96 The fourth dimension, therefore, is what We have referred to as your *subconscious* mind. It is here that the *unholy altar* is found. For it is the altar created by your mind to sacrifice itself in the hopes that God will be appeased. We use the word *unholy*, not as you are accustomed to its use, but with the implication of its true meaning. For the word *unholy* carries with it the energy of suffering, of sacrifice, of misery, and of death. And, it perfectly describes the energy associated with the torment so often associated with the word *hell*. To the *subconscious* mind, it exists in what can only be described as utter *chaos*. And, there it languishes in the agony of believing itself to be completely separate and alone, cut off from any Hope of being saved, except for the *wish* to experience its own death.

I.16.97 We use the word *chaos* to describe the *subconscious* mind, because it carries the most accurate description of its energy pattern. It is time now for you to recognize this energy signature, so that you can more readily *feel* the intentionality of the messages that your *consciousness* receives from below. The word *chaos*, like so many words in your language, have come to you via Latin. However, you have remained unaware of the true implication, the true meaning, which gives the word its energy pattern. And, this is certainly the case with the word *chaos* as well.

I.16.98 Your word *chaos* was derived from the exact same word in Latin – *chaos*. It carries with it the meanings: the *pit of Hell, the underworld*, as well as *formless/shapeless primordial matter*. Do you see, then, the implication of *chaos*? For *chaos* is *hell*. Furthermore, the messages your *consciousness* receives from the *underworld* are the thoughts – the *formless/shapeless primordial matter* – that are projected into the third dimensional realm of physicality. These thoughts, which are *formless/shapeless matter*, act upon the grand field of potentiality and possibility creating what you call matter. And, as the matter arises and takes *shape* and *form*, it becomes those things you look upon and experience.

I.16.99 In *A Course in Miracles*, you were given the *four laws of chaos*, which govern the world as you perceive it. These laws are the *Laws of Hell* made in the image and likeness of the *Spiritual Laws*. But, where the Laws of God govern Life, the *Laws of Hell* govern but one thing – *death*. And, to the *conscious* mind that sleeps and dreams of having a physical

262

experience, the *Laws of Death* seem to be the laws which govern everything. Furthermore, these same laws are believed by the consciousness to govern even the higher realms. Is there any wonder, then, as to why the mind remains *entranced by time*? For the *Laws of Chaos,* the *Laws of Hell*, were made to govern time. But, like all things you made, you have turned your power over unto them. For rather than you governing them, they now seem to control and govern you.

I.16.100 This, O Holy Brother and Sister, is the *great deceit.* For it is only your *belief* in your own powerlessness over your creations that keep you *distracted* and looking out into a world of nothingness, believing it more real than Heaven. Yet, to be powerless over your creations would mean that God is powerless over His. Is this what you truly *believe?* While the answer is less than palatable to many, this must be the case since you bow and worship yours.

I.16.101 Know, now, that none of this need be! None of it! For to *believe* that the *Laws of Chaos* govern you is true madness. And, it is this madness that We have come to expose. For the reign of the *dark lord of terror* is ending. Where you once used *denial of Love* to create the hellish experiences of this world, the time has come for to use *denial* once again. This time, rather than *denying* the Truth of What You Are, claim your Truth, and *deny* that the *Laws of Hell* have any power over you. For this, then, is but to *deny* death for that of Life. Do not let death rob you for even one more second of the Life that awaits but a change of mind.

I.16.102 The messages received from the *underworld* can only create experiences of separation. For the messages themselves are rooted in the tightly held *belief* of the *subconscious* mind that it is alone and without Love. It can but *project* this energy of a separate, personal-self into the Grand Field of Energy, thereby ensuring that it sees and experiences what it *believes* real. Yet, your salvation is at hand. And, all that is required is but this: *choose again.*

I.16.103 This is the purpose of this Course: to help you but choose Heaven rather than hell. This Course but points to the *beliefs* held within the *subconscious* mind that creates the hell experienced by the *consciousness*. It is designed to help guide you into choosing to listen to the messages coming from your *Higher Self.* This will then allow you to have experiences that will develop and strengthen the *trust* which is necessary to recognize your Completion and Wholeness. And, these experiences will but point to you of your Holiness and the Self for which you are in Truth.

Lesson 16

I.16.104 We come now to the sixteenth lesson found within this curriculum. It is one that will enable you to begin to listen more intently for those messages coming to you from your *Higher Self.* As with all that We ask of you, *feel* the energy that is behind the messages. It is but Love. It is but the Love of Self for Self.

I.16.105 On an index card write the following statements. We ask that you take five minutes each morning to reflect on the implication delivered by each statement. Then, each evening, just prior to laying your head upon your pillow to sleep that night, We ask that you silently repeat the series of statements for another five minutes. However, as you do, *feel* them. Allow yourself, if possible, to get lost in the energy of the statements. Swim in the energy that is found within them. *Feel* their Love. *Feel* their Peace. And, *feel* their Joy.

I.16.106 The statements are:

I choose now to listen to the Voice of my Higher Self.

I choose now to trust my Higher Self.

I choose now to Love my Higher Self.

I choose now to feel my Higher Self.

265

CHAPTER 17

Anger Is Not Your Friend

I.17.1   Of all the *feelings* experienced in the realm of physicality, you experience the *feeling* of *anger* more than any other. But, why is this? Quite simply – you believe that there is power in *anger*. Yet, there is an energy behind *anger* which is the most disruptive to the Grand Energy Field of Possibility and Potentiality of all the *feelings* experienced and emitted in the physical realm. And, We come to you now to share with you just how *anger* robs you of your greatest treasure – that of a mind at Peace. For anger is quite literally a thief. However, rather than this thief coming stealthily to rob you of your treasures and riches, you welcome this thief with open arms.

I.17.2   Let's begin Our discussion by examining the word *anger*. Just like other words We have shared with you, the meaning and implication of the word anger has been hidden from you. For you will find that the energy signature is more profound than first realized. And, the energy pattern of *anger,* when *felt*, acts on more than just the mind. It affects even the body for which you *believe* you inhabit.

I.17.3   While you already know that the word *anger* carries with it the meaning: *a strong feeling of displeasure and antagonism*, it also carries the meaning of *rage*, as well as that of *fury*. And, your word *anger* arose from the word *fury*, which came to you via the Latin word *furere*. In your language, the Latin word *furere* means *to be mad or furious, to be wild with rage*. Here is where the intentionality has been closely held from your current *state of consciousness* by the *subconscious* mind. For the Latin word *furere* was derived from the Latin word *furis*. This word carries with it the meanings: *the devil (personified), robber,* and *thief.*

I.17.4   Yes! You read that correctly. This means that *anger* represents what you have called *the devil*. Furthermore, the word *devil* symbolizes or represents hell. Thus, it is nothing more than your own *subconscious* mind. For *anger* is the *feeling* that arises from your *subconscious* into your *consciousness*. In other words, *anger* arises into the *consciousness,* which then creates the experiences you have come to associate with *hell*; namely those experiences where you *believe* you have been attacked and are suffering as a result.

I.17.5   However, there is a much deeper implication to the phrase, *the devil personified*. And, the implication is found within the meaning of the word *personify*, which is simply *the incarnation of.* Remember, the word *incarnation* carried with it the meaning *to be in the flesh.* Therefore, when you are experiencing the *feeling* of anger, you are quite literally being, in that moment, *the devil in flesh.* In other words, the *subconscious* mind, what We have referred to as the *dark lord of the underworld*, has risen to the level of *consciousness*, and is expressing itself through the body.

I.17.6   It is for this reason that when you, or any brother or sister, become enraged, you often will not *consciously* remember what was said or done. Why is this? The answer, while unpleasant to the *conscious* mind, is simply this: the *subconscious* mind took control of the body and acted out its *dark wishes* and *desires*. As you have also come to realize, grave consequences usually result. And, We mean this in the literal sense. For the subconscious, as described in *A Course in Miracles*, carries with it a *murderous intent.* And, this is directly attributable to the *laws of chaos.*

I.17.7   Recognize, then, in this moment, that nothing *good* can ever come from *anger.* We use the term *good*, not as a judgment, but as a descriptor only. For *anger* can only create hellish experiences. It can never create experiences of Love and oneness.

268

The Thief in the Night

I.17.8   Besides carrying the implication of *the devil incarnate*, the word *anger* also carries with it the implication of *thief* as found in the Latin word *furis*. And, this *thievery* is also described in your bible. There is a verse, in which it is written, that the man named Jesus said, *But know this, that if the master of the house had known in what part of the night the thief was coming, he would have stayed awake and would not let his house be broken into.*

I.17.9   This particular biblical passage has many inferences given within it. First, it is alerting those who read it that they are the master of their *house*. Remember, We have already shared with you the implication of the word *house*, which is that of *mind*. Therefore, in the case of this bible verse, it is simply stating that *you are the master of your mind, the master of your consciousness.*

I.17.10   Second, the passage is also alerting you to become conscious of the implication and energy of the word *thief*, which carries with it the meaning *one that steals especially stealthily or secretly.* In other words, this passage is simply reminding you that a *thief* moves stealthily under the cover of darkness. And, the *thief,* being eluded to within the biblical passage, is the *subconscious*, which works day and night to *steal* your *conscious* mind. No, the *subconscious* cannot literally steal your mind, but it can rob you of being the master of your mind, which is the function you have willingly given it. The implication then, of this verse, is: *one who has mastery over his mind would not give the subconscious the opportunity to enter his conscious mind, much less be its master.*

I.17.11   Finally, the passage is also letting the reader know that one who has mastery over his mind is awake. Therefore, the deeper implication given within the verse is this: *one who is awake knows that the thief comes under the cover of night, or darkness, to commit his thievery.* And, the master knows this, because a master listens only to the *Higher Self*. For the master has learned to live in the Light of Truth.

I.17.12   How, then, does this bible verse relate to *anger?* Recall, again, that the implication of *anger* is likened to that of a *thief.* And, *anger, like* a thief, does not announce its arrival. Therefore, only a master sound asleep would remain unaware of *anger's* approach. Because, one who has mastery over his mind knows that *anger* is the effect of a thought. And, the master remains vigilant over every thought that arises within his consciousness, which gives the master the choice of which *feelings* arise. For the master understands the power of thoughts upon the Grand Field of Energy. He *knows* that his thoughts create his experiences, because he understands that the thoughts sewn within the garden of his mind become the experiences he will harvest.

The Root of All Anger

I.17.13 As you are well versed in *anger*, you know it as the *feeling* it is. And, you are very conscious of the energy that accompanies it. However, you have yet to fully recognize what anger is and how destructive it is to you and your world. Although the world as you perceive it doesn't exist, the Real World rests along side it. While neither are Real, in Truth, you nevertheless will experience the one which aligns with your *beliefs* regarding your *state of being.* One world is governed by the Laws of God; the other is governed by the *laws of chaos.* Therefore, one is governed by Love, while the other is governed by *guilt* and *fear.* In one, you experience Peace and Joy, where the other yields experiences but of *anger* and conflict. The one you experience is directly determined by the energy signature you emit. And, the energy you emit corresponds to which you identify as - God or *not-God.* And, *anger* is only associated with one of these.

I.17.14 In your world, those who are easily *angered* can take a class in something called *anger management.* Yet, until they discover what creates *anger*, the classes can but fail them. For the world has *deceived* itself as to how *anger* first arose in the mind of man, as well as how it is maintained. And, until this is recognized, the *thief* will come again and again.

I.17.15   In order to understand how *anger* entered the mind of the Child of God, We invite you to the moment that *time* began. It is this moment, the first second of *time's* long march, for which you resist releasing. To the mind, this instant is still occurring. But, to your *Heart,* the moment was not even considered what you would call a blip on a radar screen. For, in Truth, not one note in Heaven's song was missed. However, the mind quite literally ran with it and is still running.

I.17.16   Once again, We return to a passage found within *A Course in Miracles*, where it is written: *Into eternity, where all is one, there crept a tiny, mad idea, at which the Son of God remembered not to laugh. In his forgetting did the thought become a serious idea, and possible of both accomplishment and real effects. Together, We can laugh them both away, and understand that time cannot intrude upon eternity. It is a joke to think that time can come to circumvent eternity, which "means" there is no time.*

I.17.17 Look, now, upon the words, *there crept a tiny, mad idea.* Have you ever given any thought to the word *mad* before? For you use the word to mean either *insanity* or *anger.* Yet, you do not *see* their oneness. For you still *believe* that *insanity* and *anger* are different. The time has come for you to understand that *insanity* and *anger* are the same. For those who are *insane* are *angry.*

I.17.18 We invite you, at this time, to focus on the word *crept.* For this word carries with it the intentionality of the phrase, *there crept a tiny, mad idea.* To *creep* implies a movement of something that is slow and often stealthy in its approach. However, the word *creep* carries with it a meaning that has also been kept hidden from your *conscious* mind. And, just like other words where We have exposed the deeper implication, We shall do so now with it.

I.17.19 The word *creep* came to you via the Latin word *serpere,* which simply means to *creep along.* Yet, the Latin word *serpere* was derived from the Latin *serpens.* That word may have a familiar ring to it. For it is where your word *serpent* arose. And, the word *serpent* is mentioned in your bible specifically as it relates to our current discussion with you. It is found in what you call the second creation story, after the creation of who you call Adam and Eve, where it is written:

Now the serpent was more subtil than any beast of the field which the Lord God had made. And he said unto the woman, "Yea, hath God not said, 'Ye shall not eat of every tree of the garden?' And, the woman said unto the serpent, "We May eat of the fruit of the trees of the garden: But of the fruit of the tree which is in the midst of the garden, God hath said, 'Ye shall not eat of it, neither shall ye touch it, lest ye die.' And the serpent said unto the woman, "Ye shall not surely die: For God doth know that in the day Ye eat thereof, then your eyes shall be opened, and ye shall be as gods, knowing good and evil." And when the woman saw that the tree was good for food, and it was pleasant unto the eyes, and a tree to be desired to make one wise, she took of the fruit thereof, and did eat, and gave also unto her husband with her; and he did eat.

I.17.20   O Divine Child, if your biblical passage is taken literally, you will miss the intention and implication that the narrative is offering. On the same hand, if it is dismissed as nothing more than a story of old, the intention and implication will also be missed. For contained within its narrative is the reason that *anger* crept into the mind and has been a part of it ever since. In addition, the narrative, when fully understood and realized, opens doorways that have been hidden within your own mind.

I.17.21 Before We unveil the intentionality of the biblical narrative, We would also like to share with you something the man named Jesus is quoted as having had said during His brief time in your world. In your bible, it is written that Jesus said, *For there is nothing hidden that will not be revealed, and nothing concealed that will not be made known and brought to light.* The time of knowing is at hand. All you need do is but allow your *Heart* to reveal the Truth as you read the words that We share with you. For the Light is with you and the Truth will be shown. All We ask of you is for you to *feel* this discussion.

I.17.22 Now, let's look upon the words of the biblical passage so that the intentionality and implication are revealed. In order to allow your consciousness to awaken to Truth, We invite you to question everything that you have been told or taught. You must come to question everything you have ever believed. For until you question your beliefs, they will continue to keep you in darkness. And, We are with you, so that Light can be restored to your mind.

I.17.23 Remember, that this particular narrative is after the man, Adam, has been put into a deep sleep so that Eve could be created. Ask yourself, *if it was important enough for the passage to state that Adam was placed into a "deep sleep," isn't it as equally important that the passage would also declare that he had been awakened? Also, if it is important enough to relate the detail of how God breathed into the nostrils of the man to create a living soul, wouldn't it be just as important to describe the same for Eve?* Furthermore, ask yourself, *why would the man, named Adam, give his wife the name, Eve, which carries the implication and intention of "darkness"?*

I.17.24 In addition, recall that We have already shared with you that Adam represents your consciousness. And, it is your consciousness which sleeps. Now, We ask you to allow your mind to remain open as you read these next words. *Eve represents the subconscious.* How can this be? First, your bible states that, *when God breathed into the man's nostrils, He created a living soul.* We have already shared with you that the *soul* represents the *mind,* and the *spirit* represents the *Heart.* Many believe that the *soul* and *spirit* are the same. However, in your bible, it is written: *For the word of God is living and active. Sharper than any double-edged sword. It penetrates even to dividing soul and spirit.* Therefore, as you can *see,* the two words indicate varied aspects of your being.

I.17.25 Second, in the second biblical narrative regarding the story of creation, it is written that Eve was created from a rib taken from Adam. As you know, the ribs are below the head.

276

Thus, this narrative is pointing to how the *subconscious* mind is at a level below that of the *conscious* mind, as well as describing how the *subconscious* came after the consciousness. Furthermore, the *subconscious,* as We have previously shared, is completely blanketed in darkness. It is, after all, the *underworld.* More importantly, the biblical narrative demonstrates that the *subconscious* mind didn't arise until after the *conscious* mind was asleep.

I.17.26   Before We continue, ask yourself these questions: *where is it found in your bible where God instructed Eve not to eat of the fruit from the tree in the midst of the garden;* and, *if Adam and Eve had just been created and they were created perfect, then how did they KNOW what death was?*

I.17.27   You can read for yourself that God told Adam not to eat of the fruit from the tree in the midst of the garden prior to Adam being placed into deep sleep. Yet, nowhere in your bible does it state that God told Eve not to eat the fruit from the tree. Furthermore, *see* for yourself that nowhere in your bible is it written that God awakened Adam. In addition, nowhere in your bible is it written that Adam or Eve had witnessed death, much less understood what death represented.

I.17.28 Now, We ask you to turn your attention to the *serpent* in the garden. For it plays a pivotal role in the narrative. Come to realize that the word *serpent* is what carries the intention of the passage. The *serpent* is described in the biblical verse as *more subtle than any beast of the field.* And, it is this phrase which determines the implication behind the word *serpent.* Furthermore, the implication is hidden within the words themselves. Therefore, We will look at the meaning behind each word to expose the energy pattern behind the implication of the word *serpent.*

I.17.29 The word *subtle* carries with it the meaning *ingenious,* which is defined as *calling for judgment,* or *derived from a judgment.* The word *beast* carries with it the meaning *something fearful and difficult to deal with.* And, finally, the word *field* carries with it the meaning *a complex set of forces (energy) that serves as causative agents in human behavior.* When you step back and put the pieces together, the implication and intention of the phrase, *more subtle than any beast of the field,* becomes strikingly clear. For the implication is: *the serpent is derived from a judgment, fearful and difficult to deal with, and is a complex set of forces* (energy) *that serves as causative agents in human behavior.* Although this describes the implication of the *serpent,* what is the meaning of the word?

I.17.30   The meaning of the word *serpent* is quite literally *devil*. Recall that one of the meanings of *anger* is *devil*. Therefore, the Bible verse is stating: *anger is derived from a judgment, is fearful and difficult to deal with, and serves as a causative agent in human behavior.* When you read the simple logic contained within the implication of the phrase, you can understand exactly what *anger* is. Furthermore, once you understand the intention of the verse, you can see that *anger* is an energy that serves to not only create your behavior, but your experiences as well.

I.17.31   Yet, the next question to ask is: *if this is the case, then why was Eve angry?* Not only is the answer found within the bible passage, but the answer also reveals how anger arose within the mind of those who believe they are separated from God. Remember, the verse, to which We are referring, states: *And the serpent said unto the woman, "For God doth know that in the day ye eat thereof, then your eyes shall be opened and ye shall be as gods."*

I.17.32   Haven't you ever heard the voice of your anger? It's the nonstop chatter within your mind that speaks to you every time that you become angry. And, this is one of the implications being delivered within the verse.

I.17.33 However, the deeper intention is found in the phrase, *your eyes shall be opened and ye shall be as gods.* Read that statement once again. As you do, allow yourself to *feel* the words you are reading. Do not let your mind interpret them. Rather, allow your *Heart* to speak to you of their intention. For within those words, lies the creation of *anger* – your anger!

I.17.34 When the mind asked itself the question, *What am I*, it had already judged itself as *not-God.* In that act, the mind completely identified with being only human. Now, look upon the verse once more. For there in the midst of the garden is found a tree, whose fruit will open the eyes and will make the person that eats the fruit just like God. To a mind in complete darkness, there appears to be something outside of itself that will give it the answer for which it seeks. Yet, to partake of this thing means facing certain *death.* And, it was God, Himself, that declared this thing off limits. But why would God declare this thing off limits? Is it to keep the person from being like He Is?

I.17.35 Do you yet *see* it? Better still, do you *feel* it? For you have been reading the series of thoughts that direct a reasonable mind but to the only conclusion that is logical – that of the *victim/blame* game. And, *blaming* anyone or anything for your current circumstance always leads to *anger.*

I.17.36 The biblical narrative is not to be taken literally. It was given mankind to demonstrate the implication and intention of separation and the experiences it creates. The more We draw back the veil, the more Light enters the mind, that allows it to question everything it believed to be true and real.

I.17.37 Now, We will expose the reason as to how *anger* is maintained within your subconscious. And, it too is found in that same biblical passage. For it is the *belief* in lack which always keeps *anger* at a slow rolling boil within the subconscious. Thus, it doesn't take much to make your anger spill over into your consciousness. And, it will continue to do so until you remove the root of *anger* from your mind.

I.17.38 Look lovingly once more at the biblical passage. As you return to it, focus your attention on the part of it which reads: *And the woman saw that the tree was a tree to be desired to make one wise.* Do you *see* it? For the woman looked at the tree with desire. But what does desire have to do with anger?

I.17.39 Our answer is simply this: desire has everything to do with *anger.* For *anger* is maintained by *unholy desire,* as surely as *unholy desire* is maintained by the *unholy belief* in *lack.* In the case of the passage, for Eve to look at the tree with desire because she believed it offered something outside herself that she could acquire that would make her wise, means that she *believed* she was lacking something within her. What was the something she *believed* she was missing? The answer is wisdom. But, what is the wisdom she *believed* she was missing?

I.17.40 Wisdom is simply knowledge. And, Knowledge is God. Yet, your word *wisdom* also carries with it the meaning *judgment*. Therefore, in the biblical narrative, the woman *believes* she *lacks* the ability to make *judgments* like God. For to be able to *judge* between good and evil will make her wise. In other words, it will make her like God.

I.17.41 Keeping your mind open is completely necessary now in order to understand how *lack* fosters and promotes *anger*. And, to have a complete understanding of the energy pattern of *anger*, We must expose the energy signature of *lack*, which is found in the deeper meaning of the word. *Lack* carries with it the meaning *a state of being wanting or deficient*. Note, *lack* is a *state of being*. However, the energy pattern of *lack* is found in the word *deficient*, which carries with it the implication of *being incomplete, being imperfect*, as well as *not being whole*. It is for this reason We have already shared with you that *lack* is *unholy*. This statement is not a judgment. Rather, it is nothing more than a description of the energy signature of the word *lack*. For to *believe* in *lack* means that you *believe* you aren't whole. And, if you *believe* you are *un-whole*, then you *believe* you are *unholy*. For the word *holy* simply implies *to be whole*, just as the word *unholy* carries with it the meaning *to be not-whole*, which is *to be lacking*.

I.17.42 However, the word *deficient* carries with it a hidden meaning, and the time has come for this meaning, this implication, to be rooted out. As with other words, the implication is buried within the origin of your word. For your word *deficient* came to you from the Latin word *deficere*, which carries the meaning *rebel*. And, it is here where the intention and implication lies hidden. For the word *rebel* carries with it the meaning *to feel or exhibit anger*.

I.17.43 Therefore, the very energy of *lack* is that of *anger*. It is for this reason that We have shared with you that *the belief in lack maintains anger*. Furthermore, *lack* is the *state of being angry*. For to *believe* that you are without something is to *believe* that you are in a *state of lack*. And, *to be in a state of lack IS TO BE IN A STATE OF ANGER*. This is a direct result of the Law of Being.

I.17.44   When you follow the workings of the Law of Being, you can clearly *see* the havoc that the *feeling* of *anger* has regarding what you experience. For *to be angry* is *to have anger*, and *to have anger* is to *give anger*. And, when you give *anger*, you receive *anger*. It is the proverbial hamster wheel, you might say.

I.17.45   Now, the time has come for Us to expose the deep root of *anger*. And, We will do this by inviting you to turn your attention to the Law of Cause and Effect. Recall, thoughts are causal agents, feelings are their effect. *Anger,* as you well know, is a *feeling*. And, like all *feelings, anger* arises from a thought. In the case of *anger,* the thought is a judgment. Although We have already discussed the energy field of *judging* with you, We will now expose the underbelly of the *serpent.*

I.17.46   In addition to the implication and meaning given before regarding making *judgments,* We will now call into focus the deeper, hidden intention associated behind *judging.* The word *judge* also carries with it the meaning *to think*. Furthermore, the word *think* carries with it the meaning *to reason*. And, it is from the word *reason* where the energy pattern of *judging* arises and is emitted into the Grand Field of Energy.

I.17.47 The word *reason* is defined as *the thing that makes some fact intelligible: cause.* It also carries the implication of *proper exercise of the mind: sanity.* Look now upon the first meaning given for the word *reason*, which is *cause.* For herein lies the *original error.* And, it is from this *original error* where not only was *time* born, but *anger* was born as well.

I.17.48 It is written in the curriculum of *A Course in Miracles* that *God is the First Cause and you are His Effect.* O Child of God, do you yet truly understand the implication here? For the implication is the *original error.* Listen now with your *Heart* to these words: *God is the Thought, you are His Feeling.* For were you not also taught that *you are an extension of God's Love*? You are *His Joy*, because joy is the *feeling* of a thought of love.

I.17.49 Therefore, when you asked the question, *What am I*, you *denied* your joy. For *Joy* is your True Self. *Joy* is your *True State of Being.* O Divine One, *Joy* is your Divinity. And, when you *judged* against your Self, you *denied* your *being of joy.*

I.17.50 *Judgments* are thoughts. And, thoughts are the *causal agents* of creation. Thus, the *original error* was a *thought against your Self.* This meant that you became *the cause.* And, here is where terror was born. For in that moment you *judged*

285

your Self for having usurped God's Purpose. This, too, is the root of all *guilt.*

I.17.51 Bring back into your mind where We shared with you that one of the meanings of *anger* is *madness.* And, *madness* is *insanity.* If the implication of *reason* is: *the proper exercise of mind*, which is *sanity*; then the *improper exercise of the mind* is: *insanity*, which is *madness.* And, *madness* is *anger.* Therefore, the *original error* is simply this: *the improper use of your mind* – *insanity*, or that of *anger.*

I.17.52 Come to recognize, in this most glorious moment, that you have but lived time and time again nothing but the *original error.* In other words, you have lived but in *insanity* - in *anger.* For every judgment made even unto this moment is but to continue the *insanity,* thus the *anger,* forward in time. This is why the *anger* you have experienced in the past becomes the *anger* you experience in the present, which ultimately becomes the *anger* you will experience in the future. *NOTHING CHANGES WHEN NOTHING CHANGES.* And, it is for this reason that you have yet to ever find lasting joy in your world. You seek in things for that which you believe you threw away, always *wishing* that, once in your possession, the thing will return to you the *joy* for which you so desperately yearn.

I.17.53   This is what the narrative of the biblical story regarding the fruit from the tree in the midst of the garden was to reveal unto you. For Eve saw the fruit as *something* pleasant to the eye. She *believed* it would bring her *joy*. Yet, it delivered but heartache and misery. For what else can *insanity*, can *anger*, ever return? The lesson, then, is but this: to seek for your Self, which *IS JOY,* is to never find *Joy*, to never find your Self. For your Self, your Joy, your Divinity, lies within you, exactly where it has always been. Where else could it be?

I.17.54   The subconscious is the seat of darkness. It is the host to the *unholy* thoughts of *lack*. And, it is where *anger* resides. It projects onto others, the world, and God, the *anger* which lives within it. But try as hard as it may, projection can never cast out the *anger* which boils and churns within it. *For thoughts never leave their source.* Therefore, the *anger* but churns and churns and churns creating the experiences you are so familiar with. Yet, this need not be!

I.17.55   Recognize, then, that you but re-create in each moment the *original error*. For in each moment that you *deny* your *True State of Being*, which is Joy, which is but Love, you choose to remain in *anger.* You refuse to accept the Truth of your Being. Therefore, you but choose *denial* yet again. And, the consciousness, under the control of the *subconscious,* moves thereby creating but another passing second on the clock. Thus, *time* is maintained, because *anger* is maintained.

I.17.56 We share with you now that the time of revealing the secrets you have kept hidden from your *consciousness* has come. For the awakening is upon you. It is time for you to recognize that the *subconscious* has been controlling you since the moment time began, the moment *anger* entered into the mind, the moment *insanity* became a part of the mind of the Child of God. And, even this *subconscious* control of the *conscious* mind is demonstrated in the bible passage We have been discussing. For was it not Eve who offered to Adam the fruit from the tree in the midst of the garden, and he did eat of it?

I.17.57 We have shared with you many times now that the *subconscious* is the *underworld*. It is completely devoid of Light. Therefore, it is devoid of Love, Truth, and Knowledge. And because of this, its ruler can be but a tyrant.

I.17.58 The *dark lord* has many names. But, they all mean the same. For his name is but *death*. He reigns over *time* and wields *anger* to compensate for his fear. Know this, now, O Divine Child, *Only the fearful know anger, because only the fearful perceive lack.* And to perceive *lack* means that you can only be listening to the *subconscious*.

I.17.59 Just as the purpose of the Higher Self is to guide you Home by reminding you that everything you perceive begins and ends with you, the purpose of the *subconscious* is to keep your *consciousness entranced in time.* And, it does this because of the *insanity*, the *anger*, that fuels its *state of beingness*. It is lost in a world of darkness and deceit. And, its beliefs - your beliefs - shape every experience you have ever had. Yet, the time has come for this tyrant, created by your own mind, to be exposed. For it is not a hideous beast of past legends told. It is but a frightened child, sitting alone in darkness, trembling in fear at the monsters it believes to be lurking in the dark, awaiting to torment it without mercy.

I.17.60 This child, who knows not of Love, has but created a labyrinth of dark defenses to protect itself from the *attack* it knows is coming. It keeps a close watch for any sign of the enemy's approach. It is *angry* and *fearful*. For it knows not Joy, but yearns for it. Yet, it also believes Joy to be but its enemy. For it believes Joy abandoned it, leaving it cold and lonely. It perceives its own torment, and believes it is a *victim* to a Father that does not Love it. In its pain and anguish, it becomes more isolated and frightened, which but makes it all the more angry.

289

I.17.61 For decades you have heard stories and read books on healing the child within. This child is your inner child, so often referenced by your doctors of psychology. And, it inhabits your *subconscious* mind. For it is your *subconscious* mind. However, it lives just below the level of your *conscious awareness*. And, you are completely oblivious to its whims and wishes. You only sense it when you become *consciously* afraid of something, or when you become *angry*. Although you remain unaware of its true nature or its existence, its energy field is responsible for your experiences.

I.17.62 The *anger*, which has but festered in the dark labyrinth of your *subconscious* mind, has spawned yet another, more potent defense shield in its desire to protect itself from its perceived threats. Like *anger*, which is but *insanity*, this defense shield has also become a weapon that can be used offensively. Some call it *intense rage*, while others refer to it as *hate*. Regardless of what it is called, it is the most destructive *feeling* you have created.

The Hate of Anger

I.17.63 Where Love extends, *hate* consumes. *Hate* will take everything it is offered, but will leave nothing but *death* and *destruction* in its energetic wake. *Hate* is the *child of anger*.

Remember, the *subconscious* perceives everything as a threat and believes in a first strike policy. Nothing, absolutely nothing, can get past it. For this is its purpose. And, *hate* is its weapon of choice. *Hate* rests upon emotional missiles, much like your world's nuclear warheads sit atop theirs. Hate, like nuclear weapons, serve but one purpose: the complete annihilation of what is considered to be its enemies. And, just as nuclear weapons are promoted as a deterrent to attack, the *subconscious* uses its *hate* to deter its perceived enemies. Yet, the *subconscious* mind will viciously attack anyone or anything at the slightest provocation. For its greatest fear is the loss of its *dark kingdom.*

I.17.64   You, who are but the *avatar* of the *subconscious* mind*,* serve as the launch pad for its arsenal of *hatred.* The mind cannot attack, but a body can. And, the body is the *game piece* in the *game of make-believe.* To a sleeping *consciousness*, the *conscious* mind is completely unaware that it is but an *avatar* following the dictates of a terrified child. For the *consciousness* believes it is in control. Yet, it is but the servant to its master, the *dark lord.* The consciousness recognizes *hate*, but has no idea how it came to be. For *hate* just seems to be with it. Although the *conscious* mind tries to hide the *hate* that seems to lurk just beneath its surface, the *consciousness* cannot conceal the *hate* once a trigger has been pulled. And, triggers are but the defense mechanisms of the *subconscious* in order to detect any incoming threat.

I.17.65 Once a trigger has fired, the *subconscious* reacts with anger so that the perceived attack can be fended off. However, if the reaction of *anger* is not sufficient enough to thwart the attack, the *subconscious* will immediately meet the assessment of the situation by bringing out the big guns – *hate*. And, it does so without questioning any consequences that might arise.

I.17.66 Therefore, what is the energy signature of *hatred*, and how does it affect the Grand Field of Energy? The energy pattern associated with *hatred* is buried deep within its origin. We will reveal unto you, now, the energy pattern emitted from the *feeling* of *hatred*. We invite you, once again, to read and follow Our discussion with an open mind. Allow your *Heart* to interpret for you the words and their implications. Your mind will want to recoil at what the eyes read. Therefore, We ask you to relax. Take a few deep breaths. For the veil that is *hatred* is about to be removed. Then, you will know the depths to which the *subconscious* mind has gone in order to keep hidden from your *conscious* mind the *hatred* that lives within it.

I.17.67 As We expose the implication of *hatred*, you will look upon what the *veil of hatred* was meant to hide from you. This *veil of hatred* is the ancient hatred which was written about within *A Course in Miracles.* As We approach this veil, do not turn away in disgust or fear. Do not allow what it covers to continue to control your life and experiences. We are with you. Yes, it will take great courage to look upon your own darkness, buried so deeply, that you have forgotten it. But, it has not forgotten you. For this darkness has controlled every thought, every feeling, every action, and every experience you have had. Turn, then, to your *Heart*, where your True Courage is found. Join with Us now as We draw back the veils created to keep the *ancient veil of hatred* hidden from your *conscious* mind.

I.17.68   The veils, which cover and hide the *ancient veil*, are found within the various meanings that have been ascribed to the word *hate.* The meanings of the various words are the very curtains which have obstructed the view of the *ancient veil*. Therefore, We will pull back one curtain at a time, so that We can expose the lengths to which your *subconscious* has undergone in order to keep hidden the *ancient veil* from your *conscious awareness*.

I.17.69   We will begin with the word *hate*, itself. The word carries with it the meaning *intense hostility and aversion deriving from fear, anger, or sense of injury.* The *feeling* of *hatred* is certainly derived from *fear, anger,* and the *belief you have been injured or harmed*. However, this meaning doesn't expose the origin of *hatred*. It merely demonstrates how *hatred* surfaces within an experience. Besides the meaning just given, the word *hatred* also carries with it the meaning *antipathy*. And, here is where the implication and intentionality of *hatred* lies buried.

I.17.70 While the word *antipathy* means *a strong feeling of dislike*, the implication of the word lies buried within its origin. Your word *antipathy* came to you from the Greek word *antipatheia*, which carries with it the meaning *opposite feeling*. However, the Greek word arose from combining the words *anti*, meaning *opposite*, and *pathos*, which carries the meanings *suffering*, as well as *an element in experiencing pity*. As We dive even deeper into the layers of meanings hiding the implication of *hate*, We must expose the hidden meaning of *pity*. It is here where We approach the *ancient veil of hatred*. For what lies just beyond it is where We will find what the *veil of hatred* has kept hidden from you since the moment *time* seemed to circumvent eternity.

I.17.71 Your word *pity* carries with it the meaning: *something to be regretted*. However, it is in the origin of your word *pity* where the intention lies. For the word arose from the Latin word *piety*, which along with carrying the meaning of *pity*, also carries with it the meaning of your word *piety*.

I.17.72   Now, We stand before the *ancient veil of hatred*. For it is in the word *piety* where We will uncover what your *subconscious* mind has kept hidden from you, where it lays rotting, emitting an energy that permeates the Grand Field of Energy creating the suffering experienced from the *guilt* and *fear,* as well as the *anger,* that arose from the *original error*.

I.17.73   The word *piety* carries with it the meaning *the state of being pious*. Therefore, it is a *state of being*. In the case of *hatred*, it is *being pious*. Although the word *pious* is generally looked upon as favorable, it is the dark meaning to which We point you. For the word *pious*, besides meaning *something that is seen as sacred or devotional,* carries with it the dark meaning *marked by sham or hypocrisy*.

I.17.74   Join your hand with ours as We draw back the final veil, the *ancient veil of hatred,* so that you might look upon the *thing* which has for so long induced *the reign of terror* wrought by the *dark lord*. What is this *thing* which has brought so much grief and suffering into your mind? The answer is found in the very intention of the word *sham*. For the word implies *a trick that deludes: hoax*, as well as *an imitation or counterfeit purporting to be genuine*.

I.17.75   What is *a trick that deludes*? It is but *illusion.* Yet, there is more to be shown. For there is still a deeper, even darker, side found behind the word *sham.* And, this dark intention, this dark implication, is what creates the very *illusions* you *believe* real.

I.17.76   As with so many other words where We have exposed the hidden meaning, where the dark energy hides, the darkness of the word *sham* lies within its origin. The word *sham* arose from the word *shame.* Yes! You read that correctly. And, now We have reached the *thing* for which your *subconscious* mind has so thoroughly veiled from your *consciousness.* And, it is but *shame.*

I.17.77   Let's pull back the last *veil,* so the Light of Truth may shine from your mind once again. Here is where the dark intention is found. And, it is found in the implication of the word *shame,* itself. For the word *shame* carries with it the implication and the intention, *a painful emotion caused by guilt,* as well as *a condition of humiliating disgrace.*

I.17.78   O Child of God, do you *see* it? Just as it is written within *A Course in Miracles, Guilt remains the only thing that hides the Father, for guilt is the attack upon His Son. The guilty*

always condemn, and having done so, they will still condemn,
linking the future with the past.

I.17.79 *Guilt* is the thought which has created the *feeling* of shame. And, *shame* is what has kept the *guilt* hidden. Furthermore, it is the energy of *guilt* and *shame* that are emitted within the Grand Energy Field of Possibility and Potentiality creating the very experiences you have. Come, now, to recognize that the *subconscious* has hidden its *guilt* and *shame* behind the *veil of hate*.

I.17.80 O Holy One, there is still one more *veil* to be drawn back. For it is the *veil* which has been hiding behind the veil of *guilt* and *shame*. And, what lies beyond it is the reason We are with you now. This last *veil* is the intention carried with *shame*. For there is one last meaning, thus implication, found within it. And, it is but this: *a condition of disgrace or disrepute.*

I.17.81 Look, then, with eyes wide open as We draw back the last veil. Look upon the throne of the *dark lord*. For sitting upon it is but the child We spoke of earlier. It is the *child of dis-grace*. Do you yet understand what the energy of *dis-grace* is? It is but the energy of *not-God*. It is but the energy of one who still asks the question, *What am I?* For O Holy Child, it is but you who sits upon the throne scared, lonely, angry, and bitter.

I.17.82   Yes! It is but you. For you *believe* that you are in a *state of disgrace*, which carries with it the literal implication of a *state of being without God.* And, since it is your current *belief,* under the Law of Being, *to BE without God,* is *to HAVE no God*; and, *to HAVE no God,* is *to GIVE no God.*

I.17.83   In your bible, it is written, *God is Love.* Therefore, God and Love are One. As such, look upon your *belief* in your current *state of being* as: *to BE without Love,* is *to HAVE no Love*; and, *to HAVE no Love,* is *to GIVE no Love.*

I.17.84   This is the *hoax*, the *sham*, the game you have but been playing with yourself. For if you were without Love, then the child, who but sits upon the throne would be Love-less, or *God-less.* Yet, there is nothing absent of Him, Who is but the All of Everything. Just as are you, the child, who but sits upon the throne, is without *guilt.* For you are the one who has but stood in judgment of him. And, since you and the child are one, you have but stood in judgment of yourself.

I.17.85   Go, now, unto the child. Pick him up. Look lovingly into his eyes and welcome him Home. Embrace him. Love Him. Bring him out of the darkness and into the Light. For in Loving him, you but *give* Love unto yourself. And, to *give* Love unto yourself, is to *have* Love for yourself. And, to *have* Love for yourself, is to *be* Love.

I.17.86 Yes! Welcome this child Home. O Holy Child, the veil has been rent. The Light has come! Turn and see it is but your Father Who but welcomes you Home. Fall into His Arms. *Feel His Love for you*. For there is no end to the Love He has for His Child, His Beloved *Creation* – YOU!

I.17.87 Play not, then, the game of *make-believe* any longer. Know ye, in this most Holy Moment, this Eternal Now, that YOU ARE LOVED; YOU ARE LOVING; and YOU ARE LOVE, itself. For in this moment, you are Love in the flesh – the very incarnation of Love.

I.17.88 If you are ready to lay aside your anger and hatred, then We invite you to complete this exercise. For in doing so, you will come to *feel* the *Truth of your Being*. Yet, you must first remove the obstacles of *anger* and *hate*. Ultimately, you will come to no longer give the words any consideration. For you now know that they but wreak havoc within yourself and what you experience.

Lesson 17

I.17.89 For this exercise, you will need a large index card. Upon it, you are to write the following statements. As you have done previously, spend five minutes in the morning repeating the statements quietly to yourself. Then, set aside ten minutes each evening, just prior to going to bed, for the completion of this exercise. Sit someplace where you feel relaxed.

I.17.90 During the evening session, spend five minutes silently repeating the statements. Use the remaining five minutes to *feel* the energy behind the statements. Become comfortable with the energy of each one. For they will help create new experiences in unity and wholeness.

I.17.91 The statements are:

There is nothing in anger that I want.

There is nothing in hatred that I choose to experience.

There is nothing to hate, but everything to Love.

I choose, in this Holy Moment, to love all of myself.

I welcome the Light into my subconscious.

I.17.92 Keep the index card with you throughout your day. If for any reason you feel anger arising within you, take the card and silently repeat the statements. *Feel* their healing power. *Feel* their Love. *Feel* their Joy. For you need never experience anger again.

CHAPTER 18

The Avatar and the Belief in Separation

I.18.1   The *belief* in separation, the *game of make-believe*, would be impossible without the game piece, which is the body. Thus, the body allows you to *play* the game. The *body-mind* is therefore the *avatar*. The purpose given the *avatar* is to move through the world reacting to threats by defending itself or attacking when the need arises. It does this while it searches for treasure – the treasure that it *believes* will give it the joy for which it so yearns. The *avatar* knows not where the joy will be found, so it goes seeking hither and yon, all in the hopes that it will find this *thing* before its *time* is spent.

I.18.2   We are able to have this discussion with you because of the *time* you *believe* you are in the world. For you live in a *time* where *games* are *played* by many on your planet, where the *gamer* controls an *avatar,* in something you refer to as a *virtual reality,* or *a virtual world.* Just three of your decades past, We would not be able to have this discussion, because the very words We are communicating with you would be meaningless. For you would not have a frame of reference through experience in order for the implication to be seen and understood.

I.18.3   There are currently scientists on your planet who have proposed theories ranging from the description where you live in a holographic reality to that of what is referred to as a computer simulation. While We are not with you at this *time* to point to one or the other and say that this one or that one has more merit, We can use your creations as a descriptive device, in order to aid you in removing the obstacles which stand between you and Truth. However, We can state this with absolute certainty: *whether you inhabit a virtual world or holographic world, neither of them are Real.* And, neither they nor the world you believe you inhabit can *give* you the joy for which your *heart* yearns. Yet, the word *virtual* most closely relates to the implication of the *avatar,* as well as the implication of *illusions.* For the word *virtual* carries the energy pattern of both.

I.18.4   One of the most difficult things for the mind to accept is that it looks upon nothing but *death*, or *illusions*. For the eyes but perceive the *projections* emitted from the *subconscious* mind. And, the *subconscious* can but emit the energy pattern of death, since death is its current *state of being.*

I.18.5   Let's look at the implication of the word *virtual*, in order for you to *see* and *feel* the energy pattern associated with *being* an *avatar* in the world in which you believe you inhabit. Your word *virtual* carries the meaning: *being in effect but not recognized as true or real.* Furthermore, your word came to you via the Latin word *virtus*, which carries the meaning: *character.* Here is where the intentionality arises. For the word *character* has the meaning: *symbol.*

I.18.6   It is in the word *symbol* for which the energy pattern of intentionality affects the Grand Energy Field. And, like many other words, the intention has been hidden within its origin. Your word *symbol* has its origin in the Greek word *symbolon*, which carries with it the meaning *token of identity to establish its truth by assuming the appearance of its other half with the intent to deceive.*

I.18.7   Although this meaning carries the energy signature, it becomes even more clear to the mind when We look deeper into the Greek word *symbolon.* For it arose from the Greek word *syn+ballien*, which literally means *to throw together.* It becomes even more telling once you understand that the Greek word *ballien* arose from the Greek root *bolen*, meaning to *cast out; devil.*

I.18.8   Therefore, the intention of the word *virtual* is quite literally that of *having an outward, or external, identity to*

304

establish its truth by assuming the appearance of its other half with the intent to deceive. In order to bring even greater clarity to the intentionality of the word *virtual,* let's expose the implication of the word *outward* by looking at its meaning, which is: *relating to the body rather than the mind or the inner life.* In addition, the word *external* carries with it the meaning: *apart,* which has the implication of *separation.*

I.18.9   O Holy Child, do you *feel* the implication of what We are exposing? Look at it with your eyes wide open. *Feel* the implication as you read these words: *the intentionality behind the word virtual is – to have a body as your identity in order to establish its truth by assuming the appearance of its other half with the intent to deceive.* Yet, there is still more to expose. For the word *assume* carries the implication *to pretend,* which literally means *make-believe.* And, the word *appearance* carries the meaning *to become manifest,* which has the implication - easily recognized by the mind.

I.18.10 Therefore, the energy field contained within the word *virtual* becomes much easier to understand when read as: *to have a body as your identity, in order to establish its truth by make-believe, is easily recognized by the mind of its other half with the intent to deceive.* In other words, the *body-mind* is a creation of make-believe meant to *deceive* its other half. But, who or what is creating the *deceit?* And, who or what is being *deceived?*

I.18.11   The answer is one that always creates great consternation in the *body-mind* when it is first heard. For the *conscious* mind has been *deceived* in its complete identification with the make-believe *body-mind,* which is but the *avatar* to the *subconscious.* This makes the *subconscious* mind the one *deceiving* its other half, which is the *conscious* mind.

I.18.12   Thus, the *body-mind* is a *symbol.* Recall that the word *symbol* means to *cast out; devil.* Since the *body-mind* is a symbol, it is therefore a *projection* of the *subconscious* mind meant to *deceive* the *conscious* mind. For the *deceit* lies in the complete identification of the *body-mind.* And, by identifying with it, the *consciousness* becomes the *avatar* moving about in a *virtual reality,* believing its experiences within the *virtual world* are just as real as it is. But, what is the purpose of this *game of make-believe?*

I.18.13   You need look no farther than your bible for the answer. Just prior to Adam, which represents the *conscious* mind being placed in a deep sleep so that Eve, the *subconscious,* could be created, it is written: *And the Lord God said, "It is not good that the man should be alone; I will make him an help meet for him.*" Although many believe this bible passage to mean that God created for Adam a *help mate*, this is not the implication or intention. For the word *meet* carries with it a much darker implication, which is that of *to encounter as an antagonist or foe.*

I.18.14 Here is where the implication becomes truly recognizable. For the word *foe* carries with it the implication of *one who has personal enmity for another, an adversary,* as well as *mutual hatred or ill will.* In addition, it should be noted that the word *satan* also carries with it the meaning *adversary.*

I.18.15 Many in your world believe that there is a *being*, which exists external to you, in the *nether* regions of the spiritual realm, which tempts mankind into all sorts of depravity and *evil* acts. However, We assure you that there is nothing external to you *making* you think or do the things you do. For the adversary is you, it is your *subconscious* mind, which was the *effect* of the third splitting of the mind.

I.18.16 Why does the biblical story regarding the creation of Eve detail the account of Adam being placed into a deep sleep so that the woman could be created from a removed rib? To those who take the account literally, they *believe* that the woman, named Eve, was created in form, just as the narrative portrays.

Yet, there is a hidden implication found within that narrative. And, once understood by the mind, it can then free itself of the dark intention buried deep within the wording.

The Rib of Shame

I.18.17 *And the rib, which the Lord God had taken from man, made he a woman, and brought her unto the man. And Adam said, "This is now bone of my bones, and flesh of my flesh: she shall be called Woman, because she was taken out of Man. Therefore, shall a man leave his father and his mother, and shall cleave unto his wife: and they shall be of one flesh."*

I.18.18 Although many have heard this narrative dozens of times, they have yet to understand its deeper meaning. And, this deeper implication comes via the word *rib* as found within the biblical passage. As We expose this hidden meaning, We ask that you again read the words with an open mind. For the meaning will shatter previously held beliefs. Your mind is apt to begin questioning. We invite you to simply allow the questions to arise, regardless as to the direction they may take the mind. For until you question your most closely held beliefs, you cannot release them. Therefore, you cannot create the change in your internal belief system that will create experiences of oneness. Instead, you will continue to create experiences of suffering and grief. In other words, you will continue to experience the hell of your own making.

I.18.19 In order to expose the hidden implication found within the bible passage, We must first expose what the rib represents. Your word rib, besides meaning a bone found in the thoracic cavity, also carries with it the meaning of *wife*. Hidden deep within the origins of the word *wife* is where the dark implication rests. For the word *wife* came to you from the German word *wīb*. Yet, farther back in what you refer to as your history, the German word arose from an ancient Indo-European language known as Tocharian.

I.18.20 Thus, the German word *wīb* arose from the Tocharian word *kwīpe*, meaning pudenda. Here is where We find the implication of the word *rib* as given in the biblical story. And, it is found in the origin of the word pudenda, which comes to you from the Latin word *pudendus,* and it carries the implication and meaning: *disgrace* and *shame.* Look carefully upon the implication. For it is the *shame* and *disgrace* for which We have already shared with you.

I.18.21 While it appears that the biblical narrative is detailing the *creation* of Eve from a *rib* of Adam, as you can clearly see, this is not the case. It is not, nor ever was, meant to be taken

309

literally. It was but to bring enlightenment to the mind regarding the creation of the *subconscious* mind of all who walk or have ever walked your planet.

I.18.22   The *subconscious* mind is your *help meet*. Thus, it would appear to be your *adversary*. Rather than look on it with enmity, open your mind to the Love that is your *Heart*. For the time has come for your mind to begin *healing*. But, it cannot do this if there is still a part of it that you look upon with disgust or denial.

I.18.23   There is a question that We would like to ask of you. We invite you to *feel* the implication of the question. Yes, *feel* it. For only in *feeling* it will your mind be set free. And, freeing your mind is the purpose for Our *time* together.

I.18.24   The question is but this: *since it was a "rib" from Adam which was used to create Eve, and the word rib represents disgrace and shame, then wouldn't that imply that the disgrace and shame was already with Adam?* Can you see it? Can you *feel* it? Now, ask yourself one more question: *since Adam represents your consciousness, and Eve represents your subconscious, then doesn't it stand to reason that your consciousness already felt the shame and disgrace before the third split of the mind?*

I.18.25   Allow both of these questions to permeate deep into your mind. For now We come to yet one other question. And, it is but this: *if Adam, which is your consciousness, already held disgrace and shame within him before being placed into a deep sleep, then what is the implication for Eve?* This is the question which must be answered. For only in questioning just how deep your *feelings of disgrace* and *shame* run, will you be able to release them in totality.

I.18.26   Now, We invite you to *feel* the answer to the last question for which We are going to share with you. Recognize, in this moment, Eve was created when Adam was in a deep sleep, which means the *subconscious* was created when the *conscious* mind was asleep. And, just like Eve – the *subconscious* is but a dream. This means that the *subconscious* was created by the *consciousness* in order to *throw off* its own shame and disgrace. It is for this reason that you do not have a conscious recollection of your subconscious. For you have projected your feelings of *shame* upon it.

I.18.27   In addition, the *subconscious,* having been born from *shame* and *disgrace,* can but project these onto the world in an effort to rid itself of these *feelings,* since that is the purpose for its creation. And, it does this by projecting itself as a *body-*

311

mind. Thus, the body mind becomes its *avatar* in a world which represents the *shame and disgrace* still held within the *conscious* mind. Furthermore, as a result from the *conscious* mind splitting and creating the *subconscious*, an *adversary* was created.

I.18.28 Although We have spoken with you before regarding the *Heavenly War*, it should now be abundantly evident that this is where the war rages. For it is a war held within your own mind between the aspects of your *conscious* and *subconscious* mind. And, not only are the battlefields of this war found within your mind, they are found within your world. These battlefields are found all around you – home, school, work, and beyond. And, these are the battlefields for which the *avatar*, the *body-mind,* must maneuver and defend itself. For your world is predicated on *attack*, because your mind is.

I.18.29 Yet, if your *subconscious* was created by you as an *adversary* to the *conscious* mind, then what purpose does this serve? Better yet, what is the intention? For within the intention is found the energy pattern which affects the Grand Field of Energy. And, the intention is found within the word *adversary*, itself.

I.18.30   The word *adversary* carries the meaning *one that opposes or resists*. However, the implication is found in the word's origin, like other words We have discussed. The origin of the word *adversary* is *adverse*, which implies *to direct one's attention to*. And, it is within this meaning where the intentionality lies hidden. For the word *attention* carries with it the meaning *notice*.

I.18.31   Before We continue with our discussion, We invite you to relax. Allow your mind to clear and remain open to what you will read. Allow your *Heart* to smile upon you and blanket you in Love. For We will now expose the hidden intention of the *subconscious*. And, you will discover a friend rather than an enemy.

I.18.32   The hidden intention of the *subconscious* is found in the origin of your word *notice,* which came to you via the Latin word *noscere*, and carries with it the meaning *to become cognizant of, to learn*. And, the word *cognizant* simply implies *to bear to mind*, which means *to connect with the mind*, or *to become joined with the mind*. This, then, is the purpose, the intention, of the *subconscious*: it is an aspect of you, a dimension of your self, which is to aid you in the learning of the knowledge for which your mind desired. Thus, it is to help you learn *WHAT YOU ARE* by teaching you *WHAT YOU ARE*

NOT. In other words, the *subconscious*, which is but your own inner darkness, is to guide you into playing *not-God,* so that you can learn through experience, that you are *God.* And, it does this through the use of the *body-mind,* the *avatar,* in a game of *make-believe* played in a *virtual reality.*

I.18.33 Now, look back on the bible verse which states: *therefore, shall a man leave his father and his mother, and shall cleave unto his wife: and they shall be of one flesh.* The time of revelation of this passage is upon you. For there is a deep and purposeful implication found within it. And, it is found in the word *cleave*, which carries with it the meanings: *to split*, as well as *to adhere firmly, loyally, and unwaveringly.*

I.18.34 As you know, the meaning of *split* is that of *to separate,* or to *divide.* And, the *time* of the separation between your *subconscious* and your *conscious* mind is ending. The *time* of joining has dawned. Where you once projected your darkness upon the world, by *denying* it within yourself, the *time* has come for you to *reconcile* the divisions within yourself, which simply means *to restore the friendship and harmony* within yourself. The *harmony* of which We speak is the *tranquility,* or *inner calmness,* which is but your inheritance. It is the peace that will enable you to *remember* your divinity.

I.18.35   O Divine Child, hear these words. *Feel* them. For the *time* of Light is here. Listen to your *Heart* as it speaks to you.

I.18.36   *Do you not understand that your Heart tells you but your will? Your Heart speaks for you. In Its Divinity lies your own. And all It knows is but your knowledge, saved for you that you may do your will through It. God asks you do your will. He joins with you. He did not set His Kingdom up alone. And, Heaven Itself but represents your will, where everything created is for you. No spark of life but was created with your glad consent, as you would have it be. And not one Thought that God has ever had but waited for your blessing to be born. God is no enemy to you, because you are not an enemy to your Self. Thus, He asks no more than He hear you call Him "Friend."*

I.18.37   *Look, now, once again at your "enemy," the one you have chosen to hate instead of Love. For thus was hatred and war born into the world, and thus the rule of fear and shame established there. Listen to your Heart, which but reminds you that it is not your will to hate and be a prisoner, an avatar, to fear, or a slave to death and destruction. Hear your Heart as it whispers to you of Home, of Heaven. For hell is not your will. Heaven is. Allow your Heart to share with you a friendship that lives and breathes and sees All in but Love.*

I.18.38 You cannot call God "Friend," until you make friends with every aspect of yourself. For when you make a friend of yourself, you but make a Friend of God. But, what is required of you to reunite all of the seemingly separated parts of yourself. It is but this: *come to Love yourself, every part of yourself, as God has first Loved you.*

I.18.39 O Holy Child, *what day, what hour, what moment, will you make friends with yourself? What day, what hour, what moment, will you come to truly, and We mean truly, Love yourself, even that aspect of you which appears to be the very meaning and reflection of darkness?* Do not allow one more moment of *time* to circumvent eternity within your mind.

I.18.40 Remember, *time* can waste as well as be wasted. Yet, *time* is yours, in this moment, to declare an end of the war that has raged within your mind for longer than even you can remember. The choice is yours, just as it has always been.

I.18.41 You once made a choice to experience *separation.* Now, you but need to choose again. *Separation* and the game of *make-believe* are not real. It but appears real, because of your attachment to the *body-mind.* For in this false identification lies

316

every experience of hell. But, what else could it have been? For war only creates *death* and *destruction*. For *war is hell!*

I.18.42 Look around you. For the endless strife born out in the world is but a reflection of the war that rages within your mind. Can you change the world? No! For it is but a testament to the workings of a *subconscious* created to project your *shame* and *disgrace*. Yet, you have a new purpose. One born of Love. One born of Truth. For you are to bring oneness to what seems separate and alone. You are to create a New Heaven and Earth. This is your Holy Purpose.

I.18.43 We invite you, now, to choose tranquility. We invite you to choose Heaven instead of hell. Therefore, We invite you to complete this Lesson within this curriculum. For in doing so, you will make friends with what you have but considered an adversary, an enemy. You will come to be your own *best friend.* And, then, you will know what friendship truly is.

Lesson 18

I.18.44 For this Lesson, We ask that you use one large index card. As before, write the following statements upon it. However, rather than two practice periods each day, We invite you to do just one each morning. Take ten minutes shortly after rising to start your day, and sit quietly, while you *feel* the statements. *Feel* their intention. *Feel* their energy. *Feel* their power. Do this for five minutes.

I.18.45 Then, use the remaining time to silently repeat the statements. Repeat them slowly. *Feel* each one as you slowly say it within your mind. Hear your *Heart* as it whispers them to you. Recognize the Love your *Heart* has for you. *Feel* the Love. Embrace it. Allow it to flow through your entire being.

I.18.46 The statements are:

I welcome Home all aspects of myself.

I have missed you my Father, my Friend.

I am a friend to all of my Self.

Today, I see no enemies. I only see Love all around me.

Because I see only Love, I see only Life.

CHAPTER 19

The Virtuality of Humanity

I.19.1   Although We have shared with you the implication of the meaning of the word *virtual* as it pertains to your world, We come to you now in order to expose the deeper meaning, thus the energy which allows for the manifestation of form. However, because of the intensity regarding Our purpose for this time with you, We invite you to relax as you read these words. For this discussion will be as an earthquake to your beliefs, shaking the mental ground for which they are built upon.

I.19.2   There is a verse in your bible, where it is written that the man named Jesus said: *"And great earthquakes shall be in divers places, and famines, and pestilences; and fearful sights and great signs shall there be from heaven."*

I.19.3   Although there are those who read this verse and believe it to be apocalyptic in nature, they do so because they have, as of yet, not understood the meaning of its intentionality. For they believe that it refers to what they call "the end times." Yet,

319

while the verse implies *the end of time*, it does not mean what so many have come to believe.

I.19.4   We are with you, in this moment, to reveal unto you the meaning and implication of this passage. For once understood in its proper context, you will discover that there is great hope and freedom contained within it. This passage will also allow Us to reveal unto you the fullness of creation. It has only been the *detour into fear,* for a time, that has kept it from being remembered within your holy mind.

I.19.5   Again, We invite you to keep both an open mind and heart. As you read the words in this discussion, We simply ask that you *feel* the freedom found in the passage's intention. For once the intention dawns within the mind, the *Heart* can begin the process of restoring it to the holy function given it at creation.

I.19.6   As with other biblical passages, We will expose this passage's hidden meaning by detailing the meanings of certain key words contained within it. For if the words of the passage are taken in the literal context, then fear will arise in the mind, because God is seen as being vengeful and wrathful. However, if the passage is seen within the Light of its true intention and purpose, then the obstacles, which currently stand between you and Truth, will be removed, creating the necessary pathway for the *Heart* to illuminate the mind.

I.19.7   The verse begins with the words *great earthquakes shall be in divers places.* We will begin with the word *earthquake.* For while you have visions of the earth trembling and splitting open, the intention of the word, as it is used in this biblical passage, is *upheaval.* And, it is within the word *upheaval* where the implication is found. For the word simply carries with it the meaning *to lift.* Furthermore, the word *lift* means *to rise,* which carries with it the implication of *awakening.*

I.19.8   The next word We will expose is *divers.* For it simply carries with it the meaning *various.* Again, the intention of the passage is found within the implication of this word, which is *separated.* However, it is in the word *places,* where We will expose the intention of the verse. For the word *places* carries with it the meaning *state of mind.*

I.19.9   Therefore, the beginning of this biblical passage is merely stating: *And a great awakening shall come to the minds of those (who believe they exist) in a state of separation.* Look, now, with Love upon the words you just read. For the intention is that of *hope* and *joy.* It is filled with Love and the promise of Light. And, quite simply, Our Dear Brothers and Sisters, when the mind is returned to its Natural State, there is nothing left of *time*. For in the blink of an eye, the thought of *time*, will be no more. And, when the thought of *time* has been undone within the mind, then *time* itself will simply cease to seem to be.

I.19.10 Now, turn your attention to the latter portion of the verse, where it is written, *and famines, and pestilences; and fearful sights and great signs shall there be from heaven.* To those who believe in a vengeful, wrathful God, this portion of the biblical passage creates a deepening of fear in a mind already paralyzed by it. Yet, just as with the beginning of the verse, the intention of the latter half is also one of freedom and joy. Join with Us, then, in this moment, as We expose the hidden implication of the passage.

I.19.11 While you most notably associate the implication of the word *famine* with that of *starvation*, the word has an archaic meaning of having *a ravenous appetite*, which simply implies *a deep longing for*. In addition, you associate the word *pestilence* with that of *plague*. However, the implication of the word is found in its Latin root, which is *pestis*. This word carries with it the meaning of *destruction*, or *to destroy*. And, here is where the energy of the word comes to play within the verse. For the word *destroy* carries with it the meaning *to take apart*. And, it becomes truly glorious, because the words *take apart* have the meaning: *to receive into joining.* In other words, the implication is *to become one with.*

I.19.12   The next word in the series of words that We shall reveal unto you is the meaning of the word *fearful.* Besides meaning *full of fear,* it also carries the implication of *reverential awe.* Recall, within *A Course in Miracles*, it is written, *Awe should be reserved for revelation, to which it is perfectly and correctly applicable. You are a perfect creation and should experience awe only in the presence of the Creator of perfection.* Therefore, in the case of the word *fearful*, as it is being used within the verse, it simply implies *awe*, not *fear.*

I.19.13   However, the energy signature of this portion of the passage is found in the next word, which is *sights.* It carries with it the meaning: *based on recognition or comprehension without previous study.* Furthermore, the word *recognition* simply implies *to remember.*

I.19.14   The last word in the series of words found within the passage, where We will expose the hidden meaning, is *signs.* We invite you to now clear your mind. Do not interpret what you will be reading. Instead, *feel* the words as you become consciously aware of them. For in doing this, the *Heart* can guide you into the *freedom* found within this particular passage.

I.19.15   Although your word *signs* has a multitude of meanings, the one that defines this passage is: *cross*, which carries the implication *to attain*, which means *to achieve* or *accomplish*. Here is where the energy signature of the word *signs* is made known. For the word *accomplish* carries with it the meaning *perfect*, which is defined as *sanity* or right mindedness, better understood as *God mindedness*.

I.19.16   Before We continue any farther, remember, *YOU ARE HEAVEN*. And, Heaven is your *True State of Being*. It is your *Divine State*. This is the purpose of Our time together. It is to bring you Home. It is to return your *Divine State of Being* to your mind. This is *wholeness*, which is but *holiness*.

I.19.17   Therefore, the last half of the Bible passage, *and famines, and pestilences; and fearful sights and great signs shall there be from heaven,* carries the implication: *and a deep longing for, and to receive into joining; and reverential awe will there be in remembering the Holy Mind of God.*

I.19.18　O Holy One, this is when true life begins. This is when *time* simply ceases. For only that which is eternal is remembered. Look now, once again, at the implication of the bible verse. *Feel* its hope. *Feel* your freedom, as you read it in its magnificence:

> *And a great awakening shall come into the minds of those (who believe they exist) in a state of separation, and a deep longing for, and to become one with; and a reverential awe will there be in remembering the Holy Mind of God.*

I.19.19　This is the very reason why We are with you now. For We are here to ignite the fire, the deep yearning, for the *Great Awakening*. Your becoming one with the *Holy Mind of God* is the promise – it is the Word of God. It is His Will, as surely as it is yours. This Course is to bring you into the *Awareness of your Holy Potential*. For this is Our purpose. It is Our Joy.

The Divine Feminine

I.19.20　What is this *Holy Potential* for which We speak to you? Before We reveal it, We invite you to recall the following passage from *A Course in Miracles,* where Our Brother, the man you refer to as Jesus, states: *There is nothing about me that you cannot attain. I have nothing that does not come from*

God. The difference between us now is that I have nothing else.
This leaves me in a state which is only potential in you.

I.19.21 In order for your potential to be fully understood and accepted by the mind, We invite you to take Our hand as We extend it in Love and Brotherhood. Join with Us as We once again return to the beginning. It is a *state of being* in both *Reality* and *Potentiality*. This does not describe some distant past. It but describes your current *state of being*. It is but a description of you in this moment.

I.19.22 What We are sharing with you now will bring about great earthquakes within your mind. It will create a great upheaval in your beliefs. Yet the time to release your false beliefs is upon you. They have but served to create experiences of hell. We, however, are with you now so that you may experience the *Great Awakening*, which will allow you to create experiences of Heaven. Look, then, upon the words you will be reading with Joy, rather than fear. *Feel* them. *Feel* the power contained within them. For this power is the power of Christ. It is your power. And, it is Ours.

I.19.23 Once again, We turn to the first verse as found in your bible: *In the beginning, God created the heaven and the earth.* We have already shared with you that this passage carries with it the implication of the creation of the *divine* and the *human*. However, the time has come to share with you the much deeper implication. For within the implication arose the question, *What am I?*

I.19.24 The implication becomes strikingly clear when you recognize that the word *heaven,* as it is given within the verse, refers to the creation of the *Divine Feminine*, whereas the word *earth* refers to the creation of the *Divine Masculine.* Yet, be not *deceived* in these. For your mind believes that the words *masculine* and *feminine* refers to and are related to the two genders found in form. However, We assure you that the implication is much, much deeper than your currently held belief.

I.19.25 Let's begin by exposing the hidden implications of the words *masculine* and *feminine.* For then you will but see the Truth unfold before your eyes. Yet, to look upon Truth, you must come to it willingly. And, this will require the release of the beliefs which have kept you bound to *not-God.*

I.19.26 We will begin with the intention of the word *feminine.* Like many other words, the implication is found in its origin. The word *feminine* comes from the Latin word *femininus,* which arose from the Latin word *fetus.* And, here is where the

327

hidden implication is found. For the Latin word *fetus* carries with it the meaning: *pregnant*, which means *full*. In addition, the word *full* has the following meanings: *perfect*, which means innocence; *pure*, which means to be without guilt; *complete*, which carries with it the meaning of whole or holy; and, *sane*, which means to be of right mindedness. However, the word *sane* came from the Latin term *compos mentis*, which carries with it the literal interpretation, *having mastery over one's mind.*

I.19.27 *To have mastery over the mind* is the aim of this curriculum. For *to have mastery over your mind* is what is referred to as *Christ Mindedness*, or *God-Mindedness*.

I.19.28 Yes! O Holy One, this is the meaning of *Heaven*. This is the meaning of the *Divine Feminine*. For it is what We have thus far called the *Heart*. And, this is being *Wholehearted* as described in *A Course of Love*. Simply put, it is your *True State of Being*. It is living from and for Love, always.

The Divine Masculine

I.19.29 Now, let's look at the implication of the word *masculine*. For just as the word *feminine* carries with it a deeper implication than what you believed, so too does the word *masculine*. Although We have already shared with you the meaning of the word *virtual* in a previous discussion, the word *virtual* arose from the Latin word *virtualis,* which also carries with it the meaning *manliness* or *masculine.* However, the Latin word *virtualis* carries with it a deeper implication, which is that of *potentiality.*

I.19.30   Look again at the last sentence that We shared earlier with you from *A Course in Miracles.* It reads: *This leaves me* (Jesus) *in a state that is only potential in you.* Yet, what is the implication found within those words? In order for there to be clarity in the mind, let's take a look at the meaning of the word *potential.*

I.19.31   The word *potential* carries the meaning: *something that can become actual or real.* In addition, the word also carries with it the meaning *promise.* And, it is in the word *promise* that will give you a clearer understanding of the *masculine energy field.* For the word *promise* carries with it the ancient meaning of *to betroth*, which implies *the promise to marry.* And, the intention, or the energy field found in the word *marry* is simply *to unite.*

I.19.32   Again, as with so many of your words, they were derived from Latin. And, this is certainly true of the word *unite*, which came to you via the Latin word *unus.* For *unus* means *one.* Therefore, you contain the *potential to be one.*

I.19.33 O Divine Child, the Christ is the *actualized one.* For the *Christ* is the *uniting*, the *marriage* between *Heaven* and *Earth*, between the *Divine Masculine* and the *Divine Feminine.* Come to *feel* the simplicity, the beauty, in what We have just shared with you. Until you accept this Truth, until you *re-member* your Self, then you but remain *virtual.* In other words, you but remain an *avatar* moving about in a *virtual reality.* For only by becoming *One* with your Self will you experience true unity, which is but Life, which is but to *BE WHOLE,* which is but to *BE REAL.*

I.19.34 There is a *promised land* within you. And, it is the *Christ.* Join with Us in Oneness. Awaken into the land of the living. Declare, then, this moment as the moment of your *Great Awakening.*

Lesson 19

I.19.35 If you are ready to truly live, then We invite you to complete this exercise. For in its completion, you will be standing just outside Heaven's door. We invite you to *feel* to the depth of your Being the statements We give you. You but need accept them as your Reality.

I.19.36 You will need one large index card for this lesson. Write the statements upon it. With this exercise, We ask that you commit reading the statements and allowing yourself to *feel* them once each hour. If you must, set an alarm on the hand-held device you carry with you everywhere you go. Do this lesson for as long as you *feel* it to be appropriate. However, you will find that there is no set expiration date. For these are eternal truths. Therefore, *feel* their immensity. *Feel* their power. For it is the *power* of the indwelling *Christ* that you will but *feel*.

I.19.37 The statements are:

With Love, I unite Heaven and Earth.

I unite the Divine Masculine and the Divine Feminine within me.

In truth, I know with certainty that "I and God are One."

CHAPTER 20

The Game of Make-Believe

I.20.1   The *game of make-believe* is one in which children dress up in costumes and don a mask pretending, for a while, to be something other than what they are. This, Our Dear Brothers and Sisters, is what you have been doing. Your costume is the *body* and the mask you wear is but that of *not-God*. However, you have forgotten you but play a game. For now the game seems to be real, and what is real has been forgotten. You have played in hell until Heaven seems but a dream, a fantasy that seems too good to be true.

I.20.2   You look into a mirror and believe that the *image* you see reflecting back is your truth. But, if the *image* you see is truth, then you can but see *death* in everything and everyone you look upon. For this is the *game* – a game where you believe that you can play the part in a drama and then, just as the story gets good, you *die*.

I.20.3   Deep within you, you *know* that this is but a game. But every time you give this idea any consideration, you are called back into the game to play your part within it. Now, you have heard a different call, one that asks you to look upon life rather than death, one that calls you into joy instead of misery. Your *Heart* calls out to you now, but as long as your mind remains within the cloud bank of *denial*, you can but continue the *game*.

I.20.4 *Yet, in this cloud bank it is easy to see a whole world rising. A solid mountain range, a lake, a city, all rise in your imagination, and from the clouds the messengers of your perception return to you, assuring you it is there. Figures stand out and move about, actions seem real, and forms appear and shift from loveliness to the grotesque. And, back and forth they go, as long as you would play the children's **game of make-believe**.*

I.20.5 Although We have spoken to you of the *game of make-believe*, We have not, as of yet, exposed its implication or purpose. You have been told of the game in both *A Course in Miracles* and your bible. Yet, the meaning has still remained obscured. And, as with everything We have revealed thus far, the meaning has been hidden within the intentions of the words themselves.

I.20.6 The time has come for Us to reveal unto you the game you have been but playing with yourself. For this game is what brought with it the *detour into fear*. And, the fear will remain within the mind until the mind can be shown that neither the *game* nor its *fear* are real. However, recognize that the mind will react by attempting to dismiss what the eyes read. Because to accept what it is reading means that the mind will have to look at the *deception* it has but played upon itself. Therefore, read this discussion with an open mind. Allow the meaning to filter through every area of your mind. For only in looking upon its *deception* will the mind begin to question every belief it has made and revered.

I.20.7   We will begin with the word *game.* For it carries with it the implication, thus the energy field, that keeps the mind entranced. The word *game* as you know has the implication of *play,* which in your language came about by the word *swordplay.* Here is where the intention is discovered. For the word *swordplay* carries with it the meaning *coercive power,* which implies *coercion* or *to be coerced.*

I.20.8   As with other words, the intention of the word *coerce* is found in its origin. Your word *coerce* came to you as a word combined from the prefix *co-,* which means *together,* and the Latin root *arcere,* which carries with it the meaning *to confine* or *imprison.* Thus, the implication of *game* is to be *imprisoned together.* But what is being *imprisoned together?*

I.20.9   The answer is one that may seem perplexing at first, but its implication will become evident as We continue this discussion. However, the answer is but this: your *conscious* mind is *imprisoned* with your *subconscious* mind. Remember, it is the different aspects of your mind that are at war with each other, which is the reason why your experiences are those of conflict rather than peace.

I.20.10   Therefore, the *game of make-believe* is really the *imprisonment of make-believe*. Now, We shall expose the implication of the word *make*. As you will soon discover, the word carries the very energy signature of everything you believe real. And, it is here where your mind will want to shut down and try to hide from the truth. For it will believe its very existence is being attacked. Allow, then, the *Heart* to gently embrace it, so that your mind can be healed and returned to its Natural State, which is but Love.

I.20.11   The word *make* is quite literally defined as *to form and hold in the mind*. However, the word *make* simply means *form*. With regards of being *imprisoned,* the word *form* carries the implication of the *prison*. For the word *form* means *the body especially in its external appearance*. Do you yet appreciate what you have just read? For the *body* is held in the mind. Yet, the *mind* believes it is in the *body*. Hence, this is the *game*. For it is the *game of identifying as a body*. Furthermore, it is the *imprisonment of the mind* for a mind that has *identified* itself as a *body*.

I.20.12   The mind that *believes* itself to be a *body* has but deceived itself. For the *body* did not create the mind. It was but the mind that *made* the body. And, as it is written within the curriculum of *A Course in Miracles:*

I.20.13   *If you believe that you are not-God, you lock the mind in the body, and you give its purpose to its prison house, which acts instead of it. A jailer does not follow orders, but enforces orders on the prisoner. Yet, it is the body that is the prisoner, and not the mind. The body thinks no thoughts. It has no power to learn, to pardon, nor enslave. It gives no orders that the mind need serve, nor sets condition that it must obey. It holds in prison but the willing mind that would abide in it. The sleeping mind is thus the prisoner to the snarling dogs of hate and evil, sickness and attack of pain and age, of grief and suffering.*

I.20.14   How did the belief that you are a *body* arise? How did your mind become willing to abide in a body, and then become so identified with it that the mind cannot separate itself from the body, which but seems to house it? The answers to these questions are found in your bible. And, you need look no farther than what you refer to as the sixth day of creation, where it is written, *And God said, "Let us make man in our image, after our likeness."*

I.20.15   Since We have already exposed the implication of the word *make*, which means *to form and hold within the mind,* then the verse can be read as, *And God said, "Let us form man in our image, after our likeness and hold him in our mind."* However, because the word *form* also means *body*, the verse has been interpreted as, *And God said, "Let us give man a body in our image, after our likeness."* Can you see the difference in the two versions? Better yet, can you *feel* it. For in one is found your freedom, while the other but offers you prison. But, We need to continue Our discussion regarding *form.* For here is where true freedom rests.

I.20.16   The word *form* carries with it a much deeper implication. Besides meaning *body*, the word *form* also has the implication: *an idea,* which is defined as *an entity actually or potentially present to consciousness.* Furthermore, the word *entity* carries the meaning *a separate being.*

I.20.17   If you believe in a literal interpretation of the bible verse, then you believe it reads, *And God said, "Let us form man as*

337

a separate being in our image, after our likeness." Do you yet see the error with this interpretation? For to believe that God created man as a separate being is the crux of the belief in separation. And, as long as you believe this, then you will continue to have experiences which seem to support this belief. However, the belief in separation is what creates the belief that the *body* is real. In addition, to believe that God made you as a separate being is why you feel lost and alone. We are with you now in order to reveal unto you Truth – that you are one with God. Only your belief in separation keeps you from experiencing the joy and peace of unity with All That Is. And, until you begin to experience unity, you will not believe in it, nor will you know the Truth of your Being.

I.20.18 Yet, this bible verse hinges on the word *image*. Here is where the hidden implication is found. And, it is the word *image,* which gives this verse its intentionality, thus its energy field. For the word *image* carries with it the meaning *semblance*, which has the meaning *countenance*. Furthermore, the word *countenance* carries the meaning *pretense*. And, the hidden meaning of the word *image* is found within the implication of *pretense,* which carries the meaning *make-believe.*

I.20.19 Yes! The word *image* carries with it the implication of *make-believe*. And, now the *game of make-believe* is exposed. It is revealed for what it is: a *deception* meant to keep the mind from looking at Truth. For *make-believe* is nothing more than *believing* that what is *not-real* is *real*. In other words, *make-believe* is simply the mind *pretending* that the *body* is real.

I.20.20 In addition, the word *image* also carries with it the archaic meaning of *an illusory form*. Although the word illusion is frequently used in *A Course in Miracles*, the time has come for the implication of the word to be revealed. For herein lies the *trick*, the *deception,* the *con-game* for which the mind has been playing. The mind has been hiding in darkness for so long, it has forgotten what Light is. It has forgotten what Love is. And, in its forgetting did it become fearful of its own power and of its own Self.

I.20.21 Do not shrink in fear as We expose the meaning of *illusion,* which carries the implication *a state of being intellectually deceived or misled: misapprehension.* Therefore, *illusion* is a *state of being* – of being intellectually deceived. However, the hidden implication lies in the origin of the word, which came to you via the prefix *il-,* which means *in,* and the Latin word *ludere,* meaning *to play,* as well as *to trick.* Thus, the word *illusion* simply means *to be in play.* And, We have already given you the implication of the word *play*, which is *imprisoned.*

I.20.22   When viewed in the Light of the Law of Being, it means that you are *(be) imprisoned*, because you have *imprisoned*. What does this mean? Quite simply, you are *(be) limited*, because you *have limited.* And, by *having limited*, you can but *give within limits*.

I.20.23   O Holy Child, this is but the game you play with your self: you pretend to exist by being limited by the body, its perceived frailties, by scarce and limited resources, and by even time itself. This is the intellectual deceit your mind plays with itself. For you are an *infinite* being – unlimited in every way imaginable. Yet, you but believe you are a being with limited power, limited freedom, and limited life. This, O Holy One, is but the *prison* your mind has created for itself. Is it any wonder why, at times, you feel like the walls are closing in on you?

I.20.24   Yet, the word *image* has one implication that carries with it the Truth of your Being, the Truth of Our Being. It is the Truth of Creation. For the word *image* carries with it the meaning of *concept*. As with so many other words, the implication lies within the origin of the word. Your word *concept* was derived from the Latin word *concipere,* which means *to wed* or *to unite*. And, We have already discussed that the implication of *unite* is *oneness*.

I.20.25   This brings Us to the last two words found in the Bible passage that We are here to expose. The words are *after* and *likeness*. The word *after,* as given in this verse, carries the meaning *beyond time,* while the word *likeness* means *resemblance*. Now We come to the hidden intention found in the bible verse. For its true meaning lies within the word *resemblance*, which carries with it the meaning *to be equals.*

I.20.26   Let's look upon the bible verse with its exposed intention. Read the words with Love. *Feel* the Truth as it dawns once again within your mind. For there is a description of perfection being delivered unto you within the passage. This perfection is your Truth. It is Our Truth. And, lying within the verse is Our Oneness. Read, then, the verse in its glory:

> *And God said, "Let us form and hold man in*
> *the Oneness of Our Mind, and beyond time to*
> *be Our equals."*

I.20.27   There is great comfort found within the passage. Yet, there is a deeper implication found in this verse, as well. And, until this deeper implication is brought into your mind, you will continue to play the *game of make-believe* and continue to believe that what is unreal is *real*. For contained within this verse is the escape hatch which releases the mind from the prison of its own creation. So, what is this escape hatch that offers you true freedom?

I.20.28   The freedom from the hell of your making is found in the two words *beyond time*. For until you transcend *time*, you can but continue playing the game with yourself. Remember, the energy pattern of *time* is that of death. Although you remain perfectly safe within the Mind of God, you cannot recognize your safety and freedom until your belief in *time* has been laid aside. For it is this *belief* in *time* which keeps the Truth hidden from you. Because *time*, like the *body,* is the prison house made by you to keep you in *denial.*

I.20.29   Now, ask yourself the following question: *Is there any reference to the creation of a body found within that biblical passage?* No! There isn't. Here, then, is the greatest *deception* mankind perpetrates against itself. For man believes the *body* to be in the *image* of his Creator. And, this is the single, most destructive belief held within the mind of man. Until it is released, then *time* will continue to be experienced, along with the hell created by it.

The Illusion of the Body

I.20.30 Many believe that the *body* was made in the *image* of God. Yet, We say unto you, *That the body is in the image of God is the greatest lie ever told.* And, the belief that the *body* is in the *image* of God is what creates the overwhelming attachment to it. For this is the *game of make-believe* you but play with yourself. This is the mockery spoken of in *A Course in Miracles.* Yet, God is not mocked. You are. For if you believe that the *body* was made in the *image* of God, then you but believe that you are imaginary. In other words, you believe that the illusory *body-mind* is real. Therefore, you will remain in conflict, thus hell. For what else can the belief in nothingness create?

I.20.31 However, the man you call Jesus spoke only of Truth regarding God. For it is written in your bible that He said, *God is Spirit, and they that worship him must worship him in spirit and in truth.* Now the time has come for you to understand what *God is Spirit* means. For until you do, you will continue to *believe* that you are separate from God. And, you will continue to create experiences of separation and hell.

I.20.32 Again, We ask you to *feel* what you will be reading. Lay aside your *beliefs* regarding the meaning of spirit. For it is not

343

what you have been led to *believe*. And, its meaning, its implication, has been hiding within the word itself.

I.20.33   The word *spirit* carries with it the meaning of *mood*, which is defined as *feeling*. Furthermore, your word *feeling* carries with it the meaning of *sentient*. And, the implication of the word *spirit* is found within the origin of the word *sentient*, which came to you via the Latin word *sententia*, and carries the meaning *way of thinking*.

I.20.34   Yet, the implication, the energy signature, is even more profound. And, it is found in the word *way,* which carries the meaning *possibility* or *possible*. As with other words, the origin of the word is where the implication rests.

I.20.35   Your word *possible* is derived from the Latin word *potentis,* which carries the meaning *potent*. And, the word *potent* means *husband* and *power*. Thus, the word *spirit* means *the power of thought*. Yet, the implication of *spirit* goes even deeper. And, it is found in the word *husband,* which has the archaic meaning of *mate,* or *a marriage union*. In other words, the word *husband* simply implies *oneness*.

I.20.36   Therefore, the deeper implication of *spirit* is that of the *oneness of thought*. However, there still remains a deeper, hidden meaning. And, it is found in the word *mate*, which carries the meaning *equal*. Yet, the word *mate* comes from your word *meat*, which means *heart*. Thus, the word *spirit* means the *heart of thought*.

I.20.37   Do you yet see the implication? Can you *feel*, then, the energy of *spirit*? For it is the *Heart*. It is wholeness. It is Everything. And, it is the *center of your being*.

I.20.38   There is a verse in your bible which reads, *For as a man thinketh in his heart, so is he*. In other words, a man's *thoughts* and *feelings* create his *beliefs*. And, a man's *beliefs* determines what he *is*. If a man believes he is a *body*, then a *body* will he be. For he *believes* that he is only human. Thus, the man *believes* he is *not-God* by denying his own divinity.

I.20.39   Therefore, *God is Spirit* carries the energy field of the *Heart*. It is the unity of the soul and spirit. It is your Divine Self. The Self created in the image and likeness of the Creator. It is Perfect, Pure Love. It is the union of Heaven and Earth. It is the Christ. And, it is what you are in Truth!

I.20.40 In order to help you understand the implication of the Truth of Our Beingness, We will remind you once again that God is the First Cause. And, We are His Effect. In other words, God is the Thought, We are the Feeling. This is why We are co-creators with God. It is also the reason that within *A Course in Miracles* it is written: *God Himself is incomplete without me.* And, just as a thought cannot be separated from its feeling, We cannot be separated from God – EVER! For just as thoughts and feelings create beliefs, God extends His Self through Us - His Joy – so that creation continues forever and ever.

I.20.41 Recognize, then, that God is the Desire, We are the Intention. And, when desire and intention unite in perfect harmony, then creation is extended. This is how creation flows. This is how energy flows continuously, always creating the *good*, the *beautiful*, and the *holy*.

I.20.42 However, if you believe that you are a *body*, then you believe that you are separate from God. And, rather than acting as a co-creator with God, you act as a separate being, creating the unholy. Is this a judgment against you? Certainly not! It is merely an observation. For without God, nothing is whole. And, when you believe you are without God, then you believe you are not whole. And, to be *not-whole* is to be *un-holy*.

I.20.43   It is for this reason that the body is unholy. It isn't because the body is *bad*, it's simply because the body is without God. Ask yourself, if the body was with God, could it get sick? Could it die? Could it be used for anything other than extending Love?

I.20.44   Read those questions again. *Feel* them this time as you read them. Although it appears that the body can become sick, weak, frail, and wither away, the body is not the Truth of your Being. Spirit is.

I.20.45   The body is itself neutral. It can only imprison a willing mind. And, a mind which has come under the body's spell is imprisoned indeed. For the mind has completely forgotten what it is. And, in this forgetting, has Heaven been made hell, and you made enemy but unto your own mind. For the mind believes the body is the one who attacks it, rather than recognizing that the body is just a garment meant to hide itself from Truth.

I.20.46   All who have ever walked your planet, walk it now, or will walk it yet, clothe themselves in a body so they can but play the *game of make-believe* and pretend they are *not-God*. Yet, what purpose does this game serve? For it has brought you nothing but pain and misery, loneliness and despair, as well as sorrow and grief. And, you accept these as normal, while believing true happiness, true joy, and true love are but fantasy. For you have yet to accept your own worthiness. Therefore, you settle for everything but what is already yours in Truth.

The Worth that is Worship

I.20.47   When the man you call Jesus said that God is Spirit, He also stated, *And they that worship him* (God) *must worship him in spirit and in truth.* Now, We ask you, *Do you believe that God needs or demands to be worshipped?* Know this: God neither needs nor requires worship. For this would make God what He is not – for God does not ask for anything – because God has no needs. Why would He? For God already knows you love Him. And, your love for Him He does not doubt.

I.20.48   Yet, if God does not require you to worship Him, then what was the man named Jesus referring to? The answer is found in the word *worship* itself. However, it does not mean what you have been taught. For the world teaches that to *worship* means *reverence offered a divine being.* This definition poses two problems. First, it is based on separation between you and God. Second, the meaning of the world's definition for the word *worship* is founded upon the word *reverence.*

I.20.49 Although *reverence* is neither good nor bad, its implication is why you have remained in darkness. And, you need look no farther than the origin of the word. Your word *reverence*, like so many of your words, has its true meaning hidden within its origin. *Reverence* comes to you via the Latin word *revereri,* which means *fear.*

I.20.50 Therefore, the world's definition of *worshipping God* is *to fear God.* Yet, God doesn't ask that you fear Him. How could He? For God knows not fear. He is but Love. And, He but asks that you love yourself and each other. For in loving your Brothers and Sisters, you but love Him.

I.20.51 Fear is what keeps the *game of make-believe* going. For *fear of God* is the underpinning of the game. Yet, fear is not real. It is of your making. And, since you made it, you can correct it. For in Truth – ***there is nothing to fear.***

I.20.52 What then did the man called Jesus mean when He said, *They that worship Him* (God) *must worship Him in spirit and in truth?* Do you believe that Jesus meant that you were to fear God? To believe this is to continue to cower in fear at the very thought of God. Furthermore, to fear God is to fear your Self, the Divine Self for which you are in Truth. In addition, the fear of God keeps you from knowing who and what you really are.

349

And, this is why We are with you at this time. We cannot take your fear from you, for We know it isn't real. Yet, We can point you to the insanity of fear and what your fear creates.

I.20.53 O Holy One, fear of God, Who is the Source of Everything, and for Whom nothing would have been created that was created, is undoubtedly the strangest of ideas for which your mind has made. Recognize that you love fear, because it is your creation. As such, you worship it. However, like all of your creations, you have turned your will and your life over to them, thinking they will keep you safe. You may worship fear for as long as you wish, but it will not make it real. Nor will it make your projections real.

I.20.54 Thus, what is the true implication of *worship*? In order to fully recognize its energy field, you need look no farther than the hidden meaning of the word, which is found in its origin. Your word *worship* came to you from the Old English word *weorthscipe*, where *weorth* carries the meaning of *worth*, and *scipe* carries the meaning -*ship*. Recall, that the implication of the word *worth* is *awake*. Furthermore, your suffix -*ship* carries the meaning *state* or *condition of*. Therefore, the word *worship* carries with it the implication – *an awakened state*, or the *state of being awake,* which is your Natural State of Being.

I.20.55　Read, now, the words spoken by Jesus with the true intention they carry: *And they that awaken in Him must awaken in Him in spirit and in truth.* Can you now *feel* the Truth contained in your bible passage? For rather than being invited to fear God, you are being invited to awaken in Him. But, as long as you have even the tiniest sliver of fear within you, it is impossible to awaken. For fear is not of the Kingdom of God. Fear is only found in the lower dimensions. And, it is only found in those who play *not-God* in the *game of make-believe.*

I.20.56　O Divine Child, claim your *worthiness.* For in doing so, you are declaring your desire to awaken in God. And, know with all certainty that your desire will be met. For your awakening is the Will of God. And God's Will will be done. In truth, it has already been completed. You must simply recognize and accept that His Will and your will are identical. They are the same. They are one.

The Body is the Symbol of Guilt and Fear

I.20.57　We have already spoken to you of the hell you have created for yourself by holding the shame of guilt and fear within your mind. And, the body, the body you believe is you, is the very symbol of shame, guilt, and fear. Recognize, in this Holy Moment, that what you believe to be your body *is* a *projection* from your *subconscious* mind – nothing more. Now, ask yourself, *If the body is real and created by God, wouldn't that imply that God knows of limitations and scarcity?*

I.20.58 Now, We ask that you join Us as We reveal unto you when the illusion of being a body occurred within the mind. And, We turn but unto the second creation story in your bible in order to bring the Light of Truth to it so that you will understand. As you read the following verse, ask yourself, *Does this passage detail the creation of a body?*

> *And the Lord God formed man from the dust of the ground and breathed into his nostrils the breath of life; and man became a living soul.*

I.20.59 This passage may appear to allude to the creation of a body. However, as you are becoming more aware of – appearances are deceiving. For this passage demonstrates the extension of Spirit and the beginning of *consciousness*. And, this is given within the very wording contained within the verse.

I.20.60 Although We have given the meaning of *Spirit* as that of the *Heart*, in the case of this verse, it might seem to have a different meaning. But, the two implications are the same. And, in order to demonstrate that your biblical passage is not about the creation of the body, We must look again at the word *spirit*.

I.20.61 This time We turn to the origin of the word. For its implication is that of the passage itself. Your word *spirit* was derived from the Latin word *spiritus*, which carries the meaning *breath of life*. Therefore, the verse can be read as: *And the Lord God formed man from the dust of the ground and breathed into his nostrils the Spirit; and man became a living soul.* However, the intention of the verse is found in the phrase *dust of the ground.*

I.20.62 If you read the verse and interpret it in the literal context, then it would seem that God formed the *body* from the *dust of the ground.* Yet, this is not its implication. For the implication, like everything else We have shared with you, is hidden within the words contained within the verse.

I.20.63 Now, the time has come for you to understand the implication of the phrase *dust of the ground.* For it is the Truth of your Creation. Therefore, We will reveal the meaning of two words: *dust* and *ground.*

I.20.64 Your word *dust* came to you from the Old German word *tunst*, which carries the meaning *storm*. Furthermore, your word *storm* has the meaning *paroxysm*. It is this word which carries the intention behind the word *dust* in the passage. And, like other words, the intention has been hiding in the origin of the word. The word *paroxysm* came to you from the Greek word *paroxynein*, which carries the meaning *to provoke* or *to call forth*.

I.20.65 The word *ground* also carries a hidden meaning that will bring illumination to your biblical passage. For *ground* carries the meaning *metaphysical*. And, the word *metaphysical* means *transcendent*.

I.20.66 *Feel*, then, the intention of your bible verse: *And God formed man by calling forth transcendence and breathed into his nostrils the Spirit; and man became a living soul.* Can you *feel* the freedom in the intention of this passage? For this verse has nothing to do with the creation of a body. Yet, what does the phrase *breathed into his nostrils* imply if there wasn't a body to breathe life into?

I.20.67 Although the mind will want to interpret the phrase literally, it has a much simpler implication. For the phrase

breathed in his nostrils carries with it the implication *extended.*
And, it is found in the very words themselves.

I.20.68 Before We continue this discussion, We invite you to relax your body and still your mind. Allow the *Heart* to whisper to you the truth of your creation. Your mind will want to deny what it will be reading, because it will interpret it as an attack on its belief system. If possible, simply let your *Heart,* your *Holy Self,* illuminate your mind with the Light of Love, the Light of Truth. Inhale a deep breath. For each breath, from this moment forward, is one that will be taken in true freedom.

I.20.69 Recognize that for God to breathe in the nostrils implies that God *exhaled* the *breath of Life* or *Spirit.* For the word *exhale* carries the meaning *to emit,* which is defined as *to eject.* And, *eject* came from the Latin word *eicere,* which carries the implication of *cause.*

I.20.70 Although your mind is certain that the word *nostrils* refers to the nose, We ask you, *How can the word nostrils refer to the nose if the body is not real and wasn't created by God?* It can't. And, it doesn't. So, what then does the word nostril imply if it is not referring to the nose?

355

I.20.71　The intention of the word *nostril*, as it applies to the bible passage, is found in its origin. Your word *nostril* came to you via the Old English word *thurh*, which carries the meaning *through*. And, *through* carries the meaning *extend*.

I.20.72　Read, now, the verse with its true intention. *Feel* your freedom. *Feel* the Love within it. *Feel* its joy. *Feel* its beauty. For the passage reads:

> *And God formed man by calling forth transcendence and caused the extension of Spirit into him; and man became a living soul.*

I.20.73　Allow the *Heart* to bring back to memory the Truth of your Creation, the Truth of your Being, as you read again, *God formed man by calling forth transcendence.* Yet, what does *calling forth transcendence* actually imply? How can you *feel* it to the center of your being?

I.20.74　Again, the answers lie within the words themselves. Therefore, let's look at the words *calling forth* and *transcendence*. The phrase *calling forth* carries the meaning *evoke*, which means *to bring to mind.* In addition, the word *transcendence* has the meaning *to be prior to, beyond, and above the universe and material existence.*

I.20.75 When We place the meanings into the biblical passage, it can be read as: *And God formed man to be prior to, beyond, and above material existence by bringing him into His Holy Mind and extended His Spirit; and man became a living soul.* Do you *feel* the good, the beautiful, and the holy gift that is your creation? For as the verse implies, you were formed by God prior to, beyond, and above material existence. In other words, your creation is far beyond the littleness and frailty of a body.

I.20.76 As long as you believe that you are a body, then you are *denying* your True Creation – which is an Extension of God. Yes! O Divine Brothers and Sisters, you are not a body. For the body is not the home of the Holy Child of God. Heaven is your True Home, because Heaven is your Divine Being.

I.20.77 The time of *make-believe* is behind you. The *game* has been played. And, your part of playing *not-God* is ending. The time of your awakening is here. And, We are with you to help guide you Home. Allow, then, your *Heart*, your Real Self, to awaken your consciousness. You need not experience hell again. If you are ready to awaken from the *dream of make-believe*, then We invite you to complete the following exercise.

Lesson 20

I.20.78 This lesson will help your mind accept that it is not the body, but something far greater than your mind can currently comprehend. We ask that you practice this exercise until you *feel* it deep within your being. There is not a set number of days or weeks for which you will be invited to practice this lesson. Rather, We simply invite you to practice it, until it *becomes* you.

I.20.79 You will once again write several statements on an index card. Then, repeat the statements as many times as possible every day. As you silently repeat them, *feel* them. *Feel* your release. *Feel* the unity you have with all of creation. *Feel* the gratitude that arises within you. And, more than anything else, rejoice as you repeat each statement. For your freedom from the hell of *make-believe* is here.

I.20.80 The statements to be written on the index card are:

I choose to awaken from the dream of make-believe.

I am not a body. I am free. For I remain as God created me.

I am an extension of Perfect, Pure Love.

358

CHAPTER 21

What Am I?

I.21.1   *What am I?* As We have already discussed, this was the question you asked which began your descent into the hell of your own making. While it appears that this question was asked in such a distant past that your memory of it has completely faded, recognize that your mind asks this question with each passing moment. And, with each moment it questions what it is, your mind denies the Truth of your Existence, thereby ensuring you linger another moment in *time*, another moment in *death*, and another moment in *hell*. None of this need be. Yet, as long as you harbor guilt, shame, and fear within your mind, you can but continue to play the *game of not-God*. Thus, you can but continue the same old, worn cycles of pain, misery, grief, and suffering. Always remember, **nothing changes, when nothing changes.**

I.21.2   We come to you now, in this Hallowed Moment, to show you the door out of the prison cell for which you have made. The door has always been there, but you have been unable to locate it, because of the darkness which surrounds you and seems to taunt you. We are with you to Light the Pathway Home. You need but take Our Hand. For now We venture to that moment, this moment in Truth, when darkness seemed to obliterate the Light. Yet, the Light of God is exactly where it has always been – within you. Now, We will but journey to that one tiny, mad instant, which you continue to live again, and again, and yet again, when the question, *What am I,* first entered your mind. For this question not only created *time, death, fear,* and everything else you experience in physicality, it also created something truly insidious for which you have so far refused to surrender. And, this thing is something you treasure more than anything else. What is this thing which you prize, yet has caused so much conflict and bitterness within your mind?

I.21.3   The answer is such that it always creates enmity in the mind when first heard. For it is seen as a judgment. However, the judgment is not levied by Us, but by your own mind. For the question, *What am I,* was not predicated on ignorance, but rather something far darker. And, it was the original thought which spawned the yoke which has burdened you and kept you hostage to your own darkness.

I.21.4   As We have just stated, the question, *What am I,* was not born out of ignorance. Rather, it was born out of *pride* and *arrogance.* You have a saying in your world which goes, *Pride goeth before a fall.* And, in the case of your experience, this would appear to be the truth.

I.21.5   When you recognize what *pride* and *arrogance* have created, you will be more apt to letting them go. For they are the precursor to every experience you have ever had, or will have, until you release them. *Pride* and *arrogance* are at the center of your entire belief system. And, they generate most of the inner conflict you experience, as well as the turmoil so prevalent within your world.

I.21.6   In order to understand how *pride* and *arrogance* effect the Grand Field of Energy, you must come to recognize their energy signatures. By recognizing their energetic frequency, you will be able to *feel* them rising within you long before they reach your *conscious awareness.* This O Divine Child is how you master your mind. For only through mastery can you create the good, the beautiful, and the holy.

I.21.7   The intentionality, or energy signature, is found in their meaning. And, like other words We have shared with you, the intention of each is buried within layers of other meanings, which has kept their true intention concealed. But now the time has come to expose their true intention, so that you will have a greater understanding of their destructive nature upon your peace of mind. For as long as you play with *pride* and *arrogance,* peace can be but a dream, something to strive for but never fully recognized. And, until peace returns to your holy mind, your Divine Self will remain unknown to you.

I.21.8   The word *pride* simply carries the meaning of *conceit.* However, it is within this word that you will discover a deeper insight into yourself. For the word *conceit* is defined as *the result of mental activity; thought.* Furthermore, the word *thought* is the past tense of the word *think.* And, it is here where the concealed meaning will be brought into the Light.

I.21.9   As with so many other words where We have shared the concealed intention, the intentionality of the word *think* lies within its Latin origin, which is the word *scio.* O Holy One, does the Latin word appear and *feel* familiar to you? It should. For the Latin word *scio* is where your word *conscious* comes from.

I.21.10   Therefore, *pride* is *consciousness.* And, just as *pride goeth before a fall,* the same must be true with regards to *consciousness,* since they carry the same intention. Recall that, in *A Course in Miracles,* it is written: *consciousness is correctly identified as the domain of the ego.* In other words, *consciousness* is the idea and belief that you are *not-God.*

I.21.11   Recognize, then, that as the question, *What am I,* was coming into the mind, the *conscious mind* was born. It is for this very reason that We have stated that *pride,* also known as the *conscious mind,* is the force which acts upon the Grand

Energy Field of Possibility and Potentiality creating every experience you have had.

I.21.12 Yet, how did *pride* create everything for which you believe real? The answer is neither complicated nor one that is easily misunderstood. Although your mind believes the question was born from ignorance by lacking the knowledge of what you are, come now to realize the impossibility in that belief. For how can a mind, created as perfect as is the Mind of God, lack anything, much less the knowledge of what it is? Thus, the question was one of *pride*, not ignorance.

I.21.13 As you have now come to realize that *pride* is a thought, what then is the *feeling* created by it? It is but *arrogance*. Yes, *pride* is the thought, and *arrogance* its feeling. Together, they create *hell*. And, We mean that quite literally.

I.21.14 Now, We ask that you turn your attention to the *feeling* of *arrogance*. For now We must expose the dark cornerstone of your belief system. This cornerstone acts as part of the foundation for the creation and maintenance of *hell* itself. For when the intentionality, the energy field, of *arrogance* is finally viewed from a correct perspective, you will discover that not only does it maintain the *game*, but it also creates the belief in *blame* and *victimhood*. As with other words, the energy signature of *arrogance* is found deep within the meaning of the word.

I.21.15 The word *arrogance* comes from your word *arrogant,* which arose from the Latin word *arrogare.* And, it is here where the hidden implication lies. For the Latin word *arrogare* carries with it the meaning *to make oneself right.*

I.21.16 Do you yet see the detriment to your mind by being *arrogant?* Do you *feel* its energy field? For it is the energy associated with *being right.* It is the energy of *judgment.* For by making yourself *right,* then another person, even God Himself, must be wrong. And, when you declare that you are *right,* then you must believe yourself to be a *victim* to another.

I.21.17 This is the hardest thing for a mind to accept and ultimately surrender. For the desire, the need, to be *right* is the greatest pull within your thought system. Not only does the desire to be *right* maintain the dream, it is what creates all external conflict you believe you experience.

I.21.18 In addition, the overarching need to be *right* is what blinds you to Truth. For your eyes were not made to look upon the magnificence that is God. Instead, your eyes were made only to look upon the experiences produced by *pride, arrogance, guilt, and fear.* And, these are all they can see. But, why is this?

I.21.19 The answer is found in one of your bible verses. For it states: *When pride comes, then comes disgrace, but with humility comes wisdom.* We have already spoken to you of *disgrace.* Recall that *disgrace* is *shame.* Therefore, when *pride* comes, then comes *shame.* And, it is but with *shame* you look upon in everything the eyes behold. For the *shame* that comes from *pride* is what you have projected upon the *subconscious,* which is then projected into the world. And, you *feel* this *shame* in all you experience. While you may not be *consciously aware* of it, *shame* is always with you, hiding deep within your *subconscious* mind. And, it is this *shame* which you must release if you want to experience the peace that comes from oneness.

I.21.20   Look at the bible verse once again. For it gives you the answer to releasing *pride,* thus *arrogance* and *shame.* What is the answer? It is but *humility.*

I.21.21   In the Talmud, the Jewish doctrine, the answer to the question, *What am I,* was given. Now, the time has come for the answer to be revealed to all of humanity. And, the answer is found in the very words of the scripture, which are: *Who is called a fool? One who loses what* (mah) *has been given to him.*"

I.21.22   The concept of *what has been given him* is represented by the Hebrew word *mah,* which denotes the *state of humility.* For

one who is humble says, *What am I? I am nothing without God.*
This O Holy Child is the answer to the question which will
bring you out of the *hell* you have created for yourself by
denying Truth. For by saying, *I am nothing without God,* you
will be rewriting your *belief* of what you are.

I.21.23   Recognize that *humility* is a *state of being.* And, it is your
Natural State of Being. For God is not proud, boastful, or
arrogant. He does not have an ego. And, in Truth, neither do
you. However, because of your belief that you are *not-God,* you
rely on *pride* and *arrogance* to attempt in overcoming your
feelings of littleness.

I.21.24   *Pride* and *arrogance* cannot replace the grandeur for
which is yours as an heir to the Kingdom. Grandeur doesn't
require *pride* and *arrogance* in order to be upheld. It simply
requires *humility.* But, as long as you believe in your littleness,
you will be compelled to remain *proud* and *arrogant.*

I.21.25   However, you believe it to be *prideful* and *arrogant* to
claim your True Identity. And, you have created a kingdom of
littleness, the kingdom of hell, which you defend even unto
death. Yet, you defend nothing. For, in Truth, you are nothing
without God.

I.21.26   Recall that in *A Course in Miracles* it is written: *You cannot replace the Kingdom, and you cannot replace yourself. God, Who knows your value, would not have it so, and so it is not so. Your value is in God's Mind, and therefore not in yours alone. To accept yourself as God created you cannot be arrogant, because it is the denial of arrogance. To accept your littleness is arrogant, because it means that you believe your evaluation of yourself is truer than God's.*

I.21.27   O Divine Child, it is not *arrogant* to accept your divinity. Rather, it is *arrogant* to deny it. For as We have previously shared, *denial* of your divinity is what brought forth the original judgment. And, this judgment was based upon *pride* and *arrogance*. Yet, you surrender *pride* and *arrogance* when you accept your True Self, the Self God created as Perfect as is He.

Humility is to Become as Little Children

I.21.28   Humility is not servitude. Nor is it weakness. For *True Humility*, which is Our Natural State of Being, rests upon Truth – that We are completely dependent upon God. Just as you have read before in *A Course in Miracles*: *"Except ye become as little children"* means that unless you recognize your complete dependence upon God, you cannot know the real power of the

367

Christ *in His true relationship with the Father.* What does this truly mean?

I.21.29 When you were a small child, you were completely dependent upon your parents in order to eat, have a place to sleep, as well as the rest of your basic survival needs. You were under their guidance and care. The same holds true regarding Our dependency upon God. We are as dependent upon Him as is your physical body is dependent upon its next heartbeat to continue to function. For without God's Love, We would not be. Does He Love Us? Oh yes! For His Love for Us is immeasurable and without end. His Love not only created Us - it sustains Us.

I.21.30 Yet, what is meant by *dependence?* Although the word *dependent* carries with it the meaning *relying on another for support*, the word's energy field has a much deeper implication. And, its implication is found in a broader meaning of the word, which is *contingent.* However, the deeper implication is found in the Latin origin of the word *contingent*, which is *contingere* and carries with it the meaning *come to pass.* Furthermore, your phrase *come to pass* carries the meaning *extend.*

I.21.31   Therefore, the phrase *We are completely dependent upon God* implies that *We are the complete extension of God.* Read that once again. This time, as you do, allow yourself to *feel* it. Allow, too, the energy pattern of the phrase, *We are the complete extension of God,* to be *felt* throughout the whole of your being. Yes! *Feel* it to your core.

I.21.32   O Divine One, as an extension of God, you are whole and complete. You lack for nothing. You were created perfect. You were created without any needs. To the mind of a separated one, this is utter nonsense. But, to the *Heart*, it is the sweet sound of Truth. Listen, then, to the *Heart* as it gently reminds you of the Truth of your Being.

I.21.33   However, there is a more glorious implication to being *dependent* upon God. And, it is also found in another one of its meanings. Besides the other two implications for the word *dependency* for which We have already shared, it also carries with it the meaning *equivalency*. Do you yet understand the magnificence of *equivalency?* For it means that We are coequals with God. But, what is the implication of being *coequals* with God?

I.21.34   Quite simply, the implication is that We are the *same.* In other words, We are *indistinguishable* to God, which implies that, like God, We do not have *individualizing* qualities. That is – there is nothing, absolutely nothing, that separates Us from God.

I.21.35 Although We have shared this with you previously, it demands revisiting. Recall that, in your bible, there is a verse which states: *(Jesus the Christ) Who, being in the form of God, thought it not robbery to be equal with God.* And, you must come to believe that you are equal with God. This O Holy Child is the meaning of the Atonement – to be one with the Father – to be one such that there is no degree of separation between the Father and His Holy Child.

I.21.36 It is neither blasphemous or arrogant to *be* what God created. However, it *is* arrogant to believe that you are something other than what God created. For to believe that you are *not-God* is the height of arrogance. Yet, how can this be?

I.21.37 Before We answer that question, We ask you to open your mind to what you will be reading. *Feel* it. For if you will allow it, the answer will help you to remember what you are in Truth.

I.21.38 Thus, the answer is but this – if you believe that what you have made of yourself is more real, more truthful, or even more worthy than what God made, then you are being both *prideful* and *arrogant.* For is it not *arrogant* to believe that the self you have become is more real than the Self God created? And, it is this *arrogance* which must be released so that *humility* can return to your hallowed mind. For only in *humility* will the Self that you denied so long ago return to your mind.

I.21.39 Know this, then, *humility* is the key to releasing the *denial* that has kept your mind playing the part of *not-God.* Humility is not servitude, it is simply being of service to the Kingdom. For it is through Our service to the Kingdom in which We extend God's Love. And, when We extend Love, We extend creation. This is Our Holy Function – the function given to Us by God Himself. Yet, in order to fulfill your function, you must accept the truth of your oneness with Everything That Is. And, this means that you must release all attachment and value you have placed upon being *not-God.* For until you do, you will maintain your belief that you are separate from God, separate from your brothers and sisters, and separate from every other aspect of creation. And, the belief that you are separate is the definition of *hell.*

I.21.40 If you are ready to be free from the hell of your own making, We invite you to complete the next lesson. It will help you in releasing the *pride* and *arrogance* that creates the hell for which you experience. And, it will aid you in recognizing the energy of true humility.

Lesson 21

I.21.41 This exercise has two parts to it. Both are to be completed every day for fourteen days. The first part of the lesson is to be done throughout the day, while the second portion is to be done in the morning for approximately five minutes.

I.21.42 Part One:

Before every experience, like answering your phone, responding to a message, meeting a friend, going into your work, running errands, take a moment and ask:

How can I act and respond with true humility?

After the experience, ask yourself:

Did I respond with arrogance and pride? Or did I respond in humility?

I.21.43 Be honest in your self-assessment. Trust that your *Heart* will answer the question if you will allow it. If you believe you acted out of *pride* and *arrogance,* do not judge yourself. For

372

that will only add another layer of judgment, thus guilt and shame, to a mind that is already under their effects. Instead, simply ask:

How can I respond and act with humility next time?

I.21.44   Part Two:

As with other lessons you have completed as a part of this curriculum, you will need an index card. Write the statements you will be given upon it. Then, each morning for five minutes repeat the statements silently. As you do, *feel* them. Allow your mind to *feel* the energy of each one. If you would like, you may silently repeat the statements anytime during the day. For each time you complete this portion of the exercise, you are helping the mind to remember its True Self.

I.21.45   The statements are:

I am the Self that God created.

I choose to recognize that I am whole and complete.

I relinquish the need to be right.

CHAPTER 22

The Idols of Madness

Thou shall have no other gods before me.

I.22.1   This is one of your bible verses which has been misunderstood for generations. We are with you at this time in order to bring clarity and light to this passage. For once understood, you will find freedom contained within it. This verse, as you know, is one of nine others often referred to as the *Ten Commandments* given by God to Moses following the exodus out of Egypt. Many call them laws. And, this is the problem. For the belief that the *Ten Commandments* are the Spiritual Laws has kept the Laws of God hidden within the darkness of deceit.

I.22.2   The time has come for you to understand the purpose and function of the Laws. For the Laws govern everything in all dimensions, including what you call the third dimension of physicality. Yes, you can and have denied them, but you cannot undo them. They were not created to hurt you, but to keep you safe.

I.22.3   However, here is what We invite you to come to understand and believe: the Laws cannot be broken. Period. The Laws simply determine the outcome, the effect, of every thought you have. What you have considered laws were nothing more than a *code of conduct* to aid in navigating the physical realm. A *code of conduct* can be transgressed, but the Laws of God cannot be broken or usurped.

I.22.4   Read the verse again – *Thou shall have no other gods before me.* O Child of God, in Reality, you can have no other gods before God. In Truth, that is impossible. It is laughable to believe that you could. Yet, here is where the *game of make-believe* has been made real by your mind, while that which is Real has been completely dismissed. For only in *make-believe* could a god you made come to replace God. And, herein lies the error of your current belief system.

I.22.5   You have been taught that the *Ten Commandments* are a set of laws given by God to man. Now, ask yourself this question: *do you really believe that it is possible to violate a commandment given by God Himself?* For if it were possible, then God would not be God, because God's Will is always accomplished. And, to believe that you can or have violated God's Will is both prideful and arrogant.

I.22.6   Yet, what is it that creates this belief? For without questioning this aspect of your belief system you will be unable to release it for the certainty of Truth. And, as with other aspects of your belief system for which We have exposed, it is the energy pattern found within one simple word. And, that word is *idol*.

What is an Idol?

I.22.7   Although you have been taught that an *idol* is *a representation or symbol of an object of devotion or worship*, the implication and intention is much different. However, if you use this meaning to define an idol, then it would appear that you could place something before God. However, there is an obsolete definition of the word *idol* which holds the energy pattern that has created every experience you have thus far had. Furthermore, this obsolete meaning defines everything you look upon, including who you believe you are. What, then, is this obsolete definition?

I.22.8   The word *idol* carries with it the obsolete meaning of *pretending*. Yes! The intention of *idol* is *pretending*. But, what is the implication of *pretending*? For in Truth, you have been pretending all of your life on the physical plane. And, through *pretending*, you continue to deny your very Being. But, what is the implication, the intention, the energy of *pretending*?

I.22.9   The word *pretend* carries the meaning *make-believe: feign*. Therefore, idols are *make-believe*. And, *make-believe,* as you now know, is the game for which you have been playing since you first asked the question, *What am I?*

I.22.10   Now, the time has come for you to discover exactly what *pretending* costs you. For there is a dark secret that has been hiding in your word *pretend*. And, it is this secret which you have buried so deeply that you have forgotten it. Furthermore, this is the secret for which the *subconscious* mind has guarded from your *conscious* mind with great pains. For the *subconscious* recognizes that, when this secret is exposed, you will choose against it. And, this secret is hiding within the meaning of the word *feign*.

I.22.11   Just as the implication of the word *idol* lies within an obsolete meaning, so too does the implication of the word *feign*. For the word *feign* has the obsolete meaning of *conceal*. And, it is within the implication of the word *conceal* for which the dark intention is found.

I.22.12   As with other words where We have exposed the hidden intentionality of a word, the same holds true for the word

377

conceal. For the hidden intention of the word *conceal* is found in its Latin origin, which is the word *concelare* and carries with it the meaning *to keep secret*, as well as *hell.* Thus, idols are kept secret. Therefore, the energy signature of an *idol* is that of *hell.*

The Secret of Hell

I.22.13   Are you ready to discover what the secret of *hell* is? For *hell* is not what you believe it to be. And, this is the secret. Your *subconscious* knows the secret and guards it viciously. For once you are made aware of it, the *game of make-believe* is over. So, what is this secret?

I.22.14   It is but this – the *body* is *hell.* For the implication, thus the intention, of the *body* is that of an *idol.* Even for those brothers and sisters who believe that they worship God and not *idols* know not that they worship the *body.* While nothing, in Truth, can come before God, if you believe that you are a *body*, then you have placed an *idol* before God. For you have placed *hell* before your Creator. And, through *pride* and *arrogance*, you are declaring that what you made – the *body* – is more real than what God created.

I.22.15   This, O Holy One, is the secret you have buried deep within the *subconscious.* Recall that *hell* is defined as *a place or state of misery and torment.* Thus, hell is a state of being. Therefore, if you believe that you are a body, then you are in a *state of hell*, which is your current *state of being*.

I.22.16 Nothing in Truth can come before God. However, when you believe yourself to be a body, then you have placed the body between you and God. And, whatever is between you and God is what is termed an *idol*. By believing that you are a body, rather than believing you are the Divine Self created by God, you have made of yourself an *idol*.

I.22.17 Recall that the man named Jesus stated, *Ye are but gods.* Therefore, to believe you are a body, and since *ye are a god*, then you have placed *another god before God.* While none of this is true, your *subconscious* mind believes it true. Thus, you reap the guilt and shame of believing you have committed an egregious act. This is the *game.* And, as long as you believe yourself to be a body, you will continue to live in the *hell* of your own making.

The Game of I'll Show You

I.22.18 The *game of make-believe* is the *game of I'll show you.* It is the game of *being right*, even at the expense of living in *hell*. As We have previously discussed, the *game of being right* is where *pride* and *arrogance* is maintained. For the game is impossible to play once you have accepted *humility*. Now the time is at hand for you to recall how *being right* came to be the foundation of your belief system. For until your current belief system crumbles back into the dust from which it was made, you can but continue to create a living *hell* for yourself.

I.22.19   As you have been told time and time again, you are a co-creator with God. Recall that God is the desire for creation, and you are the intention. Together, desire and intention are the force for all creation. However, when *pride* and *arrogance* entered your holy mind, you sought to create on your own, without God. Yet, where God extends in creation, you *project*. For there can be no creation where God is absent. And, projection is not the same as creation. It never has been, nor will it ever be.

I.22.20   Because your projections are without God, they are without Love. Do you yet understand what this means? Since your projections are without Love, they are projections of fear. What else could they be? And, because fear is not real, neither then are your projections.

I.22.21   Furthermore, these projections have become the *idols* you worship. For you see in them what you believe you are without. But, what can a Child of God be lacking? In Truth, he lacks nothing. But, because of the games he but plays within his mind, he has come to believe that he lacks everything and must go in search of that which will make him feel whole and complete. Yet, how can a projection give you what you believe you are lacking? For there is nothing in a projection that is real.

I.22.22　Come now, in this moment, to realize that *idols* are your attestation to bring reality to that which is not real. Although they are your creations, you bow before them in worship asking them to give to you the joy and life you yearn for. *Idols* have no life. And, that includes the body. Yet, you have come to believe the life the body offers is greater than the life given to you by your Father. And, you gladly cling to *hell* rather than accept your birthright – Heaven.

I.22.23　The body, the *idol* which has become your home, is your weapon of choice in the war you believe you wage with God. The body is the ultimate *idol* you made in the *game of I'll show you.* It is what you believe is the proof that *death* is real. But, you have not shown God anything. For He knows not of *death.* For it has never entered His Holy Mind. Therefore, because it is not in His Mind, in Truth, neither is it in yours.

I.22.24　*Idols,* such as the body, can offer you nothing. For they are nothing. Only your belief in them seems to give them power and life. But that which is not real can neither have power, nor life. *Why, then, would you bow before the lifeless, offering sacrifices unto them, praying that they will save you and offer you the heaven of your choice?*

I.22.25   This is the question you must ask yourself. For this is the question the *subconscious*, the dark lord, does not want you to answer, much less ask. Yet, it is one you must ask and answer with rigorous honesty.

I.22.26   Once you have answered that question, there is one remaining question for which you must ask yourself. For it is the question that will bring down the house of cards within the *subconscious* mind. And, the question is but this: *Why are you attached to death when you have been offered life eternal?*

I.22.27   The answer is one which will infuriate the mind. But, it is nevertheless Truth. And, the time has come for you to have the answer raised to the level of your *conscious awareness*. Therefore, We invite you to allow the *Heart* to speak to you of its truth. Allow your mind to read the words without interpretation. Simply read the words and allow them to percolate through every corner of your mind.

I.22.28   Recognize, now, that **you aren't afraid of dying; you are afraid of living.** For you are afraid of *Peace.* Recall that in *A Course in Miracles*, it is written, *"Rest in peace" is a blessing for the living, not the dead, because rest comes from waking, not from sleeping. Sleep is withdrawing; waking is joining. Dreams are illusions of joining, because they reflect the ego's* (the subconscious mind's) *distorted notions about what joining is.*

I.22.29   Only in death is there conflict. For there is no conflict in Peace; therefore, there is no conflict in Life. Yet, isn't the body rife with conflict? For the body is the home of conflict, because it is the home of the *living dead.* And, you defend the idea that you are a body to the point where the body has become your primary *idol,* thus weapon, in the war that you still believe is occurring between you and God.

I.22.30   O Child of God, there is no war. The only war there is - is the one that rages within your mind. Yet, you continue to fight a war that never was. For in truth, you are in the heavenly realms even as you read these words. And, this Truth is found in your bible, where it is written: *And God raised us up with Christ and seated us with him in the heavenly realms in Christ Jesus.*

I.22.31 Read that passage once again. This time read it with the knowledge that you are already Home. For the Truth is – you are! You are in the Heavenly Realms just as the biblical passage states. But, why do you not know this?

I.22.32 You know it not, because you have not yet accepted the inevitable. What is the inevitable? The answer to this question is found also in your bible, where it is written: *For it is by grace you have been saved, through faith – and this is not from yourselves, it is the gift of God.* Furthermore, in *A Course in Miracles,* it is written: *Grace becomes inevitable instantly in those who have prepared a table where it can be gently laid and willingly received.*

I.22.33 What is grace? It is but this – *grace is the acceptance of the Love of God within a world of seeming hate and fear.* In other words, grace is the simple fact that **you are Loved!** And, you always have been. **You need but accept that you are loved.** That is all that is asked of you. Nothing more.

I.22.34 Open your spiritual eyes, O Holy One, as you read the words of this discussion. For their implication is your accomplishment and completion. They are the inevitability for which We have been sharing with you. And, they are the last three words spoken by the man you call Jesus the Christ just prior to His giving up the ghost –

It is finished.

I.22.35   With those three words, the world of seeming hate and fear ended. The nightmare is over. Again, you but need accept this Truth. You are free. Accept the Love of God. Accept His Grace. It is yours!

Be in the World, Not of the World

I.22.36   Although the words, *be in the world, not of the world*, are not found in your scriptures, they attest to truth. For you are in the world. This was your choice. However, just because you appear to be in the world, you do not have to be of it. This, too, is a choice. But, how does this apply to *idols* like the body?

I.22.37   As long as you choose to live in your world, the world of physicality, you must do so in a body. The body is not you. It is merely the vehicle, the manifestation, which allows you to experience the physical realm. While there is nothing wrong with this, it becomes problematic only when the mind equates itself with the body. And, when this happens, as We have already explained, the body becomes an *idol*.

I.22.38 There are several passages within your bible that explains this with great clarity. The passages read: *Love not the world, neither the things that are in the world. If any man loves the world, the love of the Father is not in him. For all that is in the world, the lust of the flesh, and the lust of the eyes, and the pride of life, is not of the Father, but is of the world.*

I.22.39 While there are those in your world who have taught you that these passages are about what they call *the lust for sex*, they have taught it in error. For that is not the implication being delivered by these verses. Although your word *lust* carries with it the meaning *intense sexual desire*, it has a much deeper implication that is found in its obsolete meaning, which is *wish; to have an intense desire; craving*. And, it is within this obsolete meaning where the energy behind these passages is found. For the energy being described within those verses is the energy of *wishcraft*.

I.22.40 What is *wishcraft*? It is but the wish to be something other than what you are in Truth. It is the projection of the *body* by the mind. When the mind identifies itself as a body, then the *body* becomes a *thing* in the world which is loved. And, if you love the *things* in the world, then the love of God is not within you. While this appears harsh, it is Truth.

I.22.41 Come to realize, in this perfect moment, that you cannot love *things* and love as God loves. For God does not love things, He loves His Creation. He loves you! For you are His Creation. You are His Holy Child.

I.22.42 To identify with a body is to love a *thing*. And, to love things is the meaning of *idolatry*. And, it is this idolatry which creates the internal conflict, the internal torment, that you experience personally and in the greater world at large. For when you love *things,* you deny Truth.

I.22.43 However, there is a deeper implication here. For to love the *things* of the world, including the body, is to put your love in nothingness. It is loving that which is not real. Furthermore, when you love the world or the *things* found in it, you are declaring your love for the *game of make-believe.* And, as long as you love the *game* and those things found within the game, then it is impossible to truly love God. Why? Simply because God is not in the game. For the *game of make-believe* is the *game of madness*, the *game of insanity*. And, God is not insane. And, in Truth, neither are you.

The Miracle

I.22.44 A miracle has been defined as *a change in perception.* Now, receive the miracle for which you are being given.

Although miracles are themselves not real because they are only found in the lower realms, they are still the means by which time is collapsed. For when you withdraw your attachment and your identity with a body, you have experienced a change in perception, which is a miracle. Thus, time collapses.

I.22.45 Furthermore, by withdrawing your identification as a body, you recognize it for what it is – nothing more than a neutral experience. For the body no longer stands between you and God. And, once your perception has changed, you are able to use it in service to the Kingdom. Thus, the body becomes nothing more than a device to help you carry Truth to your brothers and sisters who are still entranced by time and the game.

I.22.46 The miracle, the change in perception regarding the body, is how you live in the world without being of the world. And this is the beginning of joining, of unity, of oneness. For to release your identity as a body is to prepare the table for the gift of grace. In addition, it allows the mind to accept the Truth of its Being, For the mind is ready to welcome Home its Divine Self.

I.22.47   Now, We invite you to complete the next lesson found in this curriculum. This lesson is designed to help facilitate the release of your identification with the body for all time. It will also facilitate the welcoming of God's Love by your mind.

Lesson 22

I.22.48   This exercise requires one large index card. We ask that you write the following statements on it. In addition, We ask that you set aside three - five minute intervals – in order to complete the practice periods.

I.22.49   Once in the morning, afternoon, and evening, look at the statements you have written on the index card. Silently repeat each one. As you do, hold the statement in your mind. *Feel* it. Become one with it. *Feel* yourself joining with it. Allow the energy field of each statement to course through your entire being. We ask that you do this for fourteen days.

I.22.50   As with the other lessons in this curriculum, enjoy it. *Feel* the freedom that is yours. And, as always, rejoice and give thanks! For the nightmare is ending.

I.22.51 The statements are:

It is finished. I am Home.

I am in the Heavenly Realms, where I belong.

CHAPTER 23

The Triune of God and Man

I.23.1   We come to you now to bring light and clarity to an aspect of creation which has remained hidden within the depth of your *consciousness*. Nothing has created such disagreement as the *triune* of God. In its least misunderstood aspect, it is used to support the belief in separation. For there are those who see three distinct entities, each with his own personality and effect. In its most misunderstood aspect, the *triune* is used by some in your world to discredit the belief that there is **only** God.

I.23.2   As We have stated before, you have the right to believe anything you would choose to believe. Yet, as you have now come to understand, belief does not make Truth. For only Truth is true. And, there are no half-truths. Anything that is not True, must therefore be a lie. This is the purpose for Our time together. For the time has come for the deception to be realized and Truth to be restored. This is God's Will, just as it is yours.

I.23.3   There is **only** God. For nothing exists outside the Mind of God, because there is nothing outside the Mind of God. To those playing the *game of make-believe*, this is meaningless. But, to the *Heart*, it is the sweet sound of Truth. As is written in your bible, *And ye shall know the truth, and the truth shall make you free.*

I.23.4   We now invite you to answer the following questions. But, before you just answer them, turn to the *Heart* and ask that the Truth be restored within your mind. For your mind cannot answer them, for it is still too dazed from its deep sleep to understand the questions being asked. The questions are: *if you have three parts, why wouldn't God? And, where do you think the three-in-one aspect originated?*

I.23.5   These two questions refer to what is termed the *Triune*. And, the implication of the word *triune* is simply three-in-one. We have already discussed with you the *triune* of man, albeit without using the term. For the *triune* of man is what We have called the *supra-conscious,* the *conscious*, and the *subconscious*.

I.23.6   This isn't hard to accept. For the *triune* of man can also be described as the *intellect,* the *emotions*, and the *body.* In addition, on a metaphysical level, the three aspects of man can also be referred to as the *mind,* the *heart,* and the *being.* Regardless as to which terms are used, they all refer to an *individual.*

I.23.7   Now, We invite you to open your mind to what you will be reading. For you will be reading Truth. However, this Truth has been hiding within the very words you use daily. Although the Truth is there, you will discover that it is hiding beneath a meaning which directly opposes it. And, this opposition between meanings is where the deception of your beingness has been buried, keeping you unaware that the Truth lies within the very words you have used most of your life.

I.23.8   We will begin with the word *individual*. For this word has two implications that are diametrically opposed. Each meaning carries with it an energy field that supports and reinforces the thought system behind it. Remember, there are two thought systems. One is the thought system of unity. The other is the thought system of separation. One is of God. The other is of the world. And, each thought system has as its cornerstone the energy pattern of the implication of just one word – *individual*.

I.23.9   Let's examine the word. For which one of the two meanings you identify with determines the energy that effects the Grand Field of Energy, thus every experience you have within the realm of physicality. The world's definition, thus the world's intention, of the word *individual* is *existing as a distinct entity: separate*. In addition, the word also carries the

393

meaning *having marked individuality.* Furthermore, the world's implication of being an *individual* is that of *personhood.*

I.23.10 However, the word *individual* has an obsolete meaning. This obsolete meaning carries the Truth of your Being. What is this obsolete meaning? It is but this - *inseparable.* Yet, it goes even deeper. For the word also carries the implication *being an individual existing as an indivisible whole.* Therefore, the implication with this definition is that of *individuation.*

I.23.11 Can you *see* the difference? Can you *see* how the world's version of *individuality* is the cornerstone of the thought system of separation? More importantly, can you *feel* it?

I.23.12 Likewise, can you *see* that what has been considered as obsolete is the cornerstone of the thought system of unity? Can you *feel* it? Can you yet *feel* the energy field of unity, of oneness, of wholeness, and of completion? For they are the same. They are identical. And, they are Our True Energy Signature.

I.23.13 Now, let's take the world's version of *individuality* deeper. Recall that the world's version creates the belief in separation. And, in order to play the game of separation, you must do so in a body. It is when the mind identifies itself completely with that of a body that the idea of *personhood* solidifies the belief in separation. And, it is the idea, the intentionality, of *personhood* that interacts with the Grand Energy Field creating your experiences.

I.23.14 The energy behind the word *person* affects every aspect of your life. Furthermore, the word *person* is the lynchpin for the entire thought system of separation. For unless you identify as a *person,* then you cannot play in the game of separation. And, the word *person* carries with it several implications that combine to create a distinctive, very strong, energy field. For this energy field is the one that is the hardest for the mind to release. Why is this? Quite simply – the *subconscious* mind is acutely aware that, when the *conscious* mind releases the idea, thus the energy, of *personhood*, it will simply cease to exist. For it is within the *subconscious* mind where the cornerstone of the thought system of separation resides.

I.23.15 Now, We ask that you allow your mind to be receptive to the implications of the word *person* so that you can begin the process of releasing its energy. The word *person* has the following meanings, thus intentions: *human, individual; a character* or part in or as if **in a play**, guise; the **body** of a human being; and, the personality of a human being, **self.**

I.23.16 Yet, there is a deeper implication of the word person. And, like so many other words, it too is found in the origin of the word. For in the origin lies the hallmark of the *game of make-believe.*

I.23.17 Your word *person* comes to you via the Latin word *persona,* which carries the meaning *character, mask,* as well as *personality.* Do you yet recognize the deeper implication and energy field of the word *person?* For your word *person* is describing the *mask* you don in order to play the character of *not-God* in the *game of make-believe.* Recognize, now, that to identify with *personhood* is to identify as the antithesis of God. And, it is this very identification which creates the inner conflict that you live with constantly. For deep within your *consciousness,* you know that identifying as *not-God* is to live a lie. And, this conflict between the Truth and the lie you live is the war that rages within your mind.

I.23.18 Slowly read the defining factors behind the word *person* once again. *Is it any wonder why you find oneness hard to fathom?* For your own language supports and strengthens the belief that you are separated from everyone and everything,

396

including God. And, as long as you are projecting the energy of *personhood,* unity and oneness will remain unknown to you. Thus, you will continue to create *hell.*

I.23.19   Look again at one of the meanings of the word *person*; the one which reads, *the body of a human being.* Recognize, in this moment, that each time you entertain the thought that you are a person, or use the word person, you are strengthening your belief and experiences of *hell.* For you are strengthening your belief that you are a *body.* And, it is the identification with a *body* which further entrenches within the mind the belief that you are a separate being, living a separate existence, a part from everyone and everything else found within the physical realm.

I.23.20   Furthermore, every time you look upon a brother or sister as a *person,* who is distinct and separate from you, you are reinforcing the idea of separation within your own mind. It is for this reason as to why you must become vigilant of every thought that enters into your mind. For each thought either strengthens your belief in separation, or it strengthens the idea of unity and oneness. One strengthens misery and suffering, while the other increases your joy. Which one you experience is directly associated with the thought system that you are strengthening.

I.23.21 The notion of *personhood* is the hardest for the mind to relinquish. In truth, without the persistence of the *Heart's* yearning to return to wholeness, to return to Love, the mind will never voluntarily release its belief system. For it is too ensconced and entranced with the idea of *personhood*, or being a body, for it to simply let the idea fade from its memory. For the *game of make-believe* has become real to the mind and Heaven has become lost. Not even the mind's suffering, misery, and conflict are enough to give it cause to seek for the Truth which will set it free, because it firmly believes that the separation is real. Unity is a foreign concept and is not born out in the mind's experiences. Therefore, the idea of oneness is never manifested or experienced by the mind until the choice is made to listen to the promptings of the *Heart.*

I.23.22 Each thought system, whether that of separation or unity, is predicated on the foundation of a triune, the three-in-one aspect of beingness. Separation is built upon the foundation of the *intellect* (the mind), *emotions* (the heart), and the *body.* Oneness is built upon the foundation of the *Mind of God* (Divine Thought – Desire), the *Heart of God* (Divine Feelings – Intention), and the *Expression of God* (Divine Creation).

I.23.23 Regarding the thought system of unity, you are more familiar with the terms, the *Father* (Divine Mind - Thought), the *Son* (Divine Idea – Feelings), and the *Holy Spirit* (Divine Expression – Manifestation). Regardless of the terminology used, they each represent what is called the *Triune of God*. And, the *Triune of God* simply refers to God's Wholeness, His Completion.

I.23.24   Furthermore, you complete God, just as He completes you. For without you, the Divine Idea, God would be incomplete. It is for this reason that, in *A Course in Miracles* it is written, *God is incomplete without me.* For even with the loss of one of His Children, God would not be Whole. He would be incomplete. And, it is God's Will to be Whole. Therefore, since His Will and your will are the same, it is your will to be Whole and complete as well.

Identification With Only A Third Of The Triune

I.23.25   Now, We ask you to relax and open your mind like you have never done before. We ask you to *feel* what you will be reading. Let the *feelings* course throughout your entire field of awareness. For you will be reading how you became identified as a separate being. Your mind may at first attempt to reject what it is reading and deny it, because what you will be reading will appear to contradict what the world has taught you. The time has come for you to recognize the Truth, so that you can finally release the false beliefs which have kept you playing the *game of make-believe.* It is time to remove the *mask* of *not-God*, so that you can once again take your seat at the table God has kept prepared for you.

I.23.26 We will begin by using words you are quite familiar with. For you will recognize them as what you refer to as the *Trinity*: the Father, the Son, and the Holy Spirit. Whether you call it the *Trinity* or the *Triune*, they both describe a three-in-one Godhead.

I.23.27 Using the *Triune* as the beginning point for this discussion, We ask that you come to recognize that before the tiny, mad idea entered into your mind, you identified completely with the part of the Godhead known as the Son. This means that you identified with only one-third of the *Triune*. And, it was identification with only the Son which was the *first degree of separation*. For by identifying as the Son, you had already believed that you were separate from the Father and the Spirit, which comprises the remaining two-thirds of the *Triune*.

I.23.28 In addition, your identification as the Son is where you denied the remaining aspects of God, thus denying the whole of your Self. Furthermore, as We have already revealed unto you, your denial was when *time*, the tiny, mad idea crept into your mind. And, from the denial with your whole Self, your Holy Self, came the question, *What am I?*

I.23.29 Although We have discussed the ramifications that arose from the denial of your Divine Self, the Self of Unity, We will now direct your attention to the greater effects created by your denial. For when you identified only as the Son, this thought rippled throughout creation, ultimately creating the lower dimensions, including the dimension of physicality.

I.23.30 One of the most misunderstood of your bible verses explains the *fall* of one-third of the heavenly hosts. Most on your planet believe that the verse *is of things to come.* But, O Holy Child, it is not what is to come, but what has already happened and is happening within your mind in this very moment. The verse simply reads, *And his tail drew the third part of the stars of heaven, and did cast them to the earth.*

I.23.31 O Child of God, mankind was the third of the stars of heaven cast to the earth. Yes! You are the third. For when you identified only as the Son, you identified only with one-third of Heaven.

I.23.32 Although your mind reads this with contempt, We ask you now, ***In the first creation story found in your bible, does it state that God created man and placed him upon the earth?*** No! It does not. It only states, *So God created man in his own image, in the image of God created he him; male and female created he them.*

I.23.33 Let's return to the first biblical passage of this discussion. It is time for the implication of this verse to be revealed. For the truth has been hiding in just four words contained within the passage. Those words are *tail, drew, stars,* and *cast.* Thus, We will reveal the implication of each of those words, and you will quickly discover that the verse has a much richer meaning than what you have been led to believe.

I.23.34 We will begin with the word *tail,* which carries the implication *retinue.* Furthermore, *retinue* carries with it the meaning *retain,* which simply means *to keep or hold in one's mind; to remember.* The word *drew* is the past tense of the word *draw,* which implies *patronage.* In addition, *patronage* carries the meaning *advowson.* Like other words, the intention of *advowson* is hidden in its Latin origin, which is *advocare.* And, the Latin word *advocare* carries with it the literal meaning *to invoke the gods.*

I.23.35 Before We look at the word *stars*, We will reveal the implication of the word *invoke*, which carries the meaning *solicit*. Again, We must look to the origin of the word *solicit* in order to uncover its true meaning. Your word *solicit* comes to you via the Latin word *sollicitare*, which simply means to *arouse*, or *to awaken from sleep*.

I.23.36 Now, We will reveal the implication of the word *stars* as written in your bible verse. As with other words in your language, the implication of the word, as it pertains to this passage, lies hidden within an obsolete definition. That obsolete meaning is *destiny*. Again, in order to uncover the true intention, We must look at the origin of the word. Your word *destiny* arose from the Latin word *destinare,* which carries with it the meaning *to fix in the mind,* or *to restore the mind.*

I.23.37 The last word of the verse for which We will reveal the implication is that of *cast*. Your word *cast* carries with it the meaning *direct,* which carries the implication *to enjoin*. Here, We must look to the origin of the word *enjoin* in order to uncover its true intention. The word *enjoin* is derived from the Latin word *injungere,* which means *to unite.*

I.23.38 Therefore, when We substitute the meanings with the words, the Bible passage becomes: *And His remembering to*

403

awaken the gods from sleep by restoring the mind of the third of heaven, and did unite them with earth. Recall, the word earth refers to *man,* or *mankind.* Thus, the verse can more correctly be read as: *And His remembering to awaken the gods from sleep by restoring the mind of the third of heaven, and did unite them with mankind.*

I.23.39 Do you yet *see* and *feel* the implication of this bible passage? For once the context of fear is removed, the verse becomes one of beauty and grace. Read it once again. This time, take note of the accomplishment the passage is invoking. For this passage clearly details the *awakening of the gods* **(you)** by *restoring the mind of the third of heaven* **(the Sonship)**. How is this accomplished? As the verse describes, it is the uniting of the divine with man. In other words, it is the *Christ.* For the *Christ* is the union of the divine with man, which is more aptly described as the union between heaven and earth. More specifically, it is the awakening of *God-man.* Thus, it is your awakening – the awakening of the Christ within you.

I.23.40 However, recognize in this most Holy Moment, you are already seated in the Heavenly Realm. You need but accept this Truth. Yet, to do so, you must recognize your Divine Self – the *Christ.* Furthermore, you immediately accepted the union of heaven and earth, of the divine and human, the very instant you entertained the tiny, mad idea. Although it appears that the tiny, mad idea had real and everlasting consequences, none of it occurred in Truth. It only seems to play out within your mind. Yet, this too has been but a choice. Why did We use the words, *was your choice?*

I.23.41 The answer was actually revealed to you in one of your movies, *The Matrix Reloaded.* It is found in the scene where the main character, Neo, meets with the Oracle, who is awaiting his arrival while seated on a park bench. After offering him a piece of candy, Neo comes to realize that the Oracle is a program within the matrix. During their brief encounter, Neo says to the Oracle, *"I don't think I can make that choice."* The Oracle simply responds with the Truth, *"You aren't here to make the choice. The choice has already been made. You are here to understand why you made the choice."*

I.23.42 Although this is from a movie, it nevertheless is a statement of truth. For O Holy Child, you aren't here to make a choice. You've already made it. You are here to understand *why* you made it. For only when you realize and understand that you made the choice between *nothing* and *everything*, between *time* and *eternity*, between *not-God* and *God*, where you chose the former rather than the latter in each case, will you recognize that you also made the choice to awaken.

I.23.43 You cannot, in Truth, choose against yourself. You can only *make-believe* that you have. For in the moment the tiny, mad idea arose in your mind, the correction was made and you accepted it. Therefore, the battle that rages within your split mind is nothing more than the battle between the correction, the choice you accepted, and the wish to be something other than what you are in Truth. This battle continues within your mind even as you read these words describing it.

I.23.44 Yet, you have already made the choice to awaken. It is accomplished. You are, in Truth, awakened and seated at your Father's table. For where else could you be?

I.23.45 Yes! You currently believe you are a separate being far removed from the Heavenly Realm. But, this is not so! For you are not separate and alone. Rather, you are united with the Whole, just as God Willed you to be.

I.23.46 Why does the Truth of your Oneness seem so foreign to your mind? The answer is actually a very simple one. It is because of the *belief* that you pulled off the impossible. For you cannot see past a choice you do not understand. And, in your misunderstanding of *what you are,* you believe you have become and remain as but the wish that you made so very, very long ago. But, your wish was just that – a wish. To believe in a wish is but to dream. And, dreaming comes only from sleep. For God did not Will you be apart from Him. And, His Will is always done, just as is yours, since they are the same.

I.23.47 But, how can you sleep and be awake at the same time? The answer is – you can't. For you are either asleep or awake, dead or alive. You cannot be both. But, you can still *pretend* you are sleeping, much like a child does when a parent opens his bedroom door to check-in on him. However, the time of *pretending* to be what you are not has come. The time to cease *pretending* to be dead has arrived. The time to stop playing games is here. And, this is done by simply acknowledging Truth – that you are the Holy Child, the Whole Creation, of a Loving God. You simply need but *believe* that you are more than just human. For in Truth, what you are is beyond comprehension. For there is nothing in your world to compare yourself with your Self. And, We state this emphatically!

The Making of Matter

I.23.48 To fully understand the concept of the *Triune*, you need look no farther than how, what you consider matter, arose from the Grand Energy Field of Potentiality and Possibility, the Energy which is God, which is but your Self. Although We will not go into great detail, We will lay before you how you believe you accomplished the impossible.

I.23.49 In *A Course in Miracles,* there is a question asked and answer given. The question is: *How will the world end?* The answer given is this: *It* (the world) *will simply seem to cease to be.* And, when you understand the simplicity of how it appeared to arise, you will understand how it will simply cease to seem to be. For as it simply seemed to be, it will simply cease to be, just as easily.

I.23.50 When you chose to identify with only one-third (1/3) of the *Triune,* you denied the other two-thirds (2/3). In other words, by identifying solely as the Son, you denied both the Father and Spirit. And, as a result of this denial, *time* was born. Furthermore, in that same instant, guilt and fear arose within the mind. For now the Whole seemed to have split into two fractions. And, in that moment, what you refer to as the Big Bang happened, firmly establishing guilt and fear within your mind. Furthermore, this guilt and fear created the splitting of the mind, as well as the thought systems which, on the surface, appear to oppose each other.

I.23.51   Where did this occur? Quite simply, it occurred in the Mind, which is where the Grand Field of Energy lives. In Truth, it is where We exist. It is where We reside.

I.23.52   We ask you now to simply read this discussion without making any interpretations or inferences as to what you are reading. Instead, We ask you to *feel* the words as your mind reads them. Allow your *feelings* to guide you through this portion of the discussion. Once you have read it, let your mind process and digest the information. Do not get tangled up in the content of what you will be reading. Rather, just simply *feel* it. Allow its energetic frequency to resonate within you. For as you recognize your oneness with the information you will be reading, you will begin to *see* oneness and unity in everything you look upon, because you will come to know your interconnectedness with everyone and everything within the third dimension of physicality, as well as all other realms.

I.23.53   When your scientific community first discovered atoms, it was believed that they were indivisible. Then, atoms were split to reveal that they were comprised of even smaller particles – protons, electrons, and neutrons – collectively referred to as subatomic particles. These seemed like the fundamental particles, until it was discovered that protons and neutrons were comprised of two quarks each.

I.23.54 Quarks, Our Dear Brothers and Sisters, are the basic, fundamental particles which come together to create the subatomic particles that comprise the nucleus of an atom. How does this relate to the triune and your identifying as one-third of Heaven? Recall that the Son is one-third of Heaven, and the Father and Spirit comprise the remaining two-thirds. Quarks come in two varieties. They are either -1/3 or +2/3. The positive or negative sign simply denotes their electric charge. In the case of the Son, when He denied the Father and Spirit, He turned in the opposing direction. Thus, quarks mimic the *first degree of separation.*

I.23.55 Furthermore, the energy associated with the -1/3 quark, which represents the Son of the *Triune,* is held in this form because of the guilt associated with the belief that He had separated from the Whole. Although there are six types of quarks, four rapidly decay to create the stable types referred to as *up* or *down.* This is where the phrase *as above, so below* comes into the picture. For quarks allow atoms to be formed. In addition, atoms allow the lower realm, the physical realm, to mimic the realms above.

I.23.56 Atoms are the building blocks of matter. For atoms come together to create molecules, which gives rise to what you call form. However, beneath the form of any object, whether it is a rock, a tree, a drop of water, or something such as a bird, a flower, or a human body, there exists the same quantum energy pattern. In this sense, everything you think you look upon with your eyes is interconnected. For it shares the same energy field as everything else.

I.23.57 In this sense, it should now be abundantly clear that nothing which appears to exist in form is separated from anything else. For beneath the appearance lies sameness, or oneness. In other words, everything you look upon is but energy. Nothing more.

I.23.58 *How then will the world end?* It will end just as it began. When the mind of the third is completely healed and restored to its natural state, free from guilt and fear, then the forms of the stable quarks will no longer be *up* or *down*. They will simply return to sameness. And, when this happens, form as you know it will simply cease to be. It really is that simple.

I.23.59 Can you yet *feel* that what you consider reality is but an illusion? One of the greatest minds of mankind, the man you refer to as Albert Einstein, once said, *Reality is merely an illusion, albeit a very persistent one.* In Truth, reality as you perceive it is nothing more than the rising and passing of form.

And, just as it is written within *A Course in Miracles*, *There is nothing so blinding as perception of form.* Why is this?

I.23.60 Your eyes were only made to see form. They were not made to look beyond form to the Truth that lies underneath. What is this Truth? It is but this – everything in form, regardless of what it is, arises from the same Quantum Energy Field. This Energy Field lies just beneath all things and is all things. For without it nothing would have been made that was made.

I.23.61 You have been taught that all minds are joined. The joining, the unity, of every mind is directly attributable to the Quantum Energy Field, or as We call it the Grand Field of Energy. For it is through this Energy Field that creation communicates with itself and the Source of Our Being. It is through this Energy Field that We communicate with you now.

I.23.62 You have never been separate from this Field. For to separate from it would mean that you would cease to exist – immediately and forever. In Truth, there would be no trace left of you, not even a memory. Why? Because nothing exists outside this Grand Field of Energy. And, this is what you must come to accept and realize. It is also the reason as to why you are never, ever alone. Furthermore, it is why nothing is ever really lost. For everything returns to the Energy Field. It is why you are never farther than the width of a thought from the man you call Jesus, or from any Brother or Sister, whether or not they are in the field of your physical presence. It is also why you are never farther than the width of a thought from God, Himself.

I.23.63   The time has come for you to remember, once again, that the Grand Field of Energy responds to intentionality. Recall that you learned in *The Way of Mastery* that communication is creation. And, communication is accomplished via the combining of thoughts and feelings. Remember, every thought gives rise to a feeling. And, as a thought arises within your field of *consciousness,* its corresponding feeling arises simultaneously. Thoughts and their feelings can never be separated. And, as We have already discussed, the thoughts you have, along with their corresponding feelings, create your beliefs.

I.23.64   In addition, beliefs act directly upon the Grand Field of Energy. This is why We have also previously stated that you will see and experience your beliefs. For beliefs determine, at every level, what you ultimately experience. It is for this reason that you believe what you see and experience. What else could happen? For your beliefs created the experience.

I.23.65 With this firmly affixed in your mind, can you now recognize that every experience you have ever had, or will have, is directly attributable to the thought system unto which you ascribe? For if your thought system is predicated in separation, then your experiences will but attest to separation. However, if your thought system is that of unity, oneness, connection, and relationship, then your experiences will be those of harmony and joy, glory and beauty. Yet, only one thought system is Real. The other is delusion. It is *make-believe*.

I.23.66 Can you yet *see* why this is? For O Holy Child, there is nothing in this dimension, or any other dimension, that *can* separate you. Yet, if you maintain the belief in separation, then you will continue to experience separation, thereby strengthening your belief that you are a separate entity, moving about isolated and apart from all other beings.

I.23.67 At the beginning of this discussion, We shared with you how the two belief systems were created by the energy pattern, the intention, of just one word – *individual*. Now, the time has come for you to recognize the greater implication of the intentionality of that word. For it has a much deeper implication than most suspect. And, this implication is what maintains both thought systems, regardless as to which one you uphold.

I.23.68 While each thought system was founded on one word, *individual,* each thought system is maintained, or sustained, by the energy field of one word as well. What is that word? It is but the word *self!*

Yourself or Your Self

I.23.69 While it may be difficult to imagine how one simple word could affect not only what you believe true about yourself, but every experience you have, the time has come for you to understand the power behind the intentionality of that one word. For nothing has created more misery, suffering, loneliness, and heartache than the energy associated with the misuse of the word *self.* Just like the word *individual*, the word *self* has what would appear to be diametrically opposed meanings. And, depending upon the meaning you ascribe to yourself regarding the energy associated behind the word *self,* you will either experience Heaven or hell. Recognize, in this perfect moment, that there is no in-between. For you can only experience Heaven or hell. And, which one you experience is directly attributable to the effects of this one word.

I.23.70   As We have done before, let's look at the meaning of the word. For you will quickly come to *see* that the word has two distinct, yet opposing implications. One implication supports unity and oneness, while the other supports isolation, thus separation.

I.23.71   The word *self* carries with it the meaning *the entire person of an individual.* It isn't difficult to understand that this meaning is the world's version of *self.* For it supports the idea of the world's version of *individuality*, which is that of *personhood.* Yet, it is the world's intention of *self* where the darkness of the mind can be found. Besides the implication you just read, the world's meaning of *self* carries with it the dark wish, the dark desire, to be something other than what you are in Truth.

I.23.72   What is this dark desire found in the world's idea of *self?* Before you read the answer to that question, take just a moment and relax. Take a deep, cleansing breath. Allow your mind to become quiet, even if only but an instant. We ask you to read the following with an open mind. Do not attempt any form of interpretation. For your mind will try to reconcile what it reads through the lens of what it believes to be the *past.* Instead, let the words bypass your mind and go to your *Heart.* Allow your *Heart* to interpret what you read. For it will but gently allow the implication of the world's version of *self* into your mind in a manner that will not cause it stress or grief. Let your *Heart* demonstrate its Love for you. *Feel* the Love it has, rather than the disbelief and fear that would be created within the mind as it reads the following words.

I.23.73   The dark wish of the world's intention of the *self* is found in an additional meaning besides the one already given. And, it is this: the word *self* also carries the implication of *belonging to oneself; **own***. Do you see the dark implication? For it is that of ownership, of possession. It is the admission that you *took* from God what belongs to God. Furthermore, the world's definition of *self* creates the belief that you make of yourself only that of your *will*.

I.23.74   O Child of God, do you yet comprehend how the intention, the energy, of the world's version of *self* could but yield guilt and fear. For the world's version is predicated on the belief that you took something, a part of God, from God. And, this is but the dark desire – that you could take from God a part of God in order to be something other than God. Whether or not you are *consciously aware* of this dark wish, your *subconscious* mind is acutely aware of it. For always remember that your *subconscious* is the seat of the original guilt and fear experienced from the original judgment you levied upon yourself. Because, the *subconscious* is the projection of your *conscious* mind in an attempt to free itself from the thought of guilt and its feeling of fear.

I.23.75   In addition, the world teaches you that you are your *own* person. In other words, it teaches you that you *own* yourself. This *own-ness* creates the belief that you *possess* a body. Thus, it creates the belief that you are a body. And, this belief creates the experiences of the body, which further strengthens the belief that you are a body, as well as strengthening the belief that you are a separate *person,* a separate *self,* distinct and unique from all others.

I.23.76   Again, can you *see* the intention behind the world's version of *self?* For the energy behind it literally creates the conflict and drama you experience both internally and externally. Hear Us O Brothers and Sisters. For how many times a day do you think or say the word *myself?* Know this: each time you think a thought or say something with the word *my,* you are projecting the energy of the world's version of the *self.*

I.23.77   Furthermore, each time you look upon a Brother or Sister as a distinct, unique, separate *self,* you are strengthening the belief that you are a separate *self –* a distinct and separate

418

individual – in a world that appears to be populated with billions of other *humans*, inhabiting a body that makes each the *person* that he or she is. ***This is the insanity, the delusion, created in the mind of those playing the game of make-believe.*** Do you yet *see* this? More importantly, can you *feel* it? Can you now *see* the dark desire, the dark wish, hiding within your mind? **For it is but the desire to be *not-God*, in order to make of your*self* what you would be, rather than simply being what God created you to be.**

I.23.78 However, just like the Truth of your Being was hidden within an obsolete meaning of the word *individual*, the same is true of the word *self*. The obsolete meaning of the word *self* is ***identical; sameness.*** Furthermore, the word *self* carries with it the meaning ***the realization or embodiment of an abstraction.***

I.23.79 Now, let's look at the implication of the word *same*. For its intention, it's energy, is that of *what you are*. The word *same* carries with it the following implications: *being **one** without addition, change, or discontinuance, **identical**; corresponding so closely as to be indistinguishable; **equal** in size, shape, **value**, or importance.* O Divine Child, herein is the Truth of your *Self*. It is the Truth of your Being.

I.23.80 Do you *feel* the freedom, the power, and the beauty of your True *Self?* For your *Self* is Everything, because it was created by the Source of All That Is. The energy behind the *Self* is the energy of Our Beingness. We are the *same*. We are *identical*, because We are the Extension of God. What does this mean?

I.23.81 In the most perfect, beautiful sense, We have been given Everything. We lack nothing. Yet, there is a greater implication in this. For just as it is given in the definition, We are without addition, change, or discontinuance. This means you have done nothing to add to your *Self,* nor have you done anything to lessen your Self. In addition, you have done nothing to change your *Self* – nothing! And, the experience for which you believe you are having in the realm of physicality has not created a discontinuance in your *Self.* This also means that what you refer to as death does not add anything, remove anything, change anything, or causes any form of discontinuance in your *Self.*

I.23.82 Recognize, in this Holy Moment, your *Self* is free. For your *Self* resides in the Heavenly Realm. Where else could your *Self* be? However, if you *believe* that you are the *self* the world teaches, then you do not know your True *Self.* And, it is your *Self* who calls you Home. It is your *Self* that knows only of unity, oneness, connectedness, and Holy Relationship with all of your Brothers and Sisters.

I.23.83 *Could you try to make God homeless and know that you are Home? Can you, who identified with the Son, deny the Father and Spirit without believing you have been denied? The Laws of God hold only for your protection, and they never hold in vain. What you experience when you deny the other two-thirds of the Triune is still for your protection, for the power of your will cannot be lessened without the intervention of God against it, and any limitation on your power is not the Will of God. For this would negate the Spiritual Law of Free Will. And, the Laws can neither be negated nor usurped. Therefore, look only to the power that God gave you in order to free your mind, remembering that it is yours because it is, and join with, unite with, all of your Brothers and Sisters in the Peace of God.*

I.23.84 You, who have identified with only one-third of the *Triune,* believe you denied the other two-thirds. Yet, We ask you, *Could you deny your right arm by severing it, and your right arm still be functional?* Although this seems like a ridiculous question, do you not yet *see* that your belief in which you separated from the Whole is just as ridiculous? For if the impossible had happened, how could you live?

I.23.85 Here O Holy Child is the paradox, the conundrum. For as We have discussed with you before, when you identified as *not-God* by denying the Father and Spirit, you identified with death, since God is Life. This is the reason why We have stated that, until you awaken and your mind is restored to its glory, you are the *walking dead.*

I.23.86 If you are truly ready to have your mind restored to its full Glory, to its True Nature, to its Magnificence, to its Freedom, then We invite you to complete the next lesson in this curriculum. During your practice periods, We ask that you not think about what this lesson asks. Rather, We ask that you *feel* every word in the statements you are asked to silently repeat. *Feel* the energy of the statements themselves. And, above all, rejoice in your wholeness. Rejoice in your freedom. Rejoice in your *Self.*

Lesson 23

I.23.87 You will need one large index card for this exercise. On it, write the following statements. Then, once in the morning, and again in the evening before going to bed, We invite you to hold the card in your hand and look upon each word in each statement. *Feel* their intention. This should only take a minute at the most.

I.23.88 After completing this portion, close your eyes and silently repeat each statement. This time, *feel* the intention, the energy, of each statement. Do this for approximately seven minutes. Then, keeping your eyes closed, take a deep breath. Slowly exhale it. Sit quietly for another three minutes. Allow the energy of each statement to sink into your mind. Try not to think of anything but the *feelings* you have become *consciously* aware of. Simply relax into the *feelings*. Let the *feelings* overcome you, rather than you trying to overcome them.

I.23.89 The statements are:

I am essential in the completion of the Triune of God.

I and the Father are one.

I choose now to identify with the Self God created.

CHAPTER 24

The Intentionality of Self-Importance

The greatest enemy to the mind of man is self-importance.

I.24.1   In our last discussion with you, We shared how the two thought systems were predicated on the word *individual*. Furthermore, We shared with you how just one word – self – sustains each thought system, as well as creates the intention, which affects the Quantum Energy Field of Possibility and Potentiality, thereby creating every experience you have. However, the idea of *self,* regardless of the thought system to which you claim, is the thought. Yet, like all thoughts, *self* must have a corresponding feeling. But, what is the feeling created by the thought of *self?*

I.24.2   We are here with you at this time to reveal the *feeling* and the associated energy field that is created from the thought of *self.* Just as the words *individual* and *self* have two implications each, one which is the world's version, while the other denotes unity, so too does the word for the *feeling* that arises from the thought of the *self* you identify with. And, these implications directly determine what arises from the Quantum Energy Field. For one identifies with the *self* of the world, while the other identifies with the *Self* created by God, your True *Self.*

I.24.3   The *feeling* created by the thought of *self* is but that of *self-importance*. And, as you will see, the word *importance* has two implications. One makes the world you believe you inhabit. It literally creates the *hell* you experience with every breath you take. The other simply creates experiences of unity and harmony, thus joy and peace. It quite literally creates experiences of Heaven. For this implication *is* your True State of Being. It is your inheritance.

The World's Version

I.24.4   We will begin by revealing the world's version of *self-importance* and its ramifications, or consequences, of the intention, the energy, of this *feeling.* Again, We invite you to set aside any predilection for judging what your mind will be reading. For your mind will perceive it is being attacked. But, your mind knows not that attack is impossible. However, your *Heart* knows the Truth, which is - **minds cannot attack, only bodies can.**

I.24.5   In order to reveal the world's version of *self-importance*, We need but turn to the meaning which has been assigned to it. Thus, the implication of the word *self-importance* is simply this: **consequence.** Furthermore, the word *consequence* carries with it the meaning *the **appearance** of importance; self-*

importance. In addition, the word *appearance* carries with it the implication *external show:* **semblance**. And, it is in *semblance* where the dark *feeling* is buried.

I.24.6 The word *semblance* carries with it the implication *outward and often deceptive appearance or show:* **form**; *a phantasmal form:* **apparition**. In addition, the implication of *phantasm* is that of *illusion*. Therefore, *self-importance* is nothing more than *feeling the deception of form*, or that of the *feeling of illusion*. But, where is the darkness behind this *feeling?* Besides, what does *the feeling of the deception of form* feel like?

I.24.7 Although you experience this *feeling* every moment of your day, your mind does not recognize what the *feeling* is. For the mind denies this *feeling* and immediately *projects* it in the attempt to assuage the heaviness this *feeling* generates. Recall, *self-importance* is the *feeling of the deception of* **form**. Thus, the *feeling* is that of the *body*, which is the projection of the mind. It is why your body *feels* heavy. Yet, the intention goes far, far deeper. For the *feeling* of the *body* is that of what you refer to as your *five senses,* which as you know are: *sight, sound, taste, touch,* and *smell.* And, these *five senses* report back to the mind the *body's* experiences. Therefore, these are the *feelings* created by the thought of *self.*

I.24.8   However, the greater implication of the intention of *self-importance* is that it is *illusory*. In other words, *self-importance* is a *lie*. For the *body* is the *lie*, the great deception of *shame,* that your mind projects into the world. Remember, *shame* is the *feeling* created by the thought of *guilt*.

I.24.9   Recognize, in this moment, that the *body* is the **consequence** *of the appearance of self-importance.* For the *body* is the home of *shame,* of *guilt*, and of *fear*. It is the home of *self-deception*. Furthermore, the *body* is the home to a mind which believes in separation. And, this home, which the mind believes to be its *self*, is the manifestation that arises from the Grand Field of Energy, because of the belief that is created from the thought of *self* and the feeling of *self-importance*.

I.24.10   The *body* functions exactly as your belief in separation would have it do. For the *five senses* further strengthens not only your belief in separation, but every experience you have in the realm of physicality. For your eyes can only see *form*. Your ears can only hear the sounds of *form*. Your sense of touch can only give you the different external characteristics *form* seems to take. Your tongue can only give you the taste of the *form* of the different foods you ingest. And, your sense of olfaction can only let you smell the varying odors associated with *form*. For the *body* is incapable of knowing Truth having been made in *self-deception*. Thus, the body can never know of unity, of oneness, for it is nothing but a projection of a mind suffering from a thought system founded upon separation.

I.24.11   The effects of the five senses simply reinforce the belief that the body is real, and that the body *is* what you are. ***If you believe yourself to be a body, because of what the five senses report back to you, then your belief is predicated on nothing more than that of electrical impulses.*** Is this what you truly believe you are? For if you do, then you believe you are just a device for sensory perception.

I.24.12   In *A Course in Miracles*, it is written that *projection leads to perception*. In the case regarding the thought of *self* and the feeling of *self-importance*, the *body* is the projection, and what the body reports back is the perception. Can you yet understand why identification with the *body* is the hardest concept for the mind to release? For the *body* was designed by you for but one purpose. And, that purpose is to keep you in *hell*, to keep you in *self-deception*, to keep you playing the *game of make-believe*, to keep you playing the part of *not-God*, to keep you in the conflict created by *guilt* and *shame*, to keep you in *personhood* and the belief that you are a separate *individual*, as well as to keep you in *death*. This O Holy Child is the only purpose given unto the body by a mind that lives with the intense *terror* it has of God, of Love, of its Holy Self.

I.24.13   It is for this reason that the feeling of *self-importance* is the greatest enemy of your mind. For *self-importance* does not affect God. It only affects a mind that is adrift in *self-delusion* and *self-deception*. And, the Mind of God does not know of *self-delusion* or *self-deception*. For the Mind of God knows not of conflict. It only knows Peace. For God does not deny His Holy Self. Only you, who denied the Whole by identifying with only one-third of the *Triune,* know of illusion. For God only identifies with Himself and His Creations, which is but Love.

I.24.14   God knows no enemies, because God does not attack. In truth, you know not of attack either. But, when you identify with a *body*, with *self-importance*, then you have become your own enemy, because you have attacked yourself. Yet, this need not be. It is but a choice you make moment-to-moment.

I.24.15   Come now, in this most Holy Instant, to recognize that the mind is incapable of awakening itself. For it is too lost in its *delusional* beliefs. Yet, you have all the help you need to awaken. And, this help is found within the *Heart*. However, you must come to trust your *Self.* For only in trust can the *Heart*

429

restore the mind to its Natural and Former State, which is but Peace.

The True Meaning of Self-Importance

I.24.16   Just as the thought system of the world, which is that of separation, has its implication of the *feeling* in the word *importance,* so too does the thought system of unity and oneness. However, rather than the end result being the projection of the *body*, the energy of the *feeling* of *Self-Importance* effects the Grand Field of Energy in such a way that creation of the good, the beautiful, and the Holy occurs. For the energy of the thought of *Self* with its corresponding *feeling* of *Self-Importance* acts with the Quantum Energy Field creating a pure and perfect extension of the *Self.* In other words, what arises from the Quantum Energy Field is recognized as identical with the *Self* from which the energy emanated. Therefore, there is complete oneness with the Extension, as well as perfect wholeness, creating a *Holy Relationship* between the *Self of Source* and the *Self of Extension.* Thus, there is no difference between the two. There is only sameness. Therefore, there is only oneness.

I.24.17   This, O Child of God, is the perfect balance between *Cause* and *Effect,* between *Source Energy* and the *Energy of the Extension.* It is the Holy Relationship that exists between

God and Us, His Beloved Extensions. There is only one thing, one energy, that obstructs the perfect *awareness* of this Holy Relationship with God and His Extensions. What is it? It is but the *self* for which you believe you are. For the world's version of *self* is as incapable of recognizing oneness with the Whole, as is the *Self* of Truth being capable of recognizing separation of any kind, on any level, or any degree.

I.24.18   What is the *feeling* of *Self-Importance* generated by the thought of the *Self* of Reality? Just as the implication of the *feeling* of the world's version of the *self* is found in the meaning of the word *importance*, so too is the implication of the energy associated with the *feeling* of *Self-Importance* with the *Self* of Wholeness, of Unity. For the word *importance* carries with it a concealed implication with respect to the Truth of Beingness.

I.24.19   Besides the implications given for the world's version of *self-importance*, the word *importance* also carries the meaning *the state of being important.* As you can *see* from the meaning, *Self-Importance* is a *state of being.* And, this *state of being* is found buried beneath several layers of meanings underlying the implication of the word *important*.

I.24.20   The implication of the word *important* lies hidden within its origin. Your word *important* comes to you from the Latin word *importare*, which carries the meaning *import*. And, the meaning of the word *import* is *to imply*. In addition, the word *imply* carries with it the implication *to contain potentially*. Recall, the word *potential* means *power*. In the case of the *feeling* of *Self-Importance* to the *Self* of Truth, the implication of *power* is *to magnify, to increase*.

I.24.21 Here is where the hidden implication of *Self-Importance* lies. For the word *magnify* carries the meaning *to extol*, which implies *glory*. O Holy Child, here is the *feeling* of *Self-Importance*. It is that of *Glory*. It is the *feeling* of Heaven, which is your Natural State. It is the *feeling* of Pure Joy. For in your meaning of the word *glory* is found your Truth, which is *the splendor and beatific happiness of Heaven – Eternity.*

I.24.22 Now, read these words from *A Course in Miracles* with an understanding of the likes you have yet to have. *As Heaven's peace and joy intensify when you accept them as God's gift to you, so too does the joy of your Creator grow when you accept His joy and peace as yours.* **True giving is creation.** *It extends the limitless to the unlimited, eternity to timelessness, and love unto itself. It adds to all that is complete already, not in simple terms to adding more, for that implies it was less before. It adds by what cannot contain itself fulfill its aim of giving everything it has away, securing it forever for itself.*

I.24.23 What then is the *feeling* of *Self-Importance* as it arises with the thought of the True *Self*? It is but the *feeling of God*. O Divine Child, it is but you. ***Let God complete Himself, and you will understand that what completes Him must complete you as well.***

The Glory of God

I.24.24 You are God's desire to extend His Joy. Because of this, you *are* joy. For what else could you be? You are the *Glory* of God, because you are the *beatific happiness of Heaven*. But, what does this mean? What is the *beatific happiness of Heaven*?

I.24.25 The time has come for you to remember *what you are*. For the time of *guilt* and *shame* is ending. The time of God's Glory is dawning. The time to *feel* your Truth is here. And, the Truth of your Being runs through the implication and energy of the word *beatific*, which carries the meaning *having a blissful appearance*.

I.24.26 Earlier in this discussion, We shared with you the meaning of the word *appearance*. Recall, it carries the implication of *semblance*. And, the implication of its energy with regards to the world's version of *self-importance* is that of the *body*. However, like other words where the energy of the word *self* is involved, the word *appearance* has an implication regarding the energy field of the *Self* of Truth, where the energy is also found in its meaning - *semblance*. For the word *semblance* also carries the meaning **image** and **likeness**.

I.24.27 The implication here is one that should elicit joy into the farthest reaches of your Being. For having been *created in the* **image** *and* **likeness** *of* God literally means you are His *Semblance*. You are His *Appearance*. Yet, to a mind that has identified as a *body*, this has no meaning. However, to a mind where the Truth of its Reality has been restored, the implication is far reaching. For it means that you are the **image** and **likeness** of Joy, of Heaven, and of Wholeness, Its *Self*.

I.24.28 Furthermore, you are the **image** and **likeness** of the *beatific happiness of Heaven*. Now, let's look at the implication of the word *beatific*. For the intentionality, the energy, of *beatific* is the energy of your True State of Being. And, it is your inheritance.

I.24.29 In order to uncover the hidden intentionality of the word *beatific,* We must look to its origin, which is the Latin word *beate* and carries with it the meaning *abundance,* or *bounty*.

434

Furthermore, the implication of *bounty* is where the intention rests. For *bounty* carries the implication *generosity*, or *generous,* which means *openhearted, liberal in giving,* and *characterized by an exalted spirit.*

I.24.30   However, the deeper implication is found in the origin of the word *generous*, which comes from the Latin word *generis* and carries with it the meaning of *offspring,* or *descendant.* Do you yet *see* the implication for *beatific*? For the implication is that of a *Child of God.* Can you *feel* it? It is your True Nature. It is the *Glory* of God. It is *what you are.*

I.24.31   Therefore, the intention, the *feeling* of *Self-Importance,* corresponding to the thought of the *Self* of Truth is the *feeling* of the *Glory* of God. In other words, where the *body* is the third dimensional manifestation of the belief arising from the separated *self* and its *feeling* of *self-importance,* a *Child of God* is the eternal manifestation arising from the belief in the *Self* of Truth and its corresponding *feeling* of *Self-Importance.* Recognize, in this most perfect moment, that you are the *Glory* of God, because you are the *Child of God.*

I.24.32   *Feel* the energy, the intention, of your Truth. *Feel* its incredible power. *Feel* its Peace. *Feel* the Joy. *Feel* the oneness between you and God. For you are the Intention of the Desire of God. And, when *Desire* and *Intention*, *Source* and *Extension*, are in alignment, then creation is increased.

True Giving is Creation

I.24.33 God gave Himself, His Whole *Self*, in Our creation. And, giving is not only creation, it is extension. Therefore, as His Extension, We are the *Self* of God. For extending is giving. Thus, true giving is the giving of your Whole *Self*. And, when you give your Whole *Self*, there can be no separation. For the Extension is whole, since it is the giving of the Whole *Self* to the Extended *Self*.

I.24.34 In other words, the Extension is both in the **image** and **likeness** of Its Source. For they are the same. They are identical. And, each Extension is a *Semblance* of the Whole *Self*. Therefore, there isn't anything lacking in the Extension, for It has everything the *Self of Source* has. Furthermore, since every Individuated *Self* is the *semblance* of the *Source Self*, recognize, then, that you have never looked upon another. How could you? For you can but look upon your *Self* in everyone you look upon.

I.24.35 Now, the time for your restoration has come. For your True Intention, your True Energy, your True Power, your True Freedom, your True Reality, your True Glory, and your saving grace, rests in the simple fact that you, the Extension of Source, did not create your *Self.* You can deny your *Self,* but you cannot destroy your *Self.* You have the right to attempt destruction as many times as you choose. Yet, aren't you tired of attempting the impossible?

I.24.36   You have a saying in your world, which goes, *Insanity is doing the same thing again and again expecting different result*s. If you are tired of doing the same thing over and over, time and time again, then We invite you to complete the following lesson being offered within this curriculum. We invite you to lay aside the *self-importance* that creates the experiences of hell, for the *Self- Importance* that creates and extends Heaven. Therefore, We are inviting you to return to **True Giving**.

Lesson 24

I.24.37   For this exercise, you will need one large index card. Upon it, write the statements that will be given. Unlike other exercises in this curriculum, only one practice period per day, for twenty-one days, is needed. We ask that you set aside fifteen minutes in the evening, just before you go to bed each night, in order to complete each practice session.

I.24.38 As you begin each practice period, read each statement aloud, three times each. Read them slowly. And, do so with intention. *Feel* the energy associated with each statement. *Feel* them to your core. Then, silently repeat each one for the remaining time. However, as you silently repeat each statement, do so slowly and with deliberation. Allow yourself to *feel* the power behind each statement. But, more importantly, allow gratitude to well up within you. Offer the Source of your *Self* your gratitude. And, know with certainty that it is received with Love by your *Self*.

I.24.39 The statements are as follows:

I am the Whole Extension of God.

My Self-Importance lies in the fact that I am a Child of God.

I can but see my Self in everyone I look upon.

Creating is my purpose and joy as the Self created by God.

CHAPTER 25

The Eternal Changeless Self

I.25.1   We are with you again to discuss the Truth of Our Being, the Truth you share with Us. Now, We come to the beauty and the glory for which We, as Extensions of God, are in Truth. This is a time for rejoicing. For the awakening of the mind is here. The joining of the mind and *Heart* has come. And with it, the restoration of Life draws near. Can you *feel* the change occurring within your mind? Can you yet *feel* the freedom associated with a mind that trusts the *Heart?* For you have reached the end of a journey of *self-imposed* exile, a journey through hell, and a journey littered with thoughts of separation and death. There is a new road before you. A road paved with gold. It is a road you travel with all of your Brothers and Sisters in union, in oneness, and in wholeness. It is a highway that We travel together. For this is the Highway to Heaven. And, Our destination is the Promised Land.

I.25.2   Just as Moses led the enslaved, ancient Hebrews out of Egypt to deliver them to the Promised Land, the time of your exodus from the enslavement and bondage to the thought system of separation has come. The time of your journey to the Promised Land is afoot. For the Promised Land belongs to every Child of God. However, unlike the biblical story, the

Promised Land of which We speak, is not in some far off, foreign land. For the Promised Land does not lie outside of you. It lies within your mind. It has always been with you, but because of your experiences within the realm of physicality, you have become lost and disoriented. We are with you at this time in order to prepare your mind for the journey to the Promised Land.

I.25.3   So much of the early portion of your biblical narrative is centered on and around the Promised Land. But, what exactly is the Promised Land? What exactly is meant by the words, *Promised Land?*

I.25.4   You have been taught that it was a destination where the ancient Hebrews traveled after leaving Egypt. Yet, while that is the story you have come to believe, you have not yet realized the greater implication contained within the narrative. For its deeper implication, its true intention, lies hidden within the very words themselves. Now, the time of their revelation and intention is upon you. Found within the words is the energetic vibrational frequency that will inundate your world with the Spirit of God.

I.25.5   This is not to be feared. This pouring forth of God's Spirit was foretold ages ago. For it is written in your bible, *In the last days, God says, I will pour out my Spirit on all people. Your sons and daughters will prophesy, your young men will see visions, your old men will dream dreams, even on my servants, both men and women, I will pour out my Spirit in those days and they will prophesy.*

I.25.6   As with so many of your words, you have been misled regarding their intention. While you believe that the word *prophesy* means *to predict with assurance on the basis of mystic knowledge*, the true intention of the word is found in another of its meanings, which is *to preach*. And, the intention, the energy, of the word *prophesy* is found in the origin of your word *preach*, which comes to you by way of the Latin word *praedicare* and carries with it the meaning *to make known*.

I.25.7   This, O Holy Child, is the reason for Our time together. The time for all things that were hidden to be *made known* has arrived. Even the man you refer to as Jesus stated that this time would come. And, this too is also found in your bible, where it is written that He said, *There is nothing hidden that will not be revealed. There is nothing kept secret that will not come to light.* For the Light has come to shine away the darkness of your mind. The time of revealing is at hand. And, this revealing will carry you to the Promised Land.

I.25.8   The Promised Land is the place that the *Christ* has prepared for you. And this too did the man you call Jesus leave with you. For it is written that He said, *When everything is ready, I will come and get you, so that you will always be with me where I am.*

I.25.9   O Child of God, everything has been made ready for your return. Yet, do not look outside yourself for the return of the *Christ.* For there is nothing outside your holy mind. Rather, the Christ comes to the mind which has made room for Him. Who is this *Christ,* whom you have summoned and made yourself ready for His return?

I.25.10   It is but you! It is but your *Self,* the Holy Extension of God. It is but the *Self* you believed you denied so very long ago. Although you believe you denied your *Self,* recognize that through *grace* your *Self* never denied you. For your Holy *Self,* the *Christ,* the One begotten Child of God, has never wavered in His love for you. He awaits with arms wide open to offer the sweet embrace to a child who has been away for far too long.

The Promised Land

I.25.11   What, then, is the Promised Land? It is more than you have ever hoped for or dreamed of. ***For hope deferred makes the heart sick, but a yearning for Truth, a yearning for Love,*** *fulfilled is a tree of life.* And, the tree of life is found in the Promised Land.

I.25.12 In order to understand what the Promised Land is, We need but uncover the meaning of the words *promised* and *land.* The word *promise* carries with it the meaning of *betroth.* Recall, the word *betroth* carries the meaning of *to unite*, or *uniting.* And, the word *land* simply carries with it the meaning of *realm.* Thus, what is the *Promised Land*? It is but this – the *Realm of Unity*

I.25.13 However, there is a much deeper and richer implication to the word *promise.* And, this implication carries the energy field of the *Realm of Unity.* For it carries the energy signature of the Truth of your Being. It is your *Glory.*

I.25.14 Besides carrying the intention of *unity*, the word *promise* also carries the meaning *word.* Take a moment. Let that sink deep within your being. For the implication, the intention, of the *Promised Land* is this – the *Realm of Christ.* And, it is in the *Realm of Christ* where the *Tree of Life* is found. *Christ* is the *Tree of Life.* This too is found in your bible, where it is written that the man Jesus said, *I am the way, the truth, and the life: no man cometh unto the Father, but by me.*

I.25.15 What does this imply? Does this mean that you cannot reach the Father unless you accept Jesus? For this is what many in your world have been taught and have come to believe. However, if this is your belief, then that would mean that the man named Jesus spoke from a position of *pride* and *arrogance.* And, We can assure you that was not the case. Therefore, what did He mean when He said, *No man cometh unto the Father, but by me?*

I.25.16 O Child of Heaven, do you not yet recognize that you are the Holy Extension of God? For your Holy *Self* is the *Christ.* How could you come unto the Father save it be but by your Holy *Self?* For God only knows of His Creations. He only knows you by the *Self* He Extended in your creation. Yet, this seemingly simple bible passage has a deeper implication than you yet know. For hidden within just one word is the intention, the energy, which is the key to understanding the true meaning of that verse. And, the key lies in the word *cometh,* or *comes.*

I.25.17 Although the meaning most people ascribe to the word *come* is that of *to move toward something; to approach,* the intention lies in another meaning. And, that meaning is *to extend.* Furthermore, the implication of the word *extend* is that of *advance,* which carries the meaning *to raise.* Here is where the intention of the words *come unto* is found. For the word *raise* literally means *to awaken*.

I.25.18   Therefore, when Jesus said, *no man cometh unto the Father, but by me,* the implication is but this – *no man awakens to the Father, but by Christ.* Do you yet *see* the implication here? Better yet, do you *feel* it? For how else could a man, one who has identified as only human, or *not-God*, awaken to God unless he does so through the *Self* he denied so very, very long ago?

I.25.19   Come now, in this most Hallowed Moment, to know that as an Extension of God, you are the Awakening of God. More specifically, the *Christ* is the Awakening of God. For the Christ is your completed *Self*, your Awakened *Self*. The *Christ* is the Whole *Self*, the *Realized Extended Self of God.*

I.25.20   Look once again at your bible passage where it is written, *In the beginning was the **Word**, and the **Word** was with God, and the **Word** was God. The same was in the beginning with God. All things were made by him; and without him was not anything made that was made. **In him was life, and the life was the light of men.** And the light shineth through in darkness, and the darkness comprehended it not.*

I.25.21 Do you yet understand that the *Promise* and the *Word* are the same? For *in the beginning was the **Promise**, and the **Promise** was with God, and the **Promise** was God.* O Divine Child, you are the *Promise* of God. You are His *Promise* to Awaken. And, He kept His **Word**. He kept you safely embraced in His Holy Mind while you slept and dreamed of hell.

I.25.22 Furthermore, the **Promise**, the **Word**, which is but the *Christ*, is Life. And the Life, which is but the *Christ*, is your Light. Where once your mind was so lost in the darkness of *Self*-denial and *self*-deception that it could not comprehend the Light, the *Christ*, your True *Self*, the time has come for the Light to once again shine through the darkness of the mind. Except this time, the Light will illuminate every darkened corner until the *Christ* – the Holy Extension of God – is fully accepted and realized by your mind.

I.25.23 Just as the first exodus, where the ancient Hebrews were set free from bondage in Egypt and delivered to the Promised Land, was to prepare man for the *First Coming of Christ,* the purpose of Our time together with you is to aid you in the exodus from the bondage of *self* and deliver you to the Promised Land within, so that you may prepare your mind for the *Second Coming of Christ.*

I.25.24 We fully recognize the misconceptions surrounding this most wonderful time in man's ascent to the higher realms. For many on your world believe that great chaos will erupt just prior to the *Christ's* return. Yet, your world, as you have known it, has always existed in chaos, because your world is built upon the laws of chaos. For the mind was not yet ready or prepared for the *Time of Christ*, for the *Time of Peace and Oneness*. But, the time has come for the triumphant return of the Holy Extension of God. The *Son* is dawning on the horizon. And, a new day is approaching – one never before experienced by man.

I.25.25 This is truly a time for rejoicing. The time of *Self*-denial and the *terror* it once spawned is closing. For the *Second Coming*, so long ago *Promised*, is now on your door step. Welcome your *Self* in by welcoming the *Christ* into your mind.

The Realms of the Triune

I.25.26 When We first began Our discussions, We shared with you the realms, or dimensions. Recall, there are three realms: the temporal realm (the realm of space/time); the transitional realm (the borderland between the temporal and Heavenly Realms); and, the Heavenly Realm (the Realm of God, the Realm of Pure Energy). Now, We will broaden the scope of

Our discussion of the realms in order for the Promised Land, the *Realm of Christ*, and its intention, to become open and welcomed into your mind.

I.25.27 The three realms correspond to the *Triune* of God. Remember, the Triune of God refers to the three aspects of the Godhood: the Father, the Son, and the Spirit. Each of the aspects of the *Triune* directly corresponds to a realm.

I.25.28 The realms are also referred to as the *Three Degrees of Glory*, or the *Three Kingdoms of Heaven*. This, too, is recorded in your bible. For in your bible, it is written: *There are also celestial bodies, and bodies terrestrial: but the **glory** of the celestial is one; and the **glory** of the terrestrial is another. There is one **glory** of the sun, one **glory** of the moon, and another **glory** of the stars: for one star differeth from another star in **glory**. So also, is the resurrection of the dead. It is sown in corruption; it is raised in incorruption. It is sown in dishonor; it is raised in **glory**: it is sown in weakness; it is raised in power. It is sown a natural body; it is raised a spiritual body. There is a natural body, and there is a spiritual body. And so, it is written, the first man Adam was made a living soul; the last Adam was made a quickening* (renewed) *spirit.*

I.25.29 Like most things in your world, this Truth has been misunderstood, as well as feared. Some use this passage as a weapon of control. But, Truth is incapable of being used. For Truth can only make one free. It cannot bind. Nor can it be controlled. For Truth is God.

I.25.30 Because there are those in your world who believe that this passage is of things to come at a future time, they fear it. For they have been taught that the future is a thing to be feared. What they do not understand is this – there is no such thing as the future. For there is no such thing as time. There is only eternity. There is only Truth. And, there is only Certainty and Love.

I.25.31 However, because you believe in time, the realms, depending on how they are interpreted, appear to describe some future event. Therefore, We invite you to allow your Heart to interpret what you will be reading. For what your mind is about to read, *will* occur in time. It does not occur in eternity. Your *Heart* knows this. But, your mind has forgotten it. For in Truth, you are already Whole and Complete. Yet, this Truth has yet to dawn within your mind. It is for this reason that your mind would interpret it through the lens of fear. However, your *Heart* will interpret it only through the lens of Love. For the *Heart* knows that only Love is Real.

I.25.32 The three Realms of the Triune, which are the *Three Degrees of Glory*, or the *Three Kingdoms* are as follows: the *Celestial Kingdom* (the Heavenly Realm), the *Terrestrial Kingdom* (the Transitional Realm), and the *Telestial Kingdom* (the Temporal Realm). Each Kingdom is governed by an aspect of the Godhead. As such, the Celestial Kingdom is governed by the Father, the Terrestrial Kingdom is governed by the Christ, and the Telestial Kingdom is governed by the Spirit.

I.25.33 Although some believe the *Kingdoms of Glory* will be assigned as a reward or punishment after what is called the *Final Judgment*, this simply is not the case. For the *Three Degrees of Glory* are nothing more than the names given to varying aspects of the ascension process. While it appears that there is *a* process, always remember that **you are already seated with Christ in the Heavenly Realm**. For this was accomplished by the resurrection and ascension of the one you refer to as Jesus. However, your mind is yet unaware of this Truth. Therefore, the ascension process simply refers to the gentle awakening of your mind to the Truth of your Holy *Self*.

The Telestial Realm

I.25.34 Because of your mind's attachment and identification with that of form, and its entrancement by time, your mind is thus associated with the lower or temporal realm, known as the *Telestial Kingdom,* also referred to as the *First Degree of Glory.* And, when the man you call Jesus was crucified, yet rose from the dead into Life, He completed the *First Coming of Christ*, thus allowing for the overcoming of the Temporal Realm, the *First Degree of Glory.*

I.25.35   Here, time and space seem real. This is the realm in which the mind inhabits, for a time, the *natural body*, or the physical body, as is written in the bible passage. Although the *Telestial Kingdom* seems far removed from the higher realms, it is still within what is referred to as the Kingdom of God. Where else could it be? For nothing exists outside the Mind of God. Furthermore, it is within the Kingdom of God, because you are His Kingdom. And, wherever you are, so too must His Kingdom be. Although you have denied it, you cannot negate or destroy it.

I.25.36   While it appears that the realm of space/time is governed by its own set of laws, the laws of physics, as well as the laws of chaos, the physical realm still remains fully protected by the Laws of God. Furthermore, the realm of physicality has not been abandoned by God, as some would have you believe. Rather, it has been governed by the Spirit of God, referred to in *A Course in Miracles* as the Voice for God. The Spirit of

God has been your Teacher, guiding and directing you as you navigate physicality.

I.25.37 You have never been separated from the Love of God, not even for a fraction of a moment. You have, however, thought you were. This is why your mind seems conflicted. And, the belief that you had separated from God, although untrue, created the terror, which has played out in the hell that you have made of and for yourself.

I.25.38 Yet, now you are becoming aware that you truly are interconnected to everything and everyone. This is the time to allow yourself to become reacquainted with the exquisite *feeling* of oneness and unity.

I.25.39 As you have already learned, **time can either waste or be wasted.** However, when seen as the gift and blessing for which all things are, time simply becomes a tool to experience unity and oneness. **For time cannot separate you from God if you use it on behalf of the eternal.** And, this is accomplished in the realm of physicality just as it is in all others – by sharing your *Self*, and the Love for which you are in Truth. In sharing your *Self*, you are giving your *Self*. And, through the giving of your *Self*, you receive your *Self*. And, it is through receiving your *Self*, that you come to know your *Self*.

452

I.25.40 When you accept the Truth of your *Self,* you will no longer be under the spell of time. For you will simply recognize time for what it is – nothing! Once this happens, you will have released your attachment to not only time, but to death, as well. And, this is when Life begins! For you will have welcomed your *Self* back into your mind.

The Terrestrial Realm: The Realm of Christ

I.25.41 The Transitional Realm is that of the *Realm of Christ.* It is the realm of brotherhood and unity. For it is the realm where the *Christ* in everyone governs. In this realm, there are no strangers, for there are no *others.* Although it is being described as if it was a place, it isn't. It is a state of mind. It is a *state of being.* And, it is the borderland. For it lies just outside the gates of Heaven, which is but Our True State of Being.

I.25.42 The *Realm of Christ* already exists within your holy mind. And, it is the Promised Land. In your bible, it is written that God told the ancient Hebrew people, *I have promised to rescue you from your oppression in Egypt. I will lead you to a land flowing with milk and honey.*

I.25.43   Since the Promised Land is one flowing with milk and honey, what does this mean? What is the implication? In order to recognize the implication, so that you can recognize the energy associated with that of the *Realm of Christ*, We must reveal the hidden meanings associated with the words *flowing, milk,* and *honey*.

I.25.44   While most believe in the metaphysical interpretation of the phrase, *flowing with milk and honey*, as meaning *all good things,* the implication and intention of that phrase has a significance that has been concealed within multiple layers of other words, thus hiding the energy signature associated with the *Terrestrial Kingdom*, or the *Second Degree of Glory*. For the vibrational frequency of the *Realm of Christ* is that of unity and oneness. It is the frequency of complete peace. For within this realm, conflict is not recognized in any form, because absolute and unconditional love has become realized.

I.25.45   Your word *flowing* is a form of the word *flow*, which carries with it the meaning *to rise*. And, it is within the meaning of the word *rise* where the intention of the word *flow* is found. For the implication of the word *rise* is: *to return from death, to ascend,* as well as *to come into being*. Thus, the implication, the intention, the energetic frequency of the word *flow* is that of the *Christ*, the *risen Son of God*. More specifically, the word *flow* implies Life, which is your True State of Being. Thus, the word flow carries the energy, the vibrational frequency, of **Life**.

I.25.46 Unlike *flow*, where the implication is more easily accessed, the implication of the word *milk* lies buried beneath layers of others that foster nothing but level confusion. We invite you, at this time, to allow your mind to be receptive to the varying words that will be given. For buried within them is the treasure you once denied when you asked the question, *What am I?*

I.25.47 Your word *milk* carries the meaning *lactation*, or *to lactate*. Again, We must turn to the origin of the word in order to reveal the hidden meaning. The word *lactate* comes from the Latin word *lactare*, which carries the implication *to induce*. Furthermore, your word *induce* carries with it the meaning *cause/effect*. However, the intention of the word *induce* is found in its origin, which is the Latin word *inducere* and carries the meaning *initiation*. And, it is within the word *initiation* where the implication of the word *milk* is ultimately uncovered. For the implication of your word *initiation* carries with it the meaning *the condition of being initiated into some experience or realm of activity:* **knowledgeableness**.

I.25.48 Therefore, the word *milk* is referring to the *return of knowledge*. In *A Course in Miracles*, it is written that *peace is the prerequisite for the return of Knowledge*. Thus, the *Realm of Christ* is a state of beingness, where the mind prepares itself for the return of what it once denied – the return of Knowledge. It is for this reason that the *Realm of* Christ is the *Time of Peace*. Since all knowledge is of God, then the return of Knowledge is the *Return of God*. However, the mind must be made ready by *being Peace*. And, in accordance with the Spiritual Law of Being, to *be* Peace, you must *have* Peace, which means you must *give* Peace.

I.25.49 Just like the implication of the word *milk* was buried beneath layers of other meanings, the implication of the word *honey* lies hidden in the same manner. For your word *honey* carries the meaning *a loved one: dear*. The implication of the word *dear* is found within the meaning *heartfelt*, which carries with it the implication *earnest*. Furthermore, the implication of the word *earnest* is *pledge*. And, within the word *pledge* is the hidden implication for the word *honey*. Although the word *pledge* carries the meaning *a token, sign, or earnest of something coming*, it also carries the meaning *troth*, which arose from the Old English word for *truth*. Thus, the word *honey* as given in your bible verse carries with it the implication of *truth*.

I.25.50　In your bible verse, which reads, *I will lead you to a land flowing with milk and honey,* when the words are substituted with their meanings, the verse can be read as, **I will lead you to a realm of Life with the return of Knowledge and Truth.** This, O Holy Child, is the *Promise* of God. It is His *Word.* It is the *Christ.*

I.25.51　Can you yet *feel* the energy of hope realized? For within the *Realm of Christ* is found the *Tree of Life.* And, the fruit from this tree is eternity. Recognize, then, that the *Terrestrial Kingdom,* the *Second Degree of Glory,* is a transitional realm. For it is eternal, because it is the Realm of Life. Yet, it is also temporal, because there is still some change involved. Although the time of learning as you know it now is ending, learning will still occur. It will simply occur through a different method – through sharing. And, the time of sharing is approaching.

I.25.52　When you think of learning, you associate it with the concept where there is a teacher and a student. As written in *A Course in Miracles,* a teacher-student relationship is founded on inequality, since it implies that one has more to offer than the other. However, once the *Realm of Christ* is fully realized within your mind, there will still be a teacher. It is the Christ. Yet, rather than being founded on inequality, it is based on perfect equality. For there is perfect sharing between every Child of God. It is within this realm where communication between God and His Extensions, His Creations, is re-established and maintained. In other words, it is the *Return to Wholeness*.

The Celestial Kingdom

I.25.53   The *Third Degree of Glory* is the Eternal Realm, or the Heavenly Realm. It is the Realm of the Most High. And, it is Our Eternal Home. This is the Realm of Exaltation. It is the realm of Our Glory, the Glory We share with God. And it is the Home of Our *Eternal, Changeless Self* who stands at the end, guiding Us gently with Love.

I.25.54   We aren't here with you to prepare you for the *Third Degree of Glory*. For that is the purpose of the *Realm of Christ*. Exaltation is the last step, which is taken by God. And that We leave to Him Whose Knowledge of His Extensions is likened unto Himself.

I.25.55   Therefore, Our time together is to aid you in preparing for the *Second Coming of Christ* and the arrival of the *Second Degree of Glory*. For it is within this Realm where We come to know Our *Self* as God Knows Us. If you are ready to awaken and begin the journey to the Promised Land, then We invite you to complete the next lesson within this curriculum.

Lesson 25

I.25.56   This lesson requires one large index card. On it, write the following statements. Although this exercise has two practice periods, keep the index card with you throughout the day. As often as you like, simply read the statements. When you do, allow yourself to *feel* the gratitude that will arise into your conscious awareness. Then, thank Him Who has kept His *Promise*, His *Word*.

I.25.57   For this exercise, We ask that you set aside seven minutes each morning and evening. During each practice period, We invite you to spend the seven minutes by silently repeating the statements provided at the end of Our discussion. To prepare for each practice period, find a place where it is quiet, but comfortable. Sit in a chair, if possible, with your feet on the floor. Close your eyes, and take three deep, cleansing breaths. Then, begin the seven minute practice period by slowly and silently repeating each statement. Continue to silently, but slowly, repeat them for the seven minutes you have set aside. As you do, *feel* the intention of each one. *Feel* its energy. *Feel* the hope within each one as it becomes realized within your mind. Above all, however, rejoice in each statement as you repeat it.

1.25.58 The statements are as follows:

I welcome the journey to the Promised Land.

I accept my Self, by accepting the Christ within me.

I am ready to Live again!

Bibliography

All quotes from *A Course in Miracles*© are from the Third Edition, published in 2007, by the Foundation for Inner Peace, www.acim.org and info@acim.org.

All definitions taken from **Merriam-Webster's** Collegiate Dictionary. www.merriam-webster.com

All references to the *Way of Mastery* are from the 10th Edition, published in 2004, by the Shanti Christo Foundation, Sacramento, CA.

All references from *A Course of Love* Combined Volume, 2nd Printing, published in 2014, by Take Heart Publications, Nevada City, CA

References from the Bible can be found in the King James, New International Version, New Living Translation.

Printed in Poland
by Amazon Fulfillment
Poland Sp. z o.o., Wrocław